MW01406109

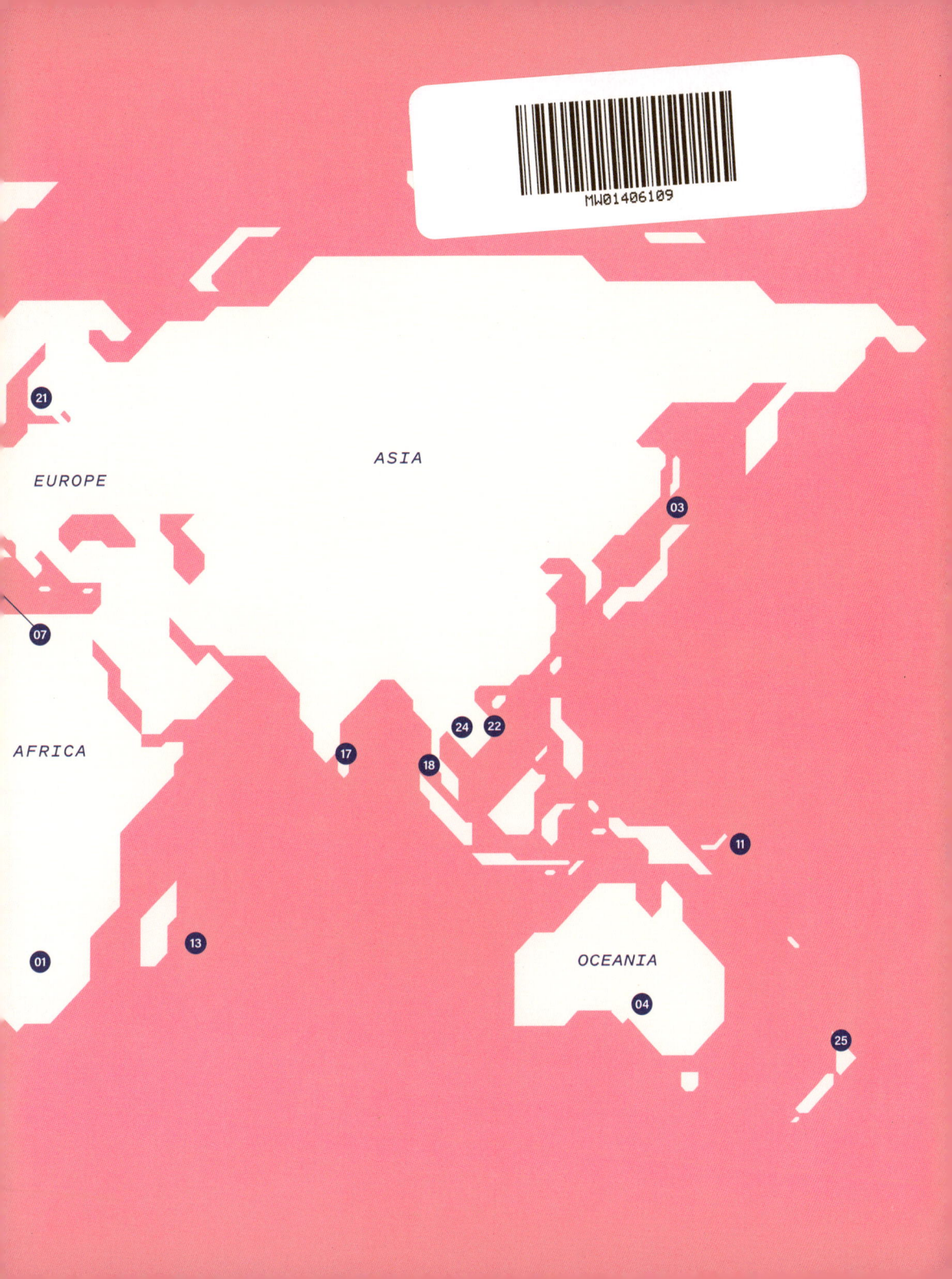

EUROPE

ASIA

21

03

07

AFRICA

17 24 22
   18

11

13

01

OCEANIA
04

25

lonely planet

BEST IN TRAVEL 2026

The 50 Best Destinations & Experiences
for the Year Ahead

CONTENTS

07 Introduction

277 About the authors
282 Photo credits
284 Index

PLACES

15	Botswana	77	Maine, USA
18	Peru	81	Mexico City, Mexico
25	Jeju-do, South Korea	87	Tipperary, Ireland
28	Ikara-Flinders Ranges & Outback, South Australia	93	Quetzaltenango (Xela), Guatemala
32	Cádiz, Spain	96	Jaffna, Sri Lanka
39	Liberdade, São Paolo, Brazil	102	Phuket, Thailand
42	Sardinia, Italy	110	Utrecht, Netherlands
48	Theodore Roosevelt National Park, USA	115	Cartagena, Colombia
52	Réunion	120	Finland
60	Tunisia	124	Quy Nhơn, Vietnam
67	Barbados, Caribbean	128	British Columbia, Canada
70	Solomon Islands	135	Siem Reap, Cambodia
		140	North Island, New Zealand/ Aotearoa

2 / BEST IN TRAVEL 2026

151	*Hike and wildcamp:* Tajikistan	
154	*Go on a cultural food tour:* Old Dubai, United Arab Emirates	
161	*Stay in a train carriage:* Kruger National Park, South Africa	
164	*Visit Eileen Gray's house:* Southern France	
168	*Spend the night in a ryokan:* Japan	
175	*Track desert elephants:* Namibia	
178	*Look for jaguars in the wetlands:* Iberá, Argentina	
182	*Watch a Flying Cholitas match:* Bolivia	
191	*Rapid-raft the Colorado River:* Grand Canyon, USA	
195	*Explore the Bathing Trail:* Victoria, Australia	
198	*Cruise the Mekong River:* Vietnam & Cambodia	
204	*Ride horses in the Andes Mountains:* Ecuador	
209	*Take a Creole trail ride:* Louisiana, USA	
214	*Go on a culinary tour:* Kerala, India	
219	*Attend a Premier League game:* England	
225	*Visit Willamette Wine Country:* Oregon, USA	
228	*Savor the exciting food scene:* Melbourne, Australia	
233	*Become a citizen scientist:* The Amazon, Peru	
238	*Party in the Caribbean:* Grenada	
247	*See the sights by bike:* Batanes Islands, Philippines	
250	*Experience the legendary nightlife scene:* Belgrade, Serbia	
257	*Stay at Hawai'i's Volcano House:* Volcanoes National Park, USA	
261	*Go whale-watching:* Azores, Portugal	
265	*Deep-dive into street art:* Bristol, England	
269	*Go stargazing:* Wairarapa, New Zealand/Aotearoa	

EXPERIENCES

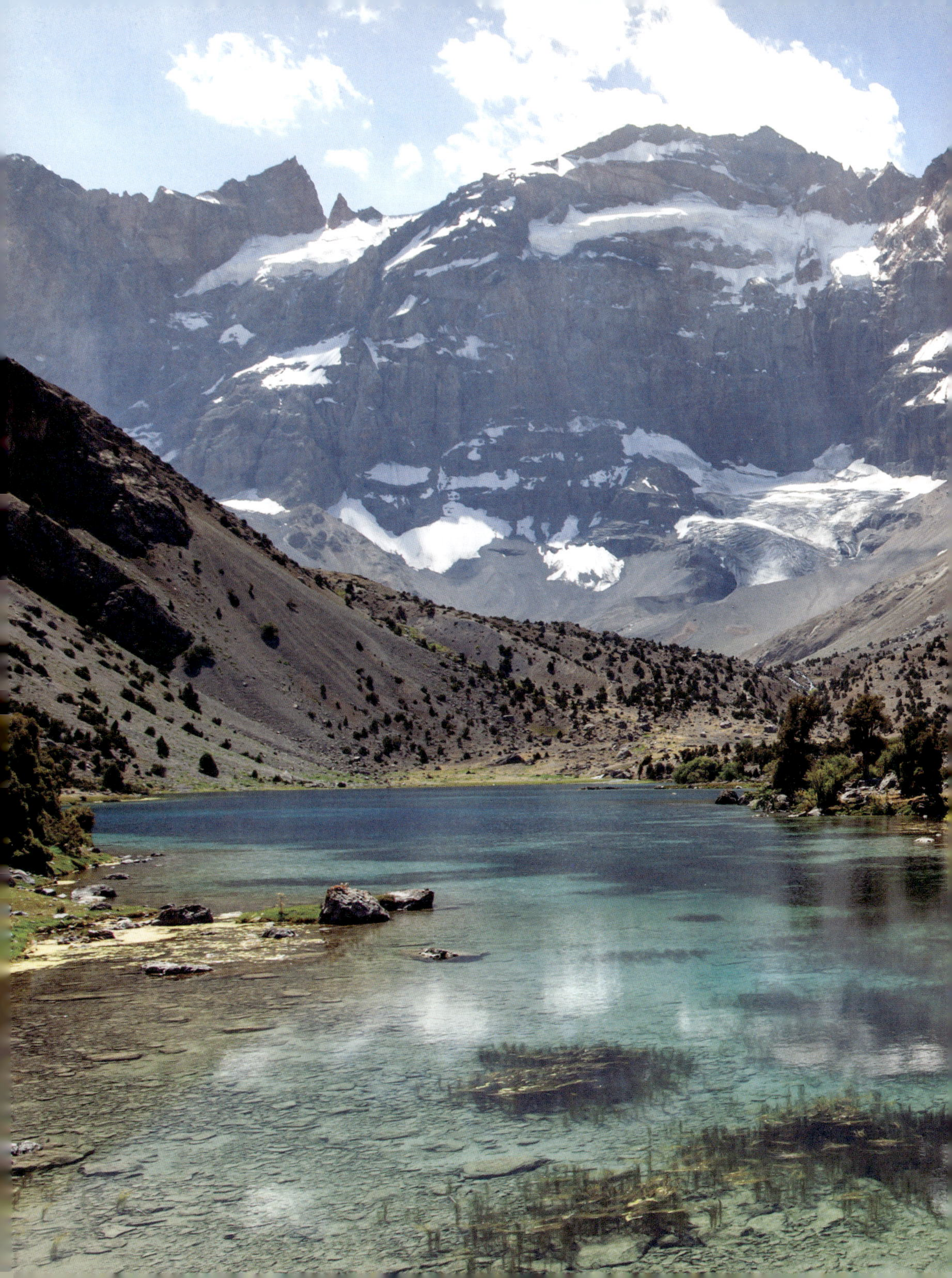

Mighty peaks frame a gin-clear glacial lake in Tajikistan's trail-laced Fan Mountains (p151).

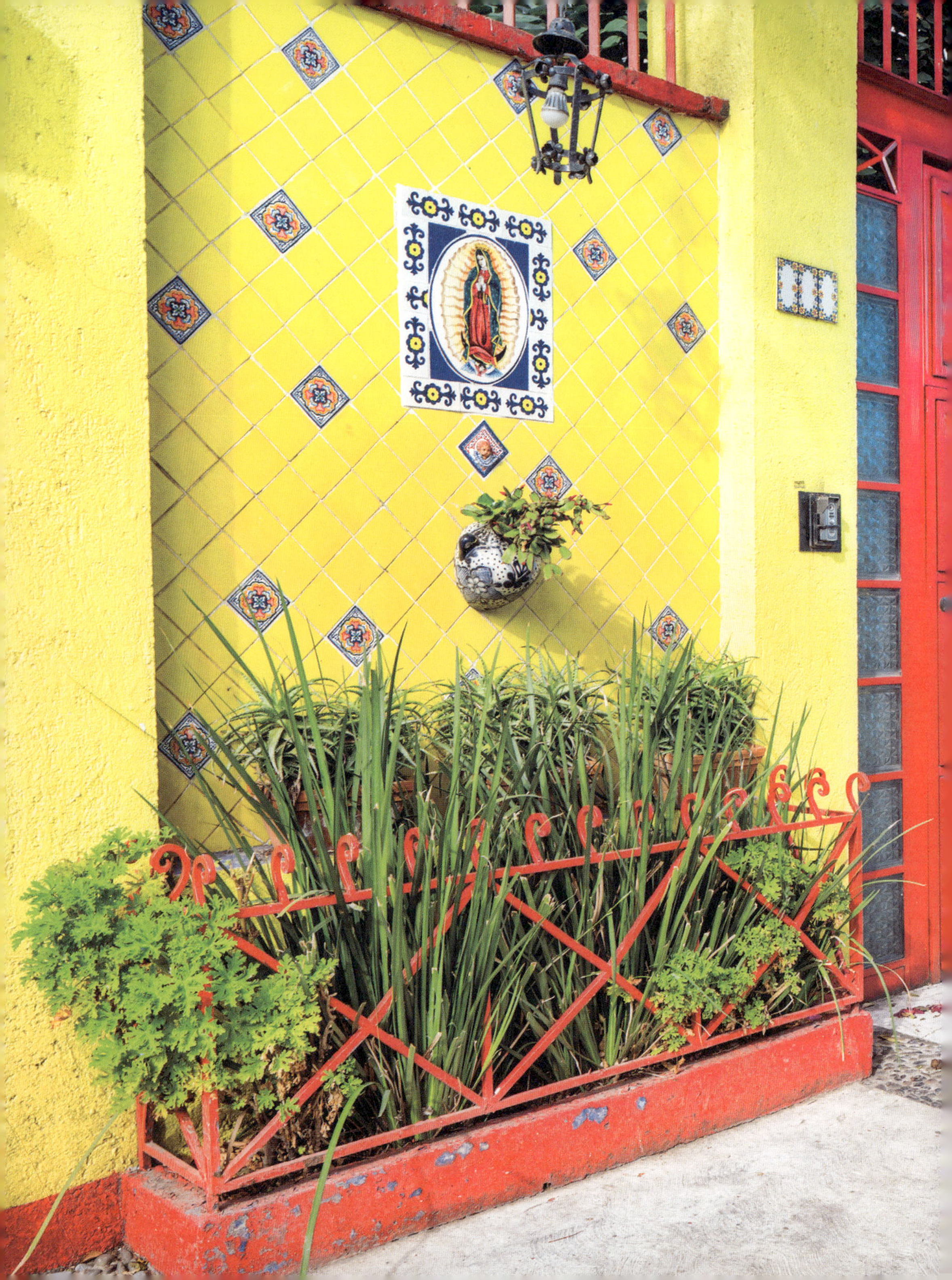

INTRODUCTION

At Lonely Planet, if we're not discussing the details of our most recent trip, we're planning our next one.

We live for travel, and spend much of our waking (and sleeping) hours talking, writing, reading and dreaming about it. Every conversation, every meeting and every gathering is filled with takes on our recent vacations, with recommendations flying back and forth between our passionate and expert team members.

As we look ahead to 2026 we find ourselves wondering: 'What is it that makes a great trip? What keeps our travels alive in our memories long after we return home?'

The truth is, it's not always the big, bucket-list travel events that linger. It's the small, often fleeting moments that elevate a trip and make it unforgettable: the delicious aromas that waft over you when walking into a local bakery on your first visit to Paris; the 20 minutes of people-watching you steal on the bus ride from Atocha Station to Museo del Prado in Madrid; the views you earn after hiking the Sintra uplands on your day trip from Lisbon. These are the memories that push a travel experience from good to great, and sustain our desire to do it all over again somewhere else. It's what next year's *Best in Travel* is all about.

Our team of writers and editors have distilled anecdotes just like this into a list of the 50 best places and experiences they've had and would recommend to fellow travel-lovers in 2026.

This year, the possibilities for travel seem bigger than ever before. So the suggestions within these pages reflect the destinations and experiences that our contributors – themselves a group scattered around the globe – are excited to recommend for the coming year and beyond.

There's something here for every type of traveler, whether you've always dreamed of an under-the-radar carnival experience like Grenada's Spicemas, of joining the fanatical chanting crowds at an English Premier League football match, or of biking the Philippines' Batanes Islands. Wildlife-lovers will find the lure of tracking desert elephants in Namibia or the Azores' awesome whale-watching irresistible. And if sleeping in a converted train carriage overlooking lions and other wonderful wildlife in South Africa is for you, we've got you covered.

Some of these destinations may be familiar, while others are just emerging as the hottest spots on the globe. Within these pages you'll find amazing reasons to visit perennial favorites like Phuket, Mexico City or Finland in 2026. Looking for something new? Let our destination experts extol the virtues of the USA's Theodore Roosevelt National Park, or the island jewel of the Indian Ocean, Réunion, or the ubercool Liberdade district of São Paulo in Brazil. In Europe, we take a deep dive into Belgrade's legendary nightlife; if daytime activities are more your thing, there's Bristol's creative and gritty street-art scene to be explored.

These are our personal passions; they may not always be picture-perfect or Instagram-grid-worthy, but they are authentic takes on the places we've been, and where we think you should go next. After all, the reason we buy the tickets, pack our bags and lace up our boots is to root down a little more: to ourselves, to one another, and to entirely new places and people that might offer us fresh eyes on the world. These pages showcase the destinations and experiences that have left a mark – the ones we can't wait to share with the other travelers we meet.

Here's to an inspired year of travel, filled with many small moments that are well worth the miles. Hopefully we'll see you along the way.

–Fionnuala McCarthy

Previous page: The colors of Coyoacán district, Mexico City (p81); *Left:* Backwater houseboats in Kerala, India's enthralling culinary capital (p214).

BEST PLA

- 15 Botswana
- 18 Peru
- 25 Jeju-do, South Korea
- 28 Ikara-Flinders Ranges & Outback, South Australia
- 32 Cádiz, Spain
- 39 Liberdade, São Paulo, Brazil
- 42 Sardinia, Italy
- 48 Theodore Roosevelt National Park, USA
- 52 Réunion
- 60 Tunisia
- 67 Barbados, Caribbean
- 70 Solomon Islands
- 77 Maine, USA

CES

81	Mexico City, Mexico
87	Tipperary, Ireland
93	Quetzaltenango (Xela), Guatemala
96	Jaffna, Sri Lanka
102	Phuket, Thailand
110	Utrecht, Netherlands
115	Cartagena, Colombia
120	Finland
124	Quy Nhdn, Vietnam
128	British Columbia, Canada
135	Siem Reap, Cambodia
140	North Island, New Zealand/Aotearoa

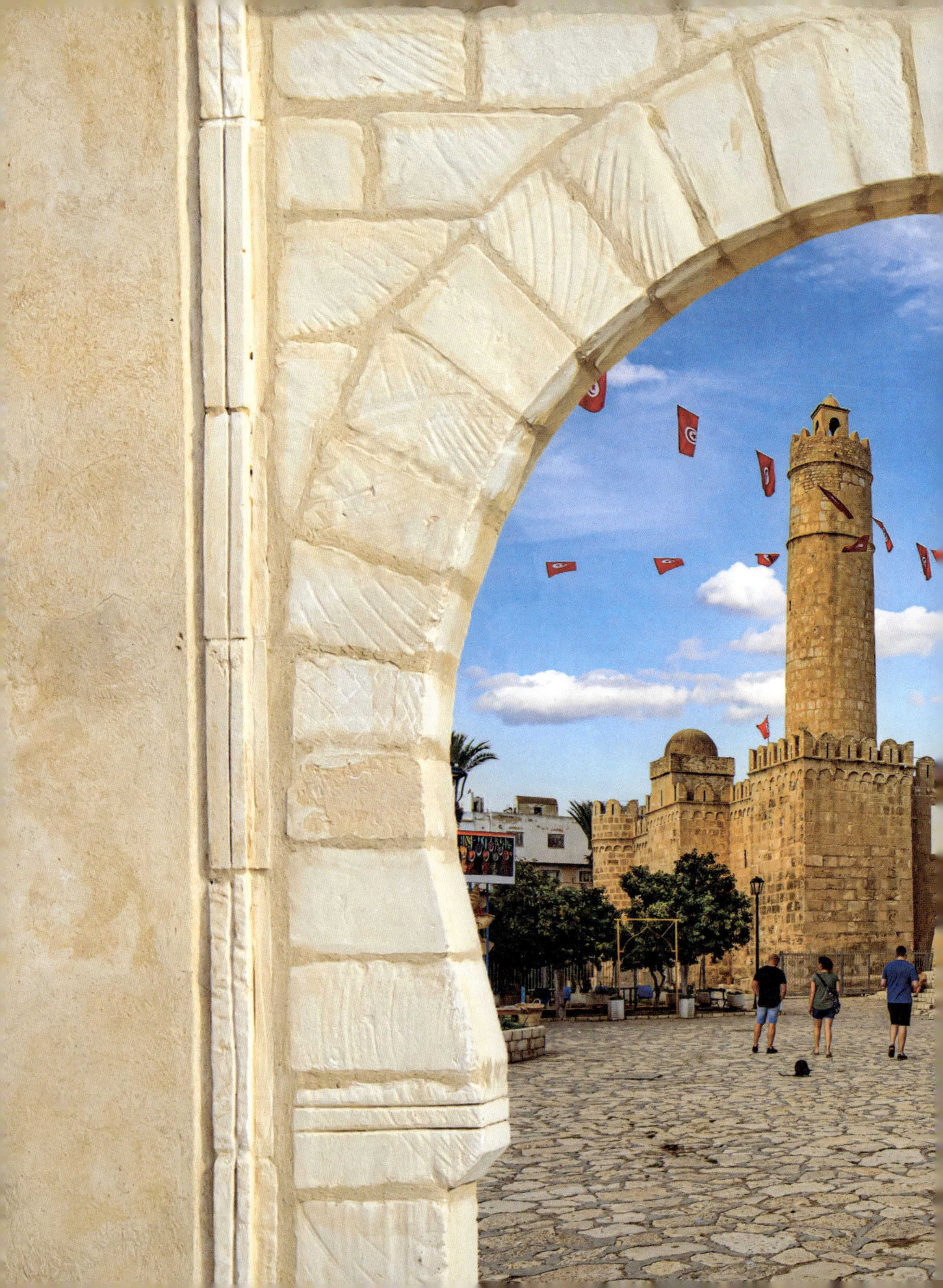

The Mediterranean resorts south of Tunisia's capital, Tunis, include centuries-old Sousse (p60).

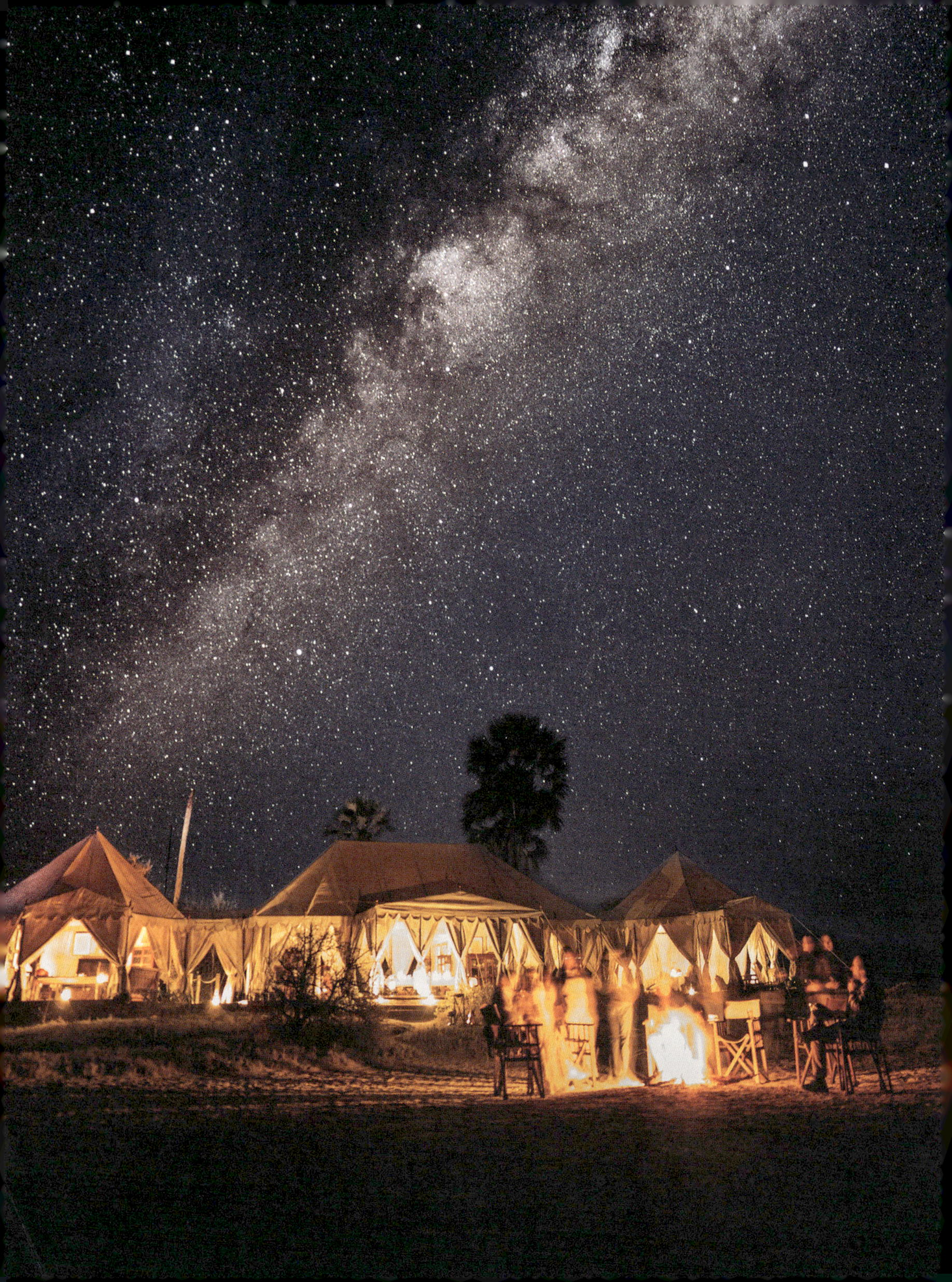

BOTSWANA

BEST FOR
Raw and real wildlife experiences

Botswana safaris are deliberately different. Reputable companies, such as &Beyond and Wilderness, operate small camps that aim to minimize visitor impact – and on game drives, this translates to dramatic wildlife sightings that serve as your own personal theatrical event. Off-roading with endlessly expert guides here is an epic adventure, each and every time.

A TRULY SPECTACULAR SAFARI

An abundance of wildlife is the first thing you'll notice after leaving the airport in Maun, which serves as the gateway to the Okavango Delta and Moremi Game Reserve, among other safari regions. Dozens of small planes and helicopters depart Maun (as well as Kasane) for the remote wilderness beyond the country's fifth-largest town.

Although it's possible to go on a safari year-round, April through September is considered the high season. You'll see tons of wildlife no matter what time of year you choose to visit, but in Botswana's north, where the Okavango Delta is located, wildlife may be slightly less abundant during the October-to-November dry season.

The Okavango Delta is often touted as Botswana's must-see attraction – and it is an awesome natural spectacle to be present during the annual flooding of the world's largest inland delta. Water from the Okavango River

Left to right: Under the stars at a Botswana tented safari camp; The Okavango's colorful avian residents include lilac-breasted rollers.

MOST MEMORABLE MOMENT

Traveling with Wilderness to Mokete – one of the longstanding safari company's newest camps, in the Mababe Depression – is practically guaranteed to include a predatory kill: a lioness catching a water buck or a wild dog snatching a baby buffalo, in the rawest display of the circle of life.

16 / BEST IN TRAVEL 2026

TOP PLACES / BOTSWANA

floods down from the Angolan highlands, creating water passages for crocodiles, elephants and hippos. Many of the safaris in this region offer both land- and water-based adventures; a huge part of the appeal is the sheer wonder and beauty of the delta, though there's plenty of game here, too.

BOTSWANA'S UNSUNG TERRITORY

Not often included in 'Best of Botswana' lists – an erroneous oversight – is the Linyanti Reserve. Bordering the lion-roamed landscape of Chobe National Park and located on a concession area leased to the operators by Botswana's Department of Wildlife and National Parks, the remoteness of this private reserve just adds to its appeal. Birdwatchers and lovers of big game alike will have trouble finding fault; budding landscape photographers will have no shortage of inspiring material. Because it's private, overland vehicles travel off-road as it's the only way around, and game drives – generally two per day, with an early start and a long siesta break in between – do not disappoint. You'll likely see majestic male lions (and hear their mighty roars), and perhaps get close to lionesses and their cubs – plus buffalo, wild dogs, giraffes, elephants, hyenas, impalas and so much more.

Most aficionados agree that the overall safari experience is dependent on a good guide. Wilderness' highly skilled guides, who train up to two years with the company before leading a drive, will teach you about the animals' habits and preferences. Botswana's low-impact, high-value tourism ethic is evident on game drives where you're unlikely to encounter another vehicle (unless it's from your lodge); the limited number of tents (around 12) at the camps is also a part of the move toward responsible tourism.

–*Stacey Lastoe*

Clockwise from top left: Botswana's 'Big Five' include African elephants; Expert safari guides lead the way; Okavango Delta residents range from tiny scorpions to prowling leopards.

BEST IN TRAVEL 2026 / 17

TOP PLACES / PERU

PERU

BEST FOR
Inca history and epic meals

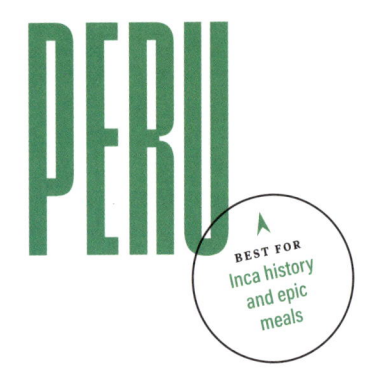

Peru is ancient ruins and modern cities; it is deep traditions and pioneering cuisines. No place in South America seems to be racing so fast toward the future while also carving out space and time to honor its illustrious past quite like Peru. Visit in 2026 to appreciate updated infrastructure, mind-bending meals, time-warping citadels and newly protected wildlands.

Left to right, from above: Pelicans gathered on the Islas Ballestas, Peru's 'miniature Galápagos'; Magical views of Machu Picchu, pinnacle of the Inca Trail trek.

PERU AT YOUR FINGERTIPS

Never before has it been so easy to travel around Peru, thanks to a slew of infrastructure developments that began in 2024 with the opening of a commercial airport in Huaraz, Peru's adventure capital. Instead of taking an eight-hour bus ride from Lima, you can now fly direct to the wild Ancash region, known for its snow-capped Andean peaks, powder-blue glacial lagoons and high-altitude treks. The Cordillera Blanca here includes several peaks above 19,685ft (6000m), including the highest mountain in Peru – and in all of the Earth's tropics – mighty Huascarán, which tops out at 22,205ft (6768m).

Peru's buzzing political capital, Lima, finally has a modern entryway into the nation with the new US$2 billion Jorge Chávez International Airport, which opened in March 2025. It can handle 30 million annual passengers, and its design features a unique hummingbird shape honoring the Nazca Lines, the mysterious geoglyphs cut into Peru's arid, rock-strewn Pampa Colorada (Red

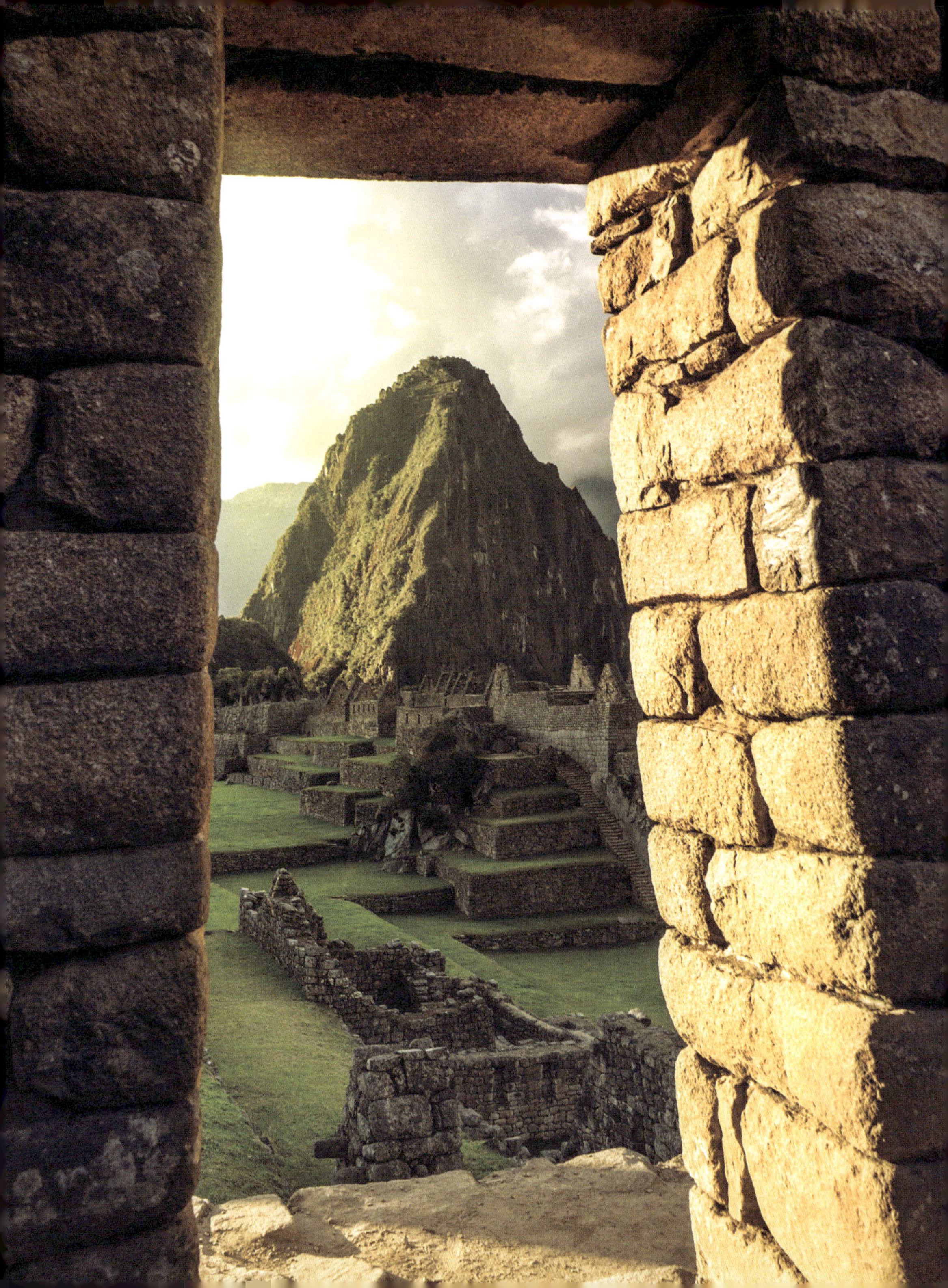

TOP PLACES / PERU

Plain). Finally, in 2026, the long-awaited Chinchero International Airport is set to open in its namesake district, about halfway between Cuzco and the Sacred Valley. Built to replace the Alejandro Velasco Astete International Airport in downtown Cuzco, it will lie at a lofty altitude of 12,200ft (3720m) above sea level.

Cuzco's new airport will be even closer to the famed Inca citadel of Machu Picchu, which recently implemented three new circuits with 10 different tourist routes in an effort to combat overtourism. Total capacity at the site has been reduced in recent years to a maximum of 5600 visitors per day, with timed entries limiting foot traffic at Peru's star attraction.

Increasingly, visitors are also hiking off-piste to lesser-visited ruins such as Choquequirao or along the stone-paved Qhapaq Ñan, the ancient Andean road system that once linked Cuzco with the vast Inca Empire.

ARCHAEOLOGY, ADVENTURE AND EPIC MEALS

Peru's archeological sites have long been its biggest draw, but food tourism isn't far behind. That's because Peruvian gastronomy has been on the cusp of global dominance for years, with Lima regularly landing more spots on the prestigious list of the World's 50 Best Restaurants than any other city.

Momentum continues to rise thanks to emerging local trends now expanding across the globe, including the Japanese-Peruvian Nikkei cuisine, whose key dishes include *tiradito* (raw sashimi-sliced fish served on colorful, piquant sauces). Completely different in style and form are the spicy Creole foods from

Left to right: Lovely Llanganuco Lakes, within Huascarán National Park; Thanks to new circuits and visitor quotas, Machu Picchu promises a less-crowded experience in 2026.

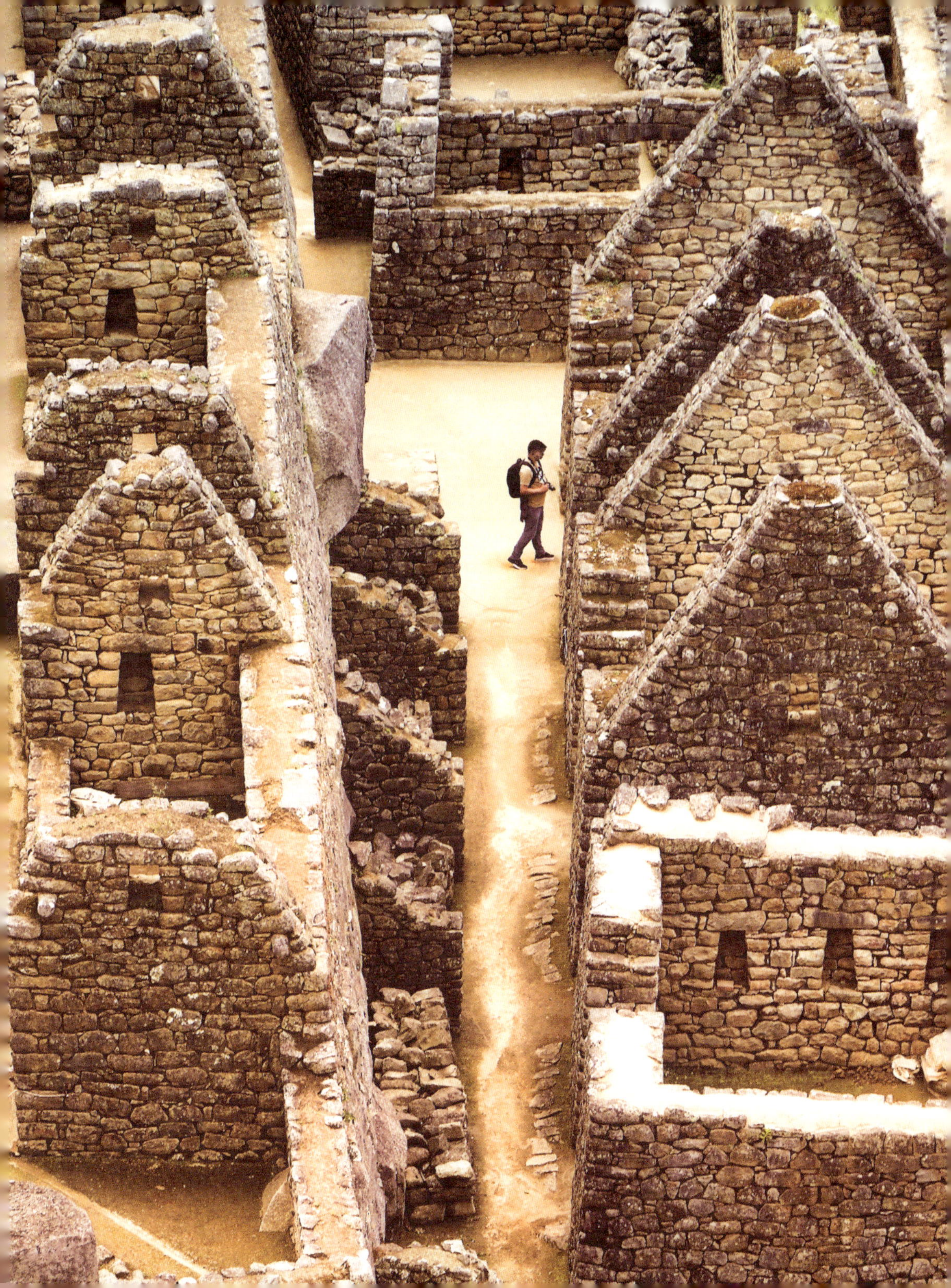

Clockwise from right: Hike off the beaten track to ravishing ruins like Choquequirao; Peruvian-style salmon ceviche; Trekking the Cordillera Blanca; Spot pelicans and other wildlife on the Islas Ballestas, near Paracas.

MOST MEMORABLE MOMENT

Hike the stone paths of the Qhapaq Ñan, an ancient 'highway' that linked the Inca empire from Colombia to Chile, covering some 19,000 miles (30,000km). All paths lead to Cuzco, uniting the various ruins on its periphery. The Inca Trail is the most famous route today, but there are many more just begging to be discovered.

22 / BEST IN TRAVEL 2026

TOP PLACES / PERU

Peru's second-largest city, Arequipa, which became a UNESCO City of Gastronomy in 2019. Arequipa is located in southern Peru, a part of the country that has seen an influx of visitors in recent years thanks to a flurry of new high-design hotels – many from local operator Andean – in remote destinations. These include properties at Lake Titicaca, the world's highest navigable lake, and above Cañón del Colca, which is twice as deep as the USA's Grand Canyon.

RAINFORESTS, SEA RESERVES AND RIVER CRUISES
Meanwhile, new river cruises are offering fresh motivation to travel into the heart of the Amazon, the world's largest rainforest.

Few international visitors spend much time along the Peruvian coast, but there are new reasons to give it a second look. Chief among them is the Grau Tropical Sea National Reserve, designated in 2024, which lies off the northern coasts of Piura and Tumbes and houses 70% of Peru's marine species, including hammerhead sharks and Humboldt penguins.

Further south, near the resort town of Paracas, the Islas Ballestas are likened to a miniature Galápagos, home to fur seals, sea lions, pelicans and blue-footed boobies. While in the area, you can also sample some unaged brandy at a pisco distillery and toast your trip with a frothy pisco sour, Peru's national drink.
–Mark Johanson

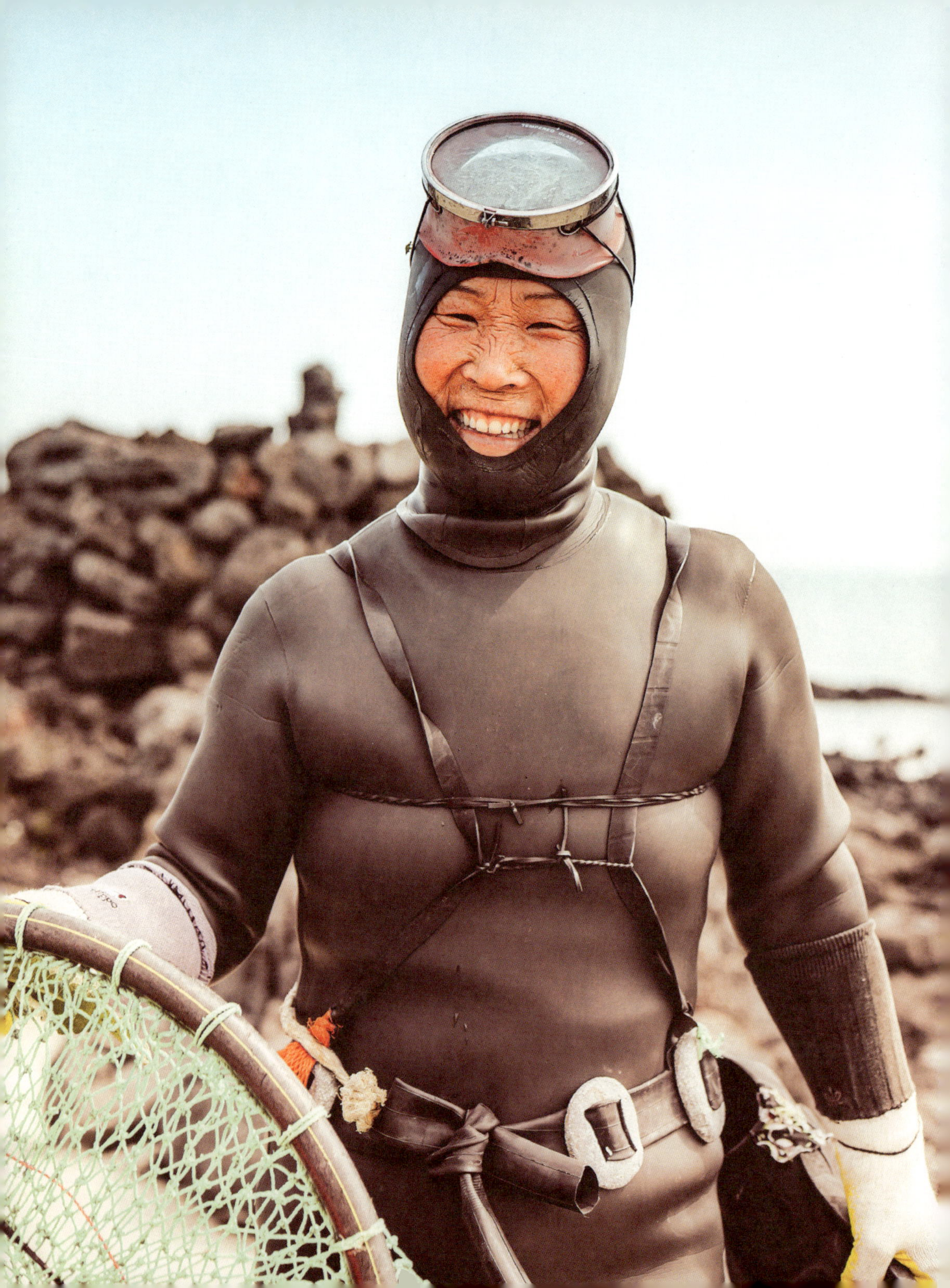

JEJU-DO

SOUTH KOREA

> **BEST FOR**
> Soothing the soul, one step at a time

The volcanic landscapes of Korea's largest island are so special that it's listed as a UNESCO Global Geopark. Many visit to climb South Korea's tallest peak, amble along the Jeju Olle Trail and dive coral reefs teeming with marine life. There's also amazing contemporary art, delicious local cuisine and blissful beaches – all just over an hour's flight south of Seoul.

LOOK TO COASTAL HIKES AND WARM WATERS

For Koreans, Jeju-do has been a popular holiday destination for decades, but since 2007 it's the hiking routes of the Jeju Olle Trail that have placed it on the wider tourist map. A chance to experience both the island's extraordinary natural beauty and its unique culture, the trail meanders mainly along Jeju's coast, as well as three smaller, outer islands including Gapado. This tiny southern island is particularly beautiful in May, when its stone-walled fields are a swaying sea of green barley punctuated by buttery yellow wildflowers.

Summiting Hallasan, the 6388ft-high (1847m) shield volcano at Jeju-do's heart, is the ultimate outdoor challenge. Two routes (neither requiring technical climbing skills) lead to a crater lake with a mirror-like surface. Alternatively, dive into the seas around the island's southern city of Seogwipo, where the warm waters are perfect for seeing soft corals, kelp and tropical fish.

Left to right: Jeju-do is famed as the home of the *haenyeo* – women freedivers who gather fruits of the sea; Fresh abalone is a local favorite.

MOST MEMORABLE MOMENT

You'll never forget your first sight of majestic Seongsan Ilchul-bong, emerging from the sea like an enormous stone-carved, moss-green-coated punchbowl. It's traditional to climb this 597ft-high (182m) extinct tuff volcano in the early hours of the morning, to catch the sunrise over the seaside village of Seongsan-ri and its crescent-shaped beaches.

TOP PLACES / JEJU-DO

DISCOVER A SURPRISING ART SCENE
Beauty comes in all forms here; just as nature inspires, so does the Jeju art scene. A former cinema is one of three unusual locations in island capital Jeju-si that comprise the Arario Museum, displaying pieces by luminaries such as Gilbert & George, Damien Hirst and Anselm Kiefer. Elsewhere on Jeju-do, a one-time factory for audio speakers and a decommissioned bunker once used to manage a submarine optical cable system now house, respectively, the Arte Museum and Bunker des Lumières, a pair of dazzling digital-art experiences.

The colorful works of Korean artists Lee Jung-seop and Lee Wal-chong feature in both the streets and museums of Seogwipo. The Bonte Museum here is a graceful set of buildings, designed by celebrated Japanese architect Tadao Ando to house traditional Korean arts and crafts as well as modern works by global names like Nam Jun Paik and Yayoi Kusama.

One-of-a-kind natural rock forms and traditional stone carvings are amassed at the Jeju Stone Park. Here, encounter armies of the carved basalt statues called *dol-hareubang* (grandfather rocks), a Jeju folk art stretching back centuries. The park's new Seolmundae Halmang exhibition hall showcases the island's fascinating mythology, history and folklore.

SAMPLE LOCAL FLAVORS
No visit to Jeju is complete without tasting freshly grilled seafood at one of the seaside shacks manned by the island's famed *haenyeo* – freediving fisherwomen who gather the ocean's bounty. And don't miss Jeju-si's lively Dongmun Market or Seogwipo Maeil Olle Market, where you can taste the island's famously juicy mandarin oranges and tuck into local delicacies such as cabbage rolls stuffed with flavorful black pork.
–Simon Richmond

Clockwise from top left: **Haenyeo** head out to freedive for seafood; Cherry-blossom season on Jeju-do; Island capital Jeju-si; Shopping for local produce at a Jeju-si market.

BEST IN TRAVEL 2026 / 27

TOP PLACES / SOUTH AUSTRALIA

IKARA-FLINDERS RANGES & OUTBACK

SOUTH AUSTRALIA

*BEST FOR
A vast pink lake, sunsets and outback adventure*

There's an otherworldly beauty to the Ikara-Flinders Ranges that is unlike anywhere else in the Australian Outback. Located at the heart of this treasured national park, the impressive Ikara (Wilpena Pound) – a vast natural amphitheater of mountains, with a cratered rim measuring a staggering eight times the size of Uluṟu – begs to be explored by air or on foot.

VENTURE TO AN OVERLOOKED SIDE OF AUSTRALIA
Take a five-hour drive north of South Australia's cute, cultured capital of Adelaide (making a detour to Riesling Country in the verdant Clare Valley if you have time), and you'll be rewarded with the vast, sprawling, lunar-like landscape of the Ikara-Flinders Ranges National Park. Often overlooked for the more internationally known

Left: The vast natural basin of Ikara (Wilpena Pound), big-ticket drawcard of fantastical Ikara-Flinders Ranges National Park.

outback destinations like Uluṟu-Kata Tjuṯa National Park or the Kimberly, this patch of South Australia delivers drama and awe in equal measure. Emus and kangaroos outnumber humans here, and sunrises and sunsets hit differently as pink, red and purple hues dance and skip across the dramatic landscape, creating an incredible intensity of shape and color.

According to land's Traditional Owners – the Adnyamathanha people – the walls of Ikara/Wilpena Pound are the bodies of two intertwined Akurra (giant serpents), further adding to the region's deeply spiritual importance. The Pound offers a variety of short day-hikes that snake alongside gumtree-lined gullies and lead wanderers to ancient Indigenous rock paintings. For those keen

DON'T LEAVE WITHOUT...

Toasting the sunset with a glass of South Australian bubbly on a guided sunset tour (make sure you pick one with charcuterie included). As the colors bleed between sky and mountaintops, the simplicity and quiet beauty of this stunning landscape is truly awesome.

30 / BEST IN TRAVEL 2026

TOP PLACES / SOUTH AUSTRALIA

to strap on the walking boots, the challenging nine-hour St Mary's Peak/Ngarri Mudlanha hike ascends the Pound's tallest mountain and rewards with the region's most breathtaking panoramic views.

MAKE TIME FOR STARGAZING, MOUNTAIN-BIKING AND SALT LAKES

Venturing deeper into the outback you'll discover the Arkaroola Wilderness Sanctuary, crowned as an official International Dark Sky Sanctuary in 2023 and boasting a selection of accommodation, including lodge rooms and camping sites. Experiences range from observatory visits to guided tours of the night sky in custom-designed robotic stargazing chairs. For those who can brave the chilly nighttime temperature drops, it's the hosted ridgetop sleep-out that offers the most immersive and intense experience. Stargazers travel by 4WD to Streitberg Range, where they're guided through the night sky by telescope before falling asleep under the stars in swags, uniquely Australian tents.

One of the region's oldest townships, quaint Melrose is fast becoming a mountain-biking phenomenon, with 50 miles (80km) of tracks weaving around the scrubbed foothills that surround the brooding Mt Remarkable. Further north, Parachilna's Prairie Hotel offers the Aussie outback on a plate – literally. The feral and native bush food (kangaroo, camel and goat) are spun into wild outback pub classics that can be washed down with a cold one from their onsite brewery.

Adding to the region's otherworldly beauty is its high-salinity pink lakes. Yes, pink! The best vantage points of the bubblegum hues – like those found at Kati Thanda-Lake Eyre, Australia's largest salt lake – are from the air.

–Chris Zeiher

Clockwise from top left: Red kangaroos survey the outback grasslands; Ruby-rock views from Razorback Lookout, Ikara-Flinders NP; Parachilna's Prairie Hotel; Cycling Melrose's MTB trails.

BEST IN TRAVEL 2026 / 31

TOP PLACES / CÁDIZ

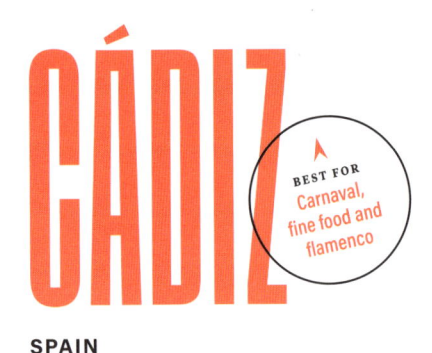

CÁDIZ

SPAIN

BEST FOR
Carnaval, fine food and flamenco

Poised to host its most exuberant Carnaval yet in the coming year, fun-loving Cádiz is once again demonstrating its 21st-century relevance – despite being Europe's oldest city. While many visitors are drawn by Spain's biggest annual party, those who explore further discover an appealing sea port with superb dining, an impassioned flamenco scene and remnants of millennia-old civilizations.

Left to right, from above: Costumed revelers celebrate Cádiz's legendary Carnaval; A bird's-eye view over the city's cathedral and beach-blessed shoreline.

START WITH CARNAVAL

It's easy to understand why Carnaval in Cádiz is Spain's biggest social event of the year. Centered on Shrove Tuesday in February or early March, it brings tens of thousands of extravagantly costumed revelers to its streets for 10 days of parades, street food, fireworks, singing and dancing. The revelry is held to the musical accompaniment of over 300 local *murgas* (bands): *coros*, lute- and mandolin-brandishing groups of 30; *comprasas*, marching bands, 15-strong; *chirigotas*, jokers singing satirical songs in Cádiz's bars; and *illegales*, small, anarchic bands composed of families and friends. Pack a costume, book your accommodation months in advance, and prepare for little sleep.

EAT AND DRINK; DRINK AND EAT

Just because Cádiz itself is not part of the so-called Sherry Triangle – the Spanish region producing highly prized fortified wines – you needn't miss out on tasting some choice tipples. Catch one of

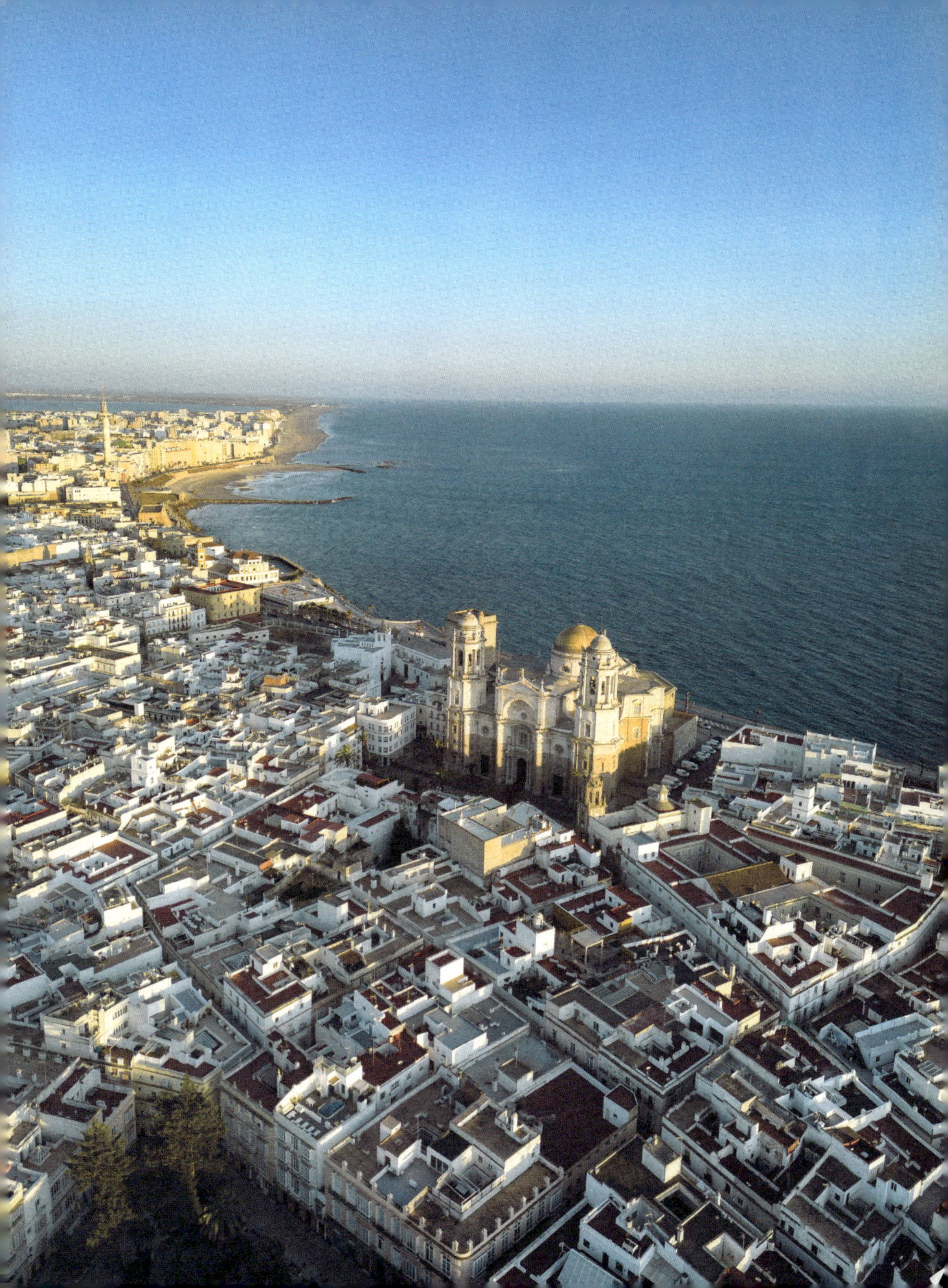

TOP PLACES / CÁDIZ

the many ferries across the bay to El Puerto and opt for a six-wine tasting at the intimate, 1838-founded Bodegas Gutiérrez Colosía. The cellars here are stacked three barrels deep, heady with the sweet aroma of maturing sherry. Or keep it local with Cádiz's atmospheric 1930s tavern, Taberna La Manzanilla, where you can sample Manzanilla, Oloroso and Amontillado directly from barrels.

And what's good wine without good food to accompany it? Cádiz's dining scene is among Andalucía's best, ranging from traditional tapas – check out the old-school tapas bars clustered around the former fishing quarter of Barrio de la Viña – to contemporary fusion, best found around Plaza Candelaria and Plaza de la Catedral.

Start your day by queuing up with the *gaditanos* (Cádiz locals) for the freshest churros at the marketside Churrería La Guapa stall, dipping them into drinking chocolate thick enough to stand a spoon in. Perhaps treat yourself to a meal at Sonámbulo, typical of Cádiz restaurants that serve farm- and sea-to-table dishes. Try a bowl of the *salmorejo* (a creamy tomato soup served cold, not unlike gazpacho); a dish made with tuna caught using the traditional Almadraba technique; or grilled artichoke with Iberian dewlap (a cut of meat from the neck of an Iberian pig). These meals celebrate the best of ingredients from the Cádiz province.

Come evening, elbow your way into the perpetually busy Casa Manteca, its 1950s interior plastered with bullfighting memorabilia. Shout your tapas order to the waiter, then wait for the *chicharrones* (pork scratchings) and local cheese with asparagus marmalade (served on pieces of waxed paper) to be passed to you by fellow diners.

Left to right: Try fresh-off-the-boat seafood snacks like *chopitos* (fried baby squid), a Cádiz specialty; Dining alfresco in the Barrio de la Viña, known for its terrific tapas bars.

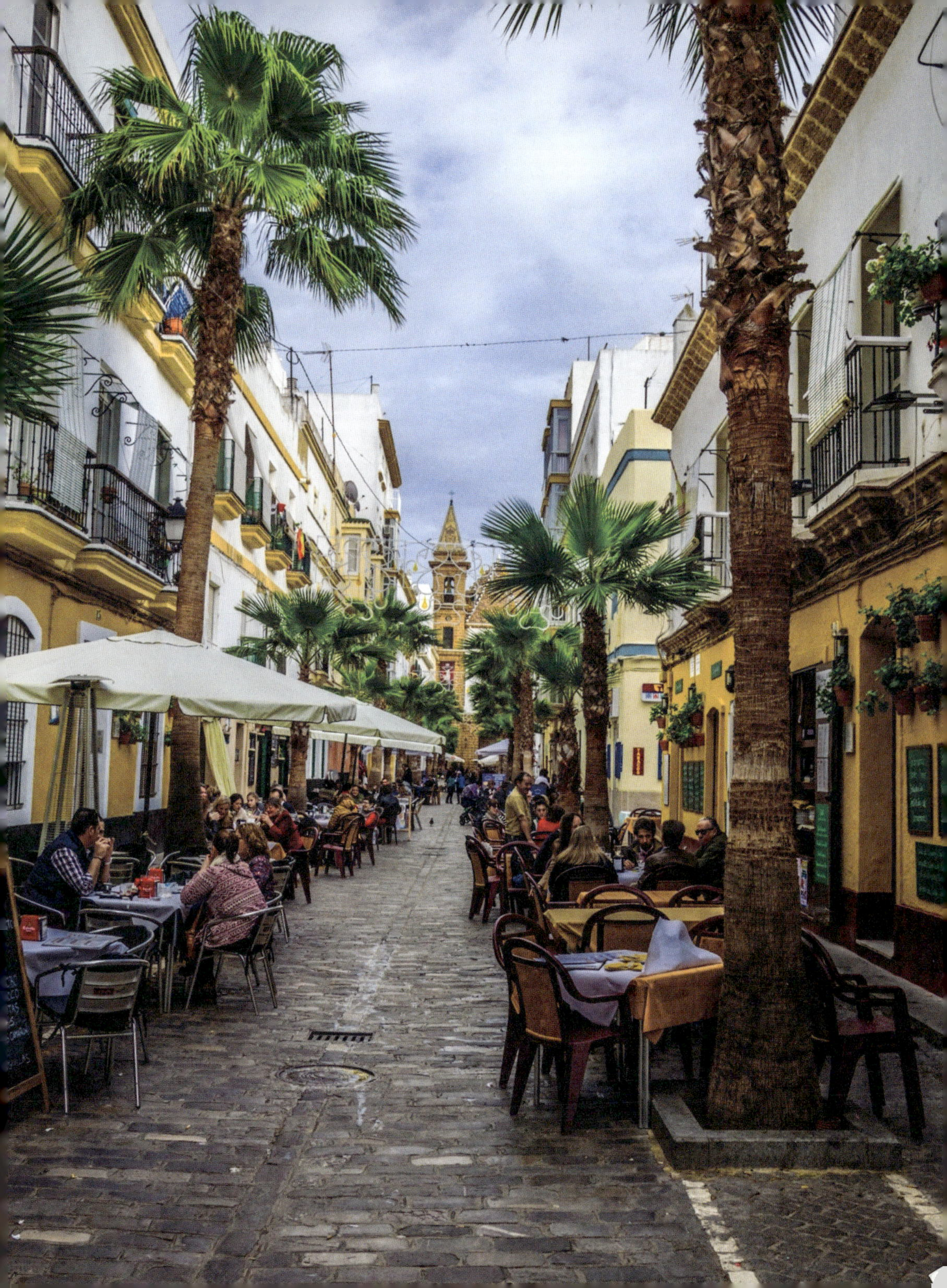

Clockwise from right: Be wowed by live flamenco in Cádiz's *peñas* (clubs); Visit Museo De Cádiz to see another side of the city's culture; Tending nets in the Cádiz Province town of Barbate; The mock-Moorish bathhouse on Cádiz's Playa de la Caleta.

MOST MEMORABLE MOMENT

Watch a flamenco performance with local aficionados at the cavernous Peña Flamenca La Perla. Alternatively, opt for a more touristy (yet no less impassioned) *tablao* (choreographed flamenco show) at the intimate La Cava. When dancers leave the audience spellbound with their footwork, express your appreciation by shouting 'Viva la máquina escribir!' (Long live the typewriter!).

TOP PLACES / CÁDIZ

COME FOR THE TAPAS, STAY FOR THE FLAMENCO
The night needn't end there. Along with Jerez de la Frontera and Seville, Cádiz is one of the cornerstones of flamenco – the unique musical genre rooted in the 15th-century arrival of the Roma people in Spain, and fused with Jewish and Moorish musical elements. The city's *peñas* (clubs) are among the best places in Spain to witness the passionate spectacle of live flamenco. The traditional vocal style of *canto jondo* (which literally means 'deep song') is accompanied by complex, rhythmic *jaleo* (clapping) and improvisation (*toque*) by guitar players, which matches with the mesmerizing staccato footwork of dancers and draws appreciative shouts of 'Ole!' from the audience.

Flamenco aside, Cádiz epitomizes Andalucía's cultural complexity, its fortunes shaped by its relationship with the sea and by its millennia-long history as an important port city – first for the Phoenicians, Carthaginians and Romans, and later for imperial Spain. Remnants of ancient civilizations are all over Cádiz: wander between the excavated remains of the Teatro Romano amphitheater, which once seated 10,000 spectators; the Phoenician marble sarcophagi at the excellent Museo de Cádiz; and the subterranean Yacimiento Arqueológico Gadir, where you can take transparent walkways above the atmospherically lit remains of Phoenician and Roman streets.
–*Anna Kaminski*

BEST IN TRAVEL 2026 / 37

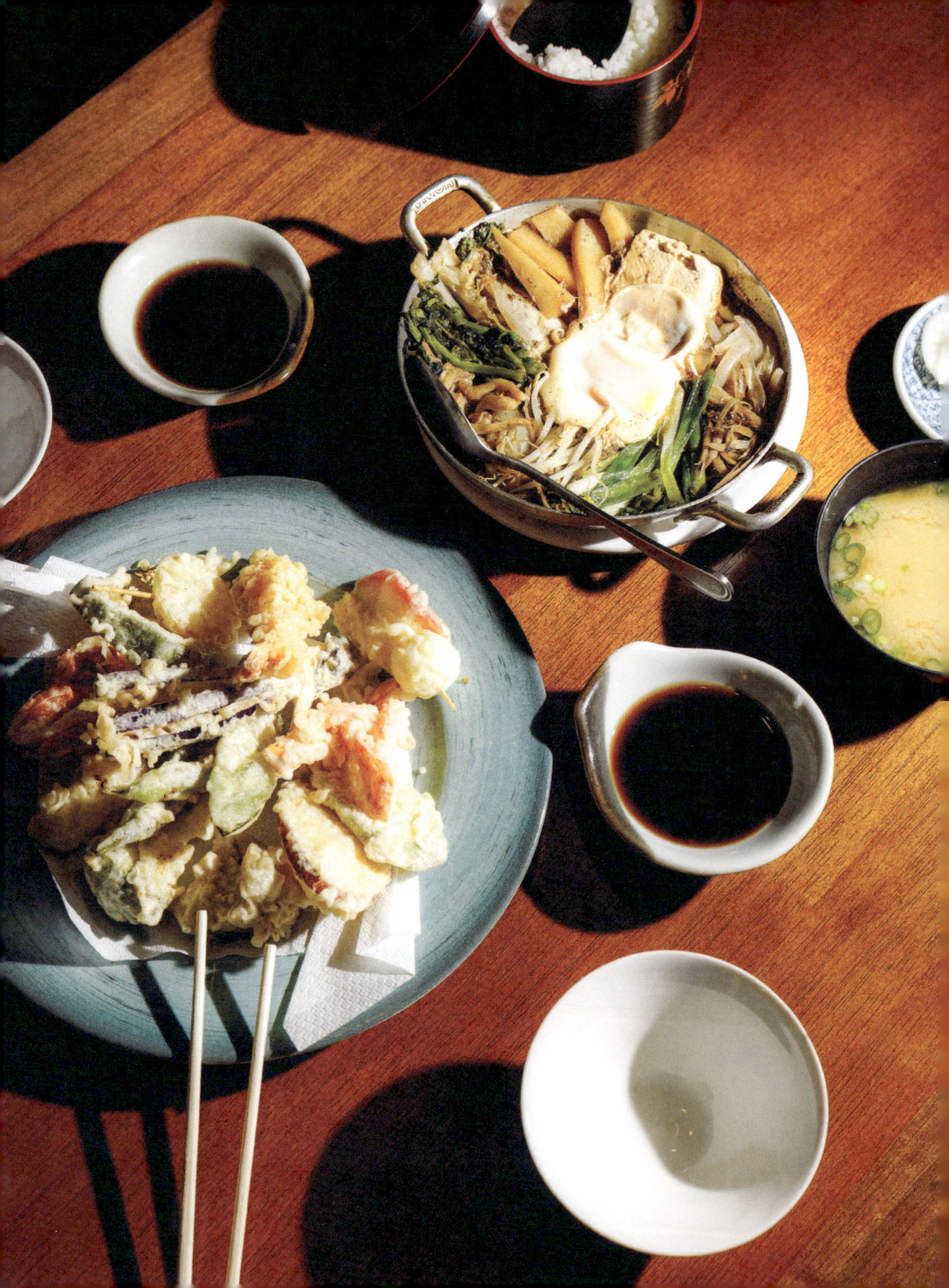

TOP PLACES / LIBERDADE, SÃO PAULO

LIBERDADE

SÃO PAULO, BRAZIL

Left to right: Savor the flavors of a Japanese meal at Liberdade's New Mimatsu; Templo Lohan, a Liberdade cultural hub for the Japanese-Brazilian community.

BEST FOR
A crossroads of culture and cuisine in Latin America

Red lanterns mark the boundaries of São Paulo's 'Little Japan', where Paulistanos enjoy diverse cuisines and shop for everything from katana sabers to Korean skincare. Liberdade's evolution from Japanese enclave to pan-Asian hub offers a new dimension to Brazil's cultural tapestry, and highlights the history of the largest Japanese community outside of Japan.

EXPLORE ASIA, IN BRAZIL

It takes some grit for travelers to really get to know São Paulo, but in the enclave of Asian cultures that is Liberdade, the city comes alive amidst the backdrop of Black- and Japanese-Brazilian history. About 60,000 people live in this cluster of blocks south of Praça de Sé, and over 600,000 Japanese-Brazilians live in the São Paulo metropolis, but the wider Japanese community expands across the country, with more than two million Japanese descendants living throughout Brazil.

When Japanese immigrants began arriving in São Paulo in the late 19th century, the land around Liberdade was one of the most inexpensive areas to live, as it was once the site of the gallows where public executions were carried out. A memorial to

BEST IN TRAVEL 2026 / 39

MOST MEMORABLE MOMENT

If you're a fan of checking out local grocery stores when traveling, you'll be delighted to know that Liberdade has perhaps the best selection of options in São Paulo. South America meets Asia in these aisles, stacked with imported snacks alongside rare combos that mix classic Brazilian ingredients into Japanese sweets and salty snacks.

40 / BEST IN TRAVEL 2026

TOP PLACES / LIBERDADE, SÃO PAULO

executed enslaved Africans still stands in the form of the Capela dos Aflitos (Chapel of the Afflicted). It was once an area many avoided, but the growing population of Japanese workers – whose stories are told in the Museu Histórico da Imigração Japonesa (Historical Museum of Japanese Immigration) – have made a home here.

If it's a weekend, go straight to Praça de Liberdade, where street-food delights beckon at Feira da Liberdade: *yakisoba* (a stir-fry noodle dish) and *taiyaki* (a fish-shaped cone filled with soft-serve ice cream) alongside *acarajé* (African-inspired fritters).

Follow the red lampposts across the overpass to the main Torii gate, but give yourself plenty of time to detour in and out of shops and narrow multi-level shopping centers like Galeria Liberdade, where you can sift through mountains of anime and pop-culture merch.

BELLY UP FOR AN UNEXPECTED AND DELICIOUS ADVENTURE

Stands selling bubble tea, *onigiri* (rice balls) and *takoyaki* (fritters) will tempt you, too, but try to save room for a full Japanese meal like the *omurice* (omelette-covered rice) at New Mimatsu, or a bowl of ramen paired with a 'sakerinha' (sake caipirinha) at Lamen Kazu.

Take your time scouring the side roads for street art, or find your way to one of the two small public gardens: the Jardim Oriental and Largo do Pólvora. Even more peaceful and private than those, Templo Lohan is a center for Buddhism and martial arts that offers tours.

At night, catch a live show at Cine Joia, housed in a former Japanese movie theater, or go for a karaoke night at Sakeria Liberdade in the Nikkey Palace Hotel.

–Jamie Ditaranto

Clockwise from top left: Seek out Asian treats in local shops; Sample Japanese food at a Liberdade diner; Inside the Jardim Oriental; Statue of samba pioneer Deolinda Madre on Praça da Liberdade.

BEST IN TRAVEL 2026 / 41

TOP PLACES / SARDINIA

SARDINIA

ITALY

BEST FOR
A wild island escape

TOP PLACES / SARDINIA

Famed for its turquoise waters and rugged coastline, Sardinia has a lot more to offer than just stunning beaches. From ancient Nuragic fortresses and protected minority languages to newly developed sustainable-tourism trails for cyclists and hikers, the island's rich history, culture and natural diversity make it a year-round destination.

DIG INTO A CULTURAL CACHE

Italians have long known Sardinia as a dreamy summer destination: the azure waters lapping the 1118-mile (1800km) shoreline are jaw-dropping. While that's no secret, the lesser-known fact about Sardinia is that its natural beauty is matched in depth and diversity by its cultural profile. An island sandwiched between Corsica to the north and Tunisia to the south, Sardinia has rugged terrain and is sparsely inhabited. With a current population of roughly 1.6 million, the island is about the size of New Jersey, USA, making it the second-largest in the Mediterranean after Sicily. However, the population increases dramatically between June and September, when the majority of its 14 million annual visitors arrive to take advantage of the abundant sunshine this land is blessed with.

Travelers who have visited Italy before will quickly notice that Sardinia's character stands apart from that of the mainland, and proudly so. This is a place with a strong sense of identity, shaped by history and customs you won't find elsewhere. Sardinia's interior is dotted with thousands of mysterious stone fortresses known as *nuraghe*, built near the end of the Bronze Age. Sardinia's only UNESCO World Heritage site is the Su Nuraxi complex, centered

Left: Explore wild and wonderful landscapes on Isola dell'Asinara, offshore of Sardinia's northwest coast and now a national park.

BEST IN TRAVEL 2026 / 43

TOP PLACES / SARDINIA

around a *nuraghe* that was constructed more than 3500 years ago. Cone-shaped archaeological treasures found only in Sardinia, *nuraghe* tell the story of the obscure Nuragic civilization, a people who inhabited the island until the late 6th century BCE, when Carthaginians began their conquest of the region. Scholars are still debating whether the title of 'Italy's first city' should go to the early Phoenician colony on Sant'Antioco, an islet off the island's southwest, rather than Rome.

Take a trip to Sant'Antioco's archaeological museum (or the one in Cagliari, the regional capital) to make this ancient history puzzle your own.

But don't be fooled: Sardinia's rich and intricate past isn't confined to museum halls or archaeological sites. Here, culture is alive, woven into daily habits. Book in at one of the many *agriturismi* (farm stays) to immerse yourself in the lifestyle that has famously made the island's rural communities part of the world's 'Blue Zones', known for the high concentration of centenarians. Feast on Sardinian pasta such as *malloreddus* (small, ridged semolina gnocchi), *culurgiones* (potato, cheese and mint ravioli) or the rare *filindeu* (semolina threads); bite into a slice of organic pecorino cheese (or if you can find it and have a strong stomach, the now-illegal *casu marzu*, in which maggots' digestive juices are used to soften the cheese). And don't forget to toast with a glass of Cannonau, the island's potent red wine.

EXPLORE A VAST CATALOG OF OUTDOOR ADVENTURE
Even if you dedicate your time to nature alone, you'll find that the island changes drastically depending on where you go. To the northeast, in and around

Left to right: Sardinian specialty pastas include *culurgiones* – ravioli stuffed with potato, cheese and mint; Sardinia's superlative shoreline.

44 / BEST IN TRAVEL 2026

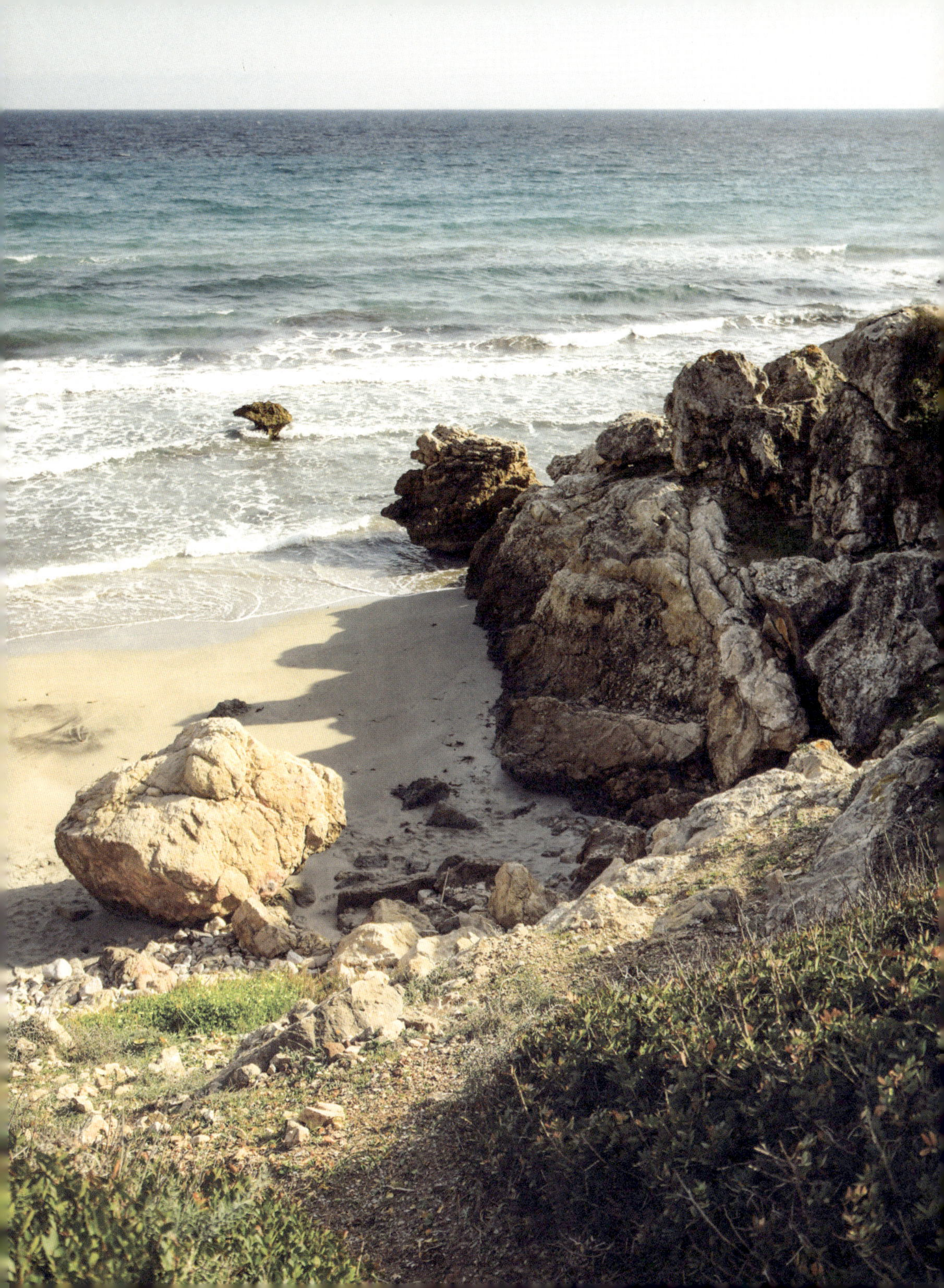

Clockwise from right: Wild donkeys roam Isola dell'Asinara; Catch masked masqueraders at folk festivals in small towns like Mamoiada; The ancient compound of Nuraghe Su Nuraxi; Sardinian *casu marzu* cheese, a specialty for gutsy gourmands.

DON'T LEAVE WITHOUT…

Taking in a folk festival. Forget about Venice's Carnevale and head to the small town of Mamoiada where every year, on January 17, the eerie procession of Mamuthones takes place. Covered in furs and hiding behind dark wooden masks, these spine-chilling figures maintain a tradition believed to date back to the Middle Ages, whose exact origin remains a mystery.

46 / BEST IN TRAVEL 2026

TOP PLACES / SARDINIA

Porto Cervo, and along the coastline of the Gallura region and out to the protected archipelago of La Maddalena, luxury resorts, yacht clubs and exclusive venues have attracted opulence-thirsty VIPs since the 1970s. Offshore of Sardinia's northwest corner, you'll find the wild Isola dell'Asinara, a fascinating national park that was once a maximum security prison; it's now an oasis for white donkeys and horses, and is uninhabited by humans most of the year.

Diving, snorkeling and caving opportunities abound around the coast. There's plenty to do outdoors off the water, too, especially in early spring and autumn. Sustainability has guided investments in tourism infrastructure in recent years, and long-distance hiking itineraries – such as the 310-mile (500km) Cammino di Santa Barbara – are gaining popularity thanks to improved mapping and accommodation options. Construction of a 715-mile (1150km) network of cycling paths, known as the Ciclovia della Sardegna, has just begun this year, promising to be one of Europe's most thrilling two-wheel journeys.

Don't be discouraged by the crowds and prices in popular hotspots in July and August. Sardinia's charm hides at the end of the roads less traveled, in gestures of genuine hospitality, and in natural wonders that shine outside the peak holiday season.
–Angelo Zinna

BEST IN TRAVEL 2026 / 47

TOP PLACES / THEODORE ROOSEVELT NP

THEODORE ROOSEVELT NAT

USA

TOP PLACES / THEODORE ROOSEVELT NP

BEST FOR
Seeing where vast prairies meet open sky

Visitors to US national parks can avoid the crowds at this ravishing North Dakota wonderland of geology, history and natural splendor. In 2026, the park will tie into the newly opened Theodore Roosevelt Presidential Library, which aims to 'show what we can learn from, not about' one of America's most influential leaders – the man who laid the foundation for the country's National Park Service.

SEE WHAT ROOSEVELT SAW

That the vast prairies and painted canyons of North Dakota are preserved in the name of Theodore Roosevelt is the perfect tribute. A great American naturalist, Roosevelt served as the 26th US president and spent several years here. During his first visit in 1883, the native New Yorker came to learn the terrain, hunt bison and ranch cattle. A year later, in 1884, Roosevelt lost his mother and new wife on the very same day (Valentine's Day), and spent the next two years here.

Roosevelt was drawn to the spellbinding serenity of the Great Plains, where herds of roaming bison and prairie-dog 'metropolises' (networks of underground burrows) meet windswept buttes and Little Missouri River gorges. It's a geologists' wonderland, with colorful rock layers, petrified forests, hoodoos (tall, thin rock spires) and other bizarre natural monuments that began forming 65 million years ago.

Left: River Bend Overlook in the hiking-trail-laced North Unit of Theodore Roosevelt National Park.

BEST IN TRAVEL 2026 / 49

MOST MEMORABLE MOMENT

Adjust your sleep schedule for dark-sky stargazing to see planets, constellations, meteor showers and maybe even the aurora borealis. The park's annual Dakota Nights Astronomy Festival in September welcomes volunteers, who can look through mighty telescopes to tour the night sky in search of astronomical wonders.

50 / BEST IN TRAVEL 2026

TOP PLACES / THEODORE ROOSEVELT NP

A NEW WINDOW TO THE PAST

In time for America's semiquincentennial on July 4, 2026, Theodore Roosevelt National Park – the country's only national park named for an individual – will be accompanied by the new Theodore Roosevelt Presidential Library, located just outside the park's South Unit and home to immersive galleries and displays of personal artifacts that invite you into TR's life. This entirely sustainable 'living building' features an earthen roof sloped into the hill, which visitors can ascend to view the surrounding Badlands. Guests can also stroll a mile-long (1.6km) boardwalk loop to soak up the grandeur of land and sky. This ties into several longer paths as well as to the rugged, 144-mile-long (232km) Maah Daah Hey Trail, established by the Mandan-Hidatsa Nation.

The national park occupies more than 110 sq miles (285 sq km) of southwest North Dakota in three areas. From the cowboy town of Medora, enter its South Unit and hit the robust Visitor Center. Nearby is TR's Maltese Cross Cabin, the tiny log structure where he stayed in 1883. Drive on to reach mesmerizing overlooks, trails and wildlife-rich valleys. The North Unit is about an hour's drive from Medora, home to rustic campgrounds and panoramic wilderness trails.

The Elkhorn Ranch Unit is an hour-long drive from any direction, mostly on a gravel road – though it's an easier journey than TR's five-hour horseback route from Medora. Elkhorn is the quiet part of the park where the then-future president lived from 1884, but only the foundations of his house remain. Still, its location at the base of foothills, near a bend in a river, summons solace. For Roosevelt, who embodied action and determination, this grassy pocket of the Great Plains offered a simple, contemplative break – the same natural gift it gives today.
–Kelsy Chauvin

Clockwise from top left: Medora, gateway to TRNP; Inside Roosevelt's Maltese Cross Cabin; The park's wonders include wind-sculpted hoodoos; Bison roam North Dakota's Great Plains.

BEST IN TRAVEL 2026 / 51

TOP PLACES / RÉUNION

RÉUNION

Despite being unlike anywhere else on Earth, the Indian Ocean island of Réunion has stayed under the global travel radar. Packed into a land area of just 965 sq miles (2500 sq km) are 400 microclimates and maybe half as many endemic species, across a breathtaking natural backdrop. The Réunionnais motto – '*Florebo quocumque ferar*' (I will flourish wherever I'm carried) – is mirrored in the island's unique multicultural Creole heritage and spectacular landscapes: UNESCO-listed mountain ranges, deep amphitheater-like valleys and a legendary volcano.

Photographs by Romain Philippon; Text by Fabienne Fong Yang

TOP PLACES / RÉUNION

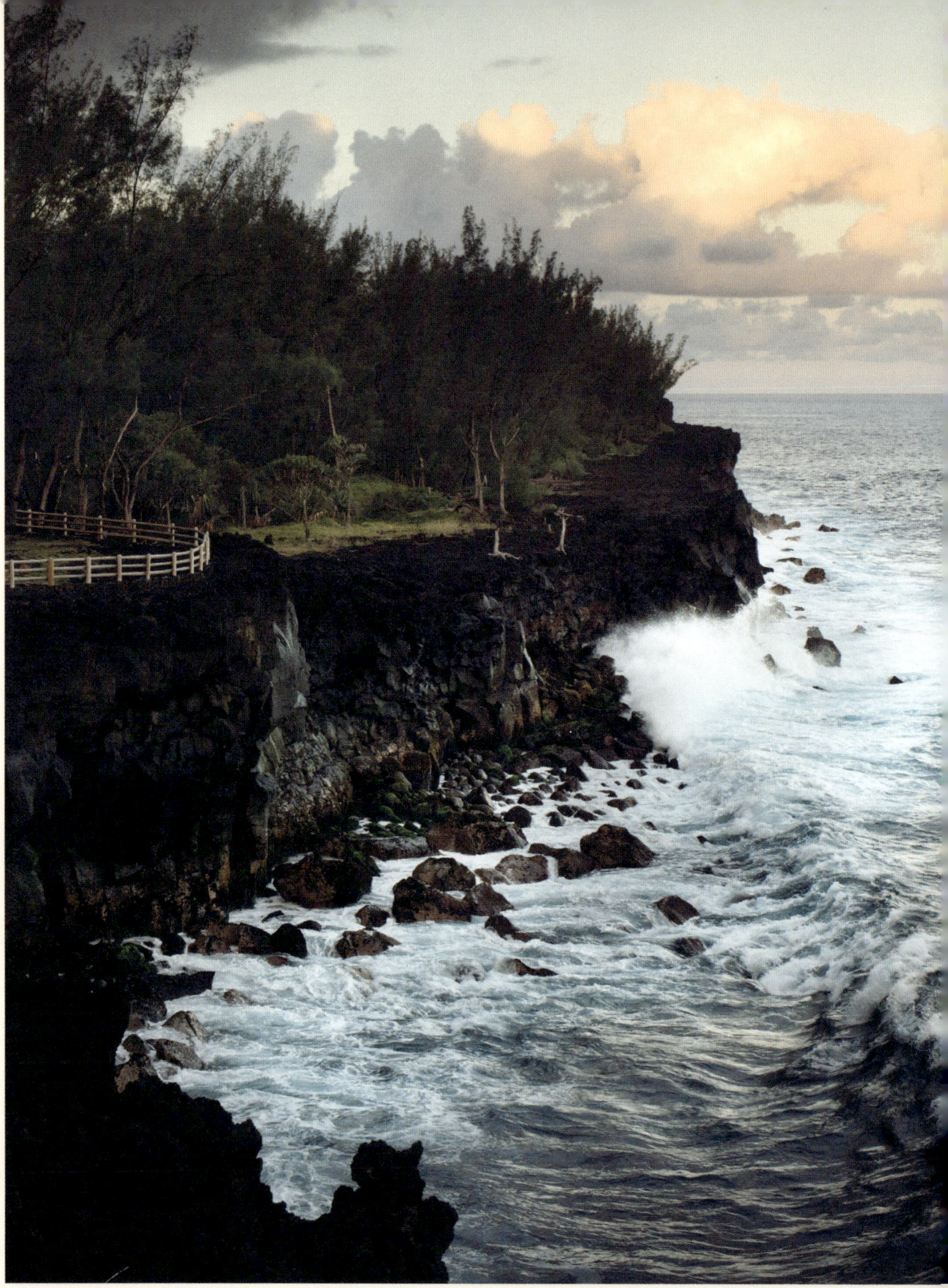

TOP PLACES / RÉUNION

Previous spread: The deep, amphitheater-like Mafate is one of Réunion's three central cirques, rugged caldera valleys born from the collapse of ancient volcanos. Each offers a different experience: untouched wilderness in Mafate, rich history in Salazie's Hell-Bourg Creole village, breathtaking ridges and waterfalls in Cilaos.

This spread: Réunion's natural experiences are exceptional. Take a morning trip to stroll lava cliffs on Cap Méchant's coastal path or visit active volcano Piton de la Fournaise, dive into one of many waterfall basins in the afternoon, and sip a cocktail on a white-sand beach by evening.

Hike into remote Mafate cirque, where family-run guesthouses in Creole mountain villages welcome trekkers with home-cooked meals. Fall asleep under the peaceful watch of the Southern Cross constellation, and wake to resident roosters welcoming the rising sun.

Blending African, Malagasian, Indian, Chinese and European traditions, Réunion's richly diverse Creole culture is celebrated in festivals such as November's Dipavali, the Hindu celebration of light.

BEST IN TRAVEL 2026 / 55

TOP PLACES / RÉUNION

Outdoor enthusiasts adore Réunion for its amazing hiking trails, which range from family-friendly to legendarily tough. The most challenging tracks form the route of the world-famous Grand Raid ultramarathon, staged here each October and taking in all three of Réunion's rugged cirques.

Visitors can dip in to the island's trails on routes like the Îlet à Malheur in Mafate. Accessible only on foot or by helicopter, this wild and wonderful valley is named after the leader of a group of escaped enslaved people who made it their resistance camp, protected and hidden by the lush wilderness.

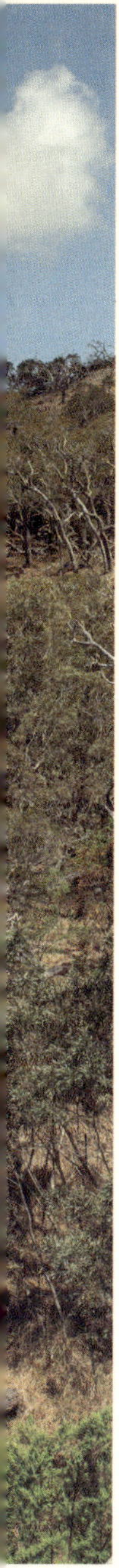

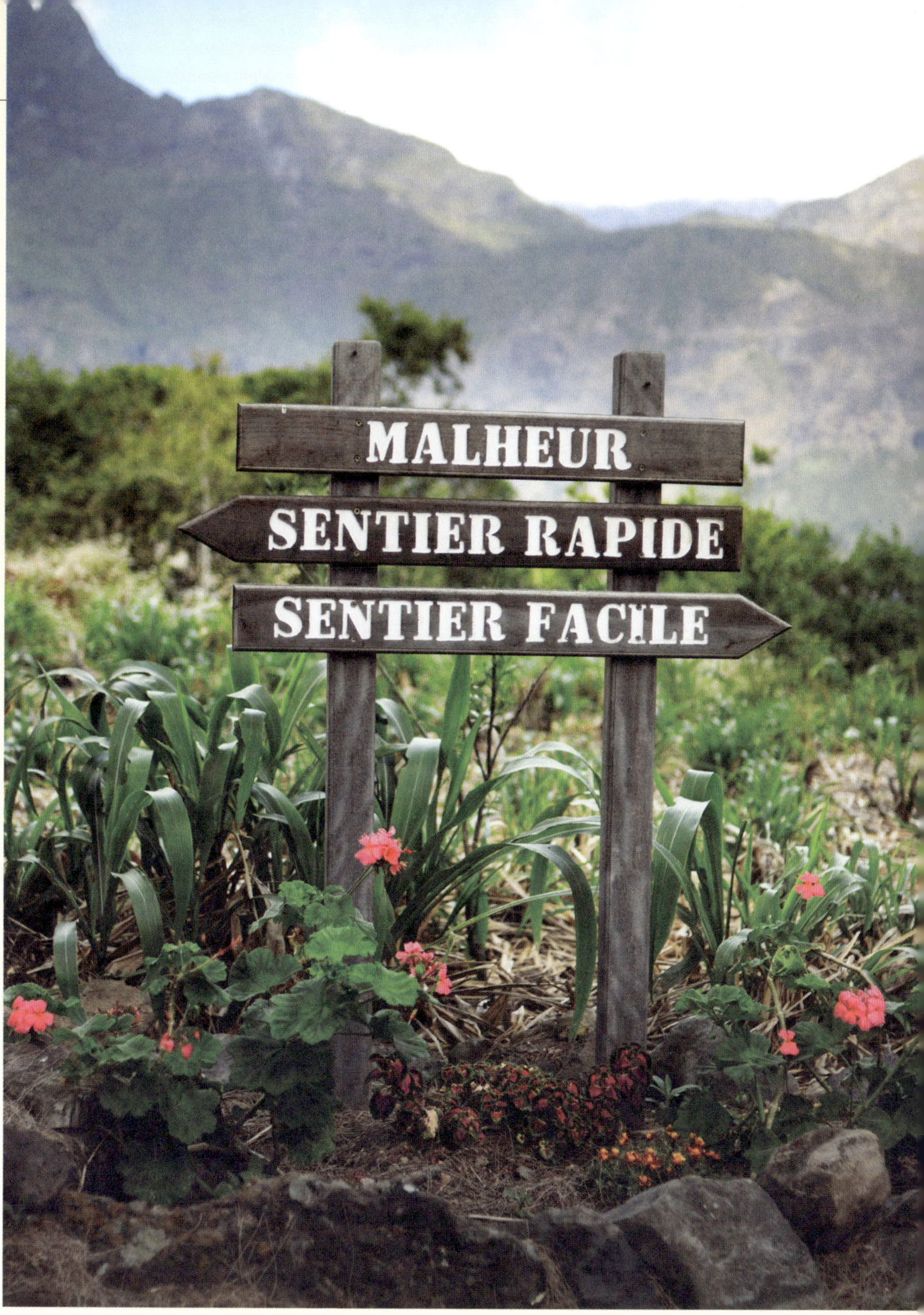
MALHEUR
SENTIER RAPIDE
SENTIER FACILE

TOP PLACES / RÉUNION

58 / BEST IN TRAVEL 2026

In this melting-pot island, it's common to see a Catholic church spire rise near a mosque's minaret, and a mesmerizing, brightly colored Hindu temple opposite a Chinese pagoda. Festivals like Dipavali are a highlight of Réunion's cultural calendar.

Réunionnais kitchens cook up *caris*, traditional dishes of meat or fish, slow-cooked cooked in a spicy sauce: look for *cari poulet* (chicken), *rougail saucisse* (pork sausage) and *cabri massalé* (Indian masala goat). And don't leave without sampling market-fresh fruit and vegetables; Réunion's Victoria pineapples are especially sweet.

This seafront Le Barachois park in Réunion's capital, St-Denis, is a picture-perfect place to catch the sea breeze or a superlative sunset.

TOP PLACES / TUNISIA

TUNISIA

Tunisia is the smallest country in North Africa, but it delivers an impressive cultural punch, effortlessly condensing Indigenous Amazigh, Jewish, Roman, Islamic and French influences in its UNESCO-heritage medinas, antiquity sites, seaside resorts, offshore islands and picturesque desert oases. And the solid road and rail infrastructure means it's easy to enjoy it all.

BEST FOR
A desert and coast adventure

Left to right, from above: Troglodyte buildings in Tataouine, southern Tunisia; Head inland to discover fascinating small towns like Testour, in Tunisia's north.

EXPERIENCE THE WAKE OF A CULTURAL SHIFT

These are interesting times in Tunisia, a country that feels suspended between an old world of romantic Roman ruins, vintage beach resorts and dated 2000s autocracy and a new world of possibilities birthed by the 2011 Arab Spring. That social upheaval opened a door for young Tunisian entrepreneurs and creatives to realise a new vision of the country – one that surfaces in its rich Arab, African and European history, its fusion food, its evolving craft traditions, and its vibrant contemporary music scene. The result is a growing buzz around Tunisia, which attracted a record-breaking 10 million tourists in 2024.

Many of them headed to the country's beautiful beaches, where the fish is always fresh on your plate and jasmine scents the night air. But beyond these honeypots, Tunisia has a wealth of history and an incredible variety of landscapes to occupy weeks of travel. Tunis is fashioning itself into a relaxed, multiethnic, modern Arab capital, and the coast is

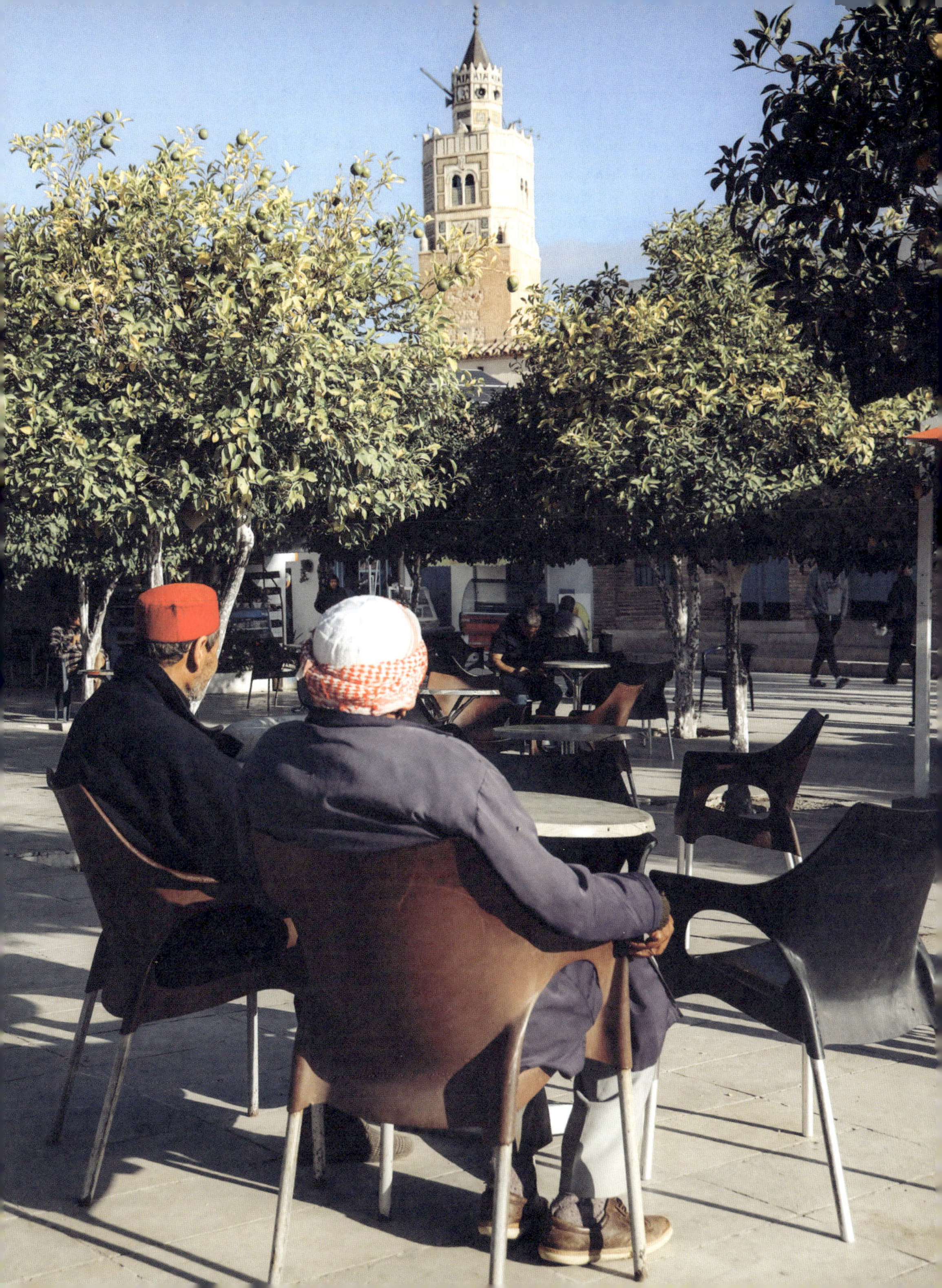

TOP PLACES / TUNISIA

dotted with period medinas, each with its own character. Around them, you'll find lakes teeming with pink flamingos, surprising oak and pine forests, sun-struck golden plains covered in olive trees, and vineyards where you can sip spicy wines. Further south, weathered mountains harbor ancient Amazigh villages that served as surreal locations for Hollywood movies – and you'll pinch yourself at the sight of the immense Saharan dunes that disappear deep into Africa across the southern border.

REVEL IN THE PLAYFUL BLEND OF OLD AND NEW

Landing in Tunis, find your way to the historic mansion of Dar Ben Gacem, buried in the 7th-century UNESCO-listed medina. There, explore a labyrinth of souks, where craftspeople still hand-make red Fez hats and handloom textiles. Then, visit the romantic ruins of Carthage, Rome's one-time rival; and the Bardo Museum, housed in a splendid palace built under the Hafsids and extended by the Ottomans in the 18th century, and holding the world's largest collection of Roman mosaics. In summer, the Festival of Carthage hosts events in the L'Acropolium, a deconsecrated Moorish-Gothic cathedral built by the French in 1884, and the music cranks up at Gammarth's alfresco nightclubs.

The woodsy headland of Cap Bon sits east of Tunis, covered in fragrant cypresses and looking out to Sicily, just 100 miles (160km) across the water. In nearby Nabeul's thriving food market, the glossy olives, bright oranges and silvery sardines highlight how closely knit Mediterranean cultures are (although the town's famous spice, harissa, is uniquely good). It's wise to eat here, then seek out a glass of deep-red Syrah at the Domaine Neferis vineyard, which continues a 2000-year-old

Left to right: Homemade flatbread for sale from a medina doorway; The peachy beachy view of Monastir, near Sousse, from its magnificent *ribat* (coastal fort).

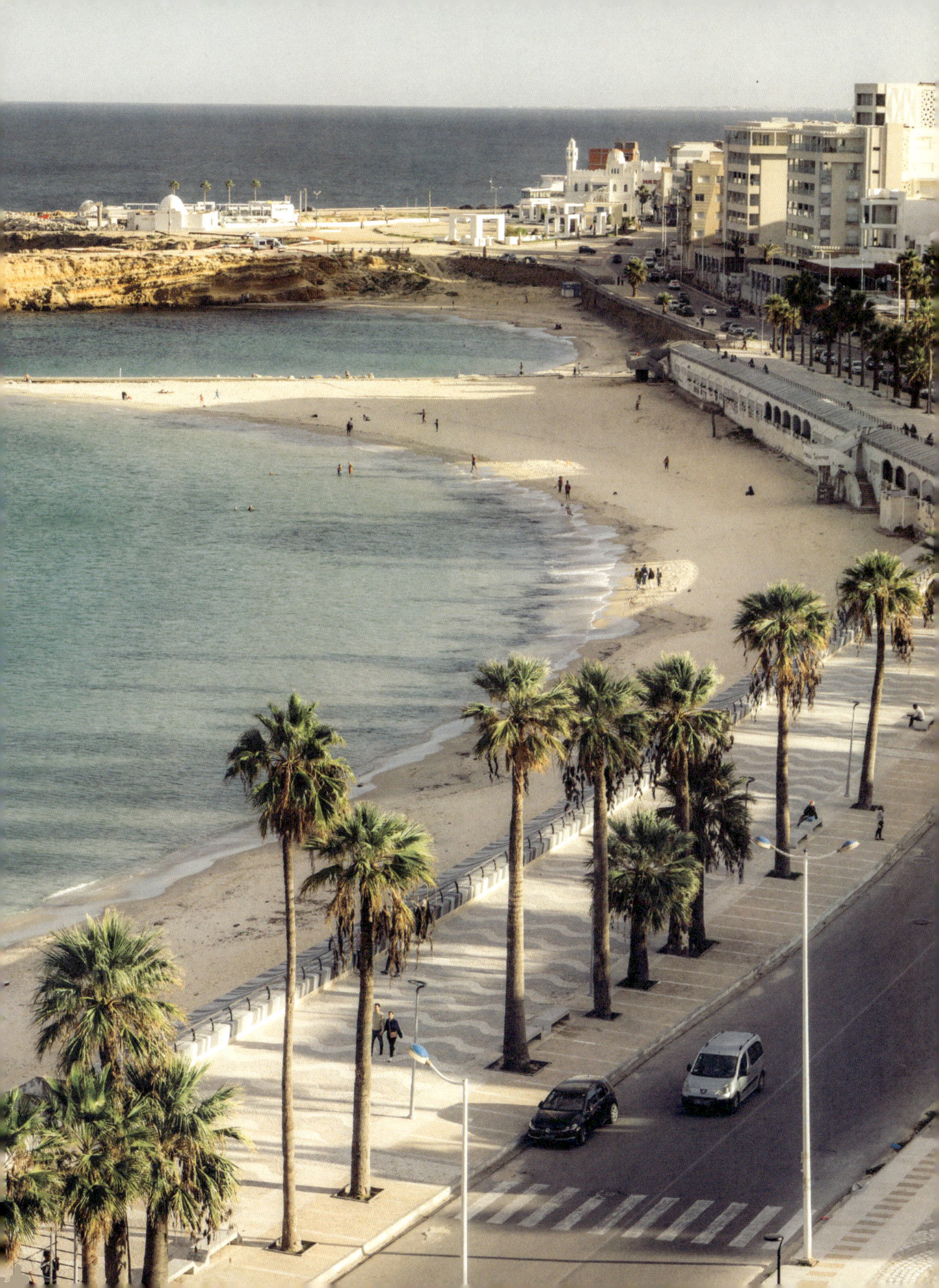

DON'T LEAVE WITHOUT...

Booking an immersive culinary journey with Sawa Taste of Tunisia to experience cooking classes, market tours and seasonal tastings. With North African and Sicilian heritage, Lamia Temimi is a fabulous guide to Tunisia's complex fusion cuisine, which blends Arab, African, Mediterranean and Jewish influences. The four-day Foundouks & Souqs of Tunis tour is a great place to start.

TOP PLACES / TUNISIA

tradition of winemaking. For more drama, there's the stony, storybook kasbah of El Kef, which rises above the Roman ruins of Dougga; or, swap those for hiking in Ichkeul National Park, a UNESCO-protected forest harboring unique North African freshwater lakes where water buffalo roam.

SWING BETWEEN STUNNING COASTAL RESORTS AND MYTHICAL MOUNTAIN SCENES

More famous, though, are the seductive sandy beaches that lie south of Tunis, lined with frosty white holiday resorts such as Hammamet, where Sophia Loren and friends once partied. You can do the same at bougie escapes like La Badira, but explore further and you'll discover Christian catacombs and an 11th-century kasbah in Sousse, and an idyllic nature reserve on the Kerkennah Islands. It's also well worth seeking out North Africa's most holy Islamic city, Kairouan, and the almost perfectly preserved Roman colosseum of El Djem. Most surprising, perhaps, is the Jewish-influenced island of Djerba, where pilgrims still flock to celebrate the 33rd day of Passover at El Ghriba, one of the oldest synagogues in the world.

There's no doubt, summer on the coast is a blast, but come fall and winter, turn inland to explore the troglodyte villages of the Dahar Mountains – a landscape so otherworldly it's where the Tatooine (named after the Tunisian city Tataouine) scenes in *Star Wars* were filmed – or venture to the oases of Tozeur and Douz. From here, desert adventures depart into the shifting sand-sea of the Grand Erg Oriental and onto the glittering Chott el Jerid salt pan, while December festivals bring the oases to life with storytelling, traditional music and camel racing in a celebration of desert culture.
–*Paula Hardy*

Clockwise from top left: Rural traditions remain in Tunisia's hinterlands; Desert dunes around Douz; Carthage's ancient Antonine Baths; Try Tunisian specialties like *houria* (carrot salad).

BEST IN TRAVEL 2026 / 65

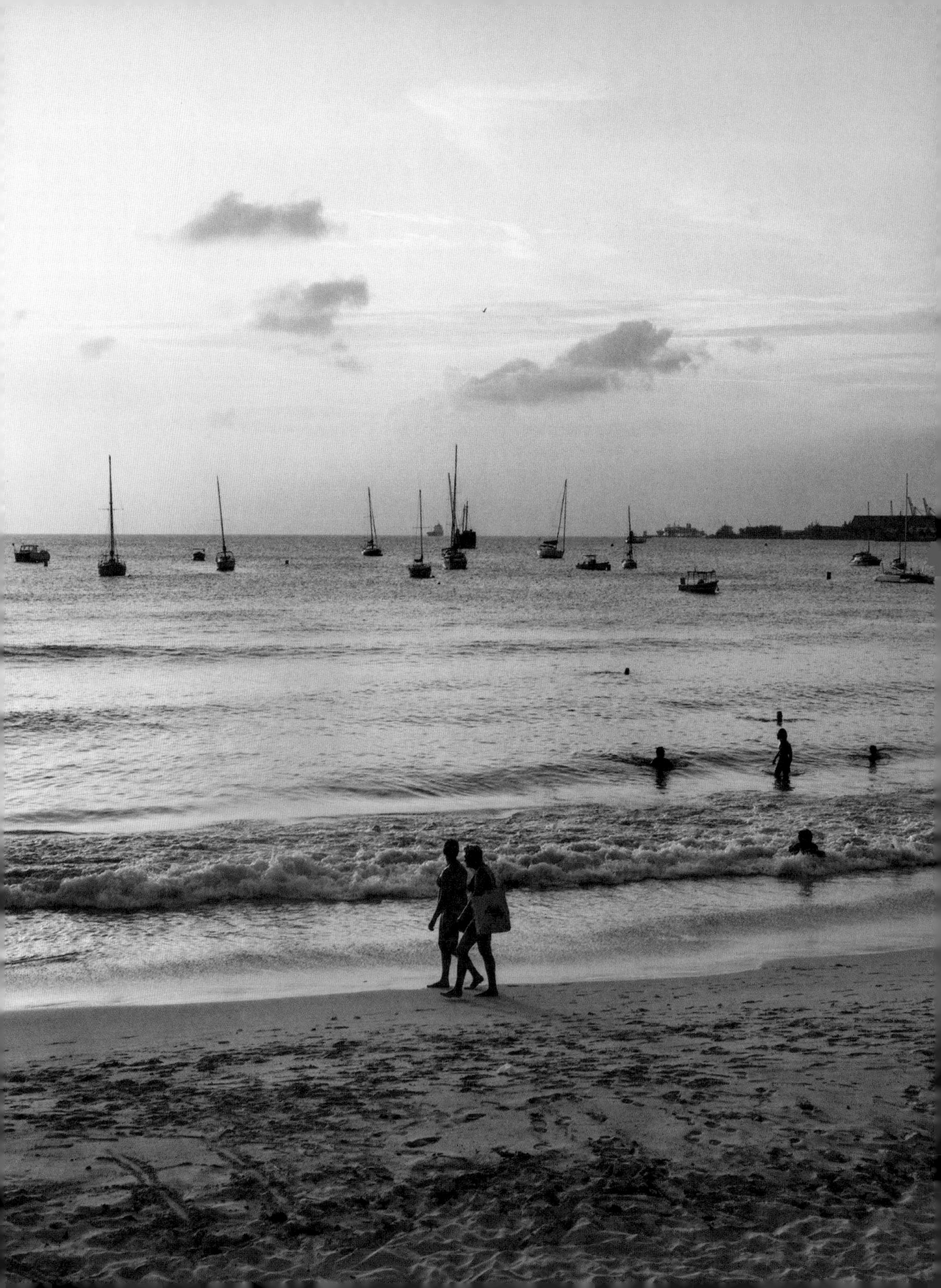

BARBADOS

BEST FOR
Culture, coastlines and celebrations

CARIBBEAN

Barbados is a harmonious symphony of luminous seascapes, sun-drenched adventures and magnetic melodies. Its heartbeat is Crop Over, with revelry and parades originating from the country's sugarcane-producing past. In 2026, Barbados celebrates 60 years of independence with nationwide festivities and the indomitable Bajan pride that defines the island.

TAKE YOURSELF ON A WALKING TOUR

Covering just 166 sq miles (430 sq km), Barbados is small but mighty. It's a panoply of sun-soaked beaches, spirited fishing villages, centuries-old sugar plantations reimagined as rum distilleries, and distinctive cultural landmarks.

The streets hum with energy in Bridgetown, where cricket-loving crowds gather near the legendary Kensington Oval ground and the waterfront sparkles with bobbing catamarans. Getting around is simple in the walkable UNESCO-listed capital. Stroll Broad St, where duty-free shops and local boutiques sit alongside historic landmarks. Head to Chamberlain Bridge for quiet and shaded Independence Sq, and on to the historic Garrison, home to 18th-century military barracks and the Barbados Museum and Historical Society.

Visit Mount Gay Distilleries for a glimpse of the world's oldest commercial rum distillery. Sign up for a tasting to sample the island's

Left to right: Golden hour at Pebbles Beach in the historic capital, Bridgetown; Relax over drinks at one of Barbados' buzzing outdoor bars.

MOST MEMORABLE MOMENT

A visit to Harrison's Cave feels like stepping into a secret passage that reveals the natural artistry hidden beneath Barbados' lush surface. In this enchanting underground world, a canopy of stalactites and stalagmites shape a labyrinth of glittering limestone caverns, laced with gentle streams that reflect the ethereal beauty. It's like something plucked from a fantasy novel.

TOP PLACES / BARBADOS

signature rums or attend a mixology class to master Caribbean-inspired cocktails. On the island's southern edge, Carlisle Bay beckons with pillowy white sands and tranquil turquoise waters, perfect for snorkeling among shipwrecks and spotting sea turtles. After sunset, locals and visitors mingle at the lively Oistins Fish Fry, where 80-plus food stalls dish up flying fish, cornmeal-and-okra cou-cou, jerk chicken and dolphin (mahi-mahi), while raucous domino and card games unfold to the rhythm of calypso music.

SPAN THE COUNTRY'S CULTURAL AND NATURAL WONDERS

Inland, the magical Harrison's Cave tram tour guides visitors through shimmering limestone chambers filled with stalactites and pellucid pools. On the east coast, Bathsheba Beach attracts surfers with its dramatic waves. Nearby, Andromeda Botanic Gardens offers a lush oasis filled with more than 600 plant species believed to have healing properties.

Summertime in Barbados buzzes with Crop Over. The months-long festival is a mélange of music, revelry and colorful costumes. Between February and April, you might even spot humpback whales from the open-deck viewing area at Animal Flower Cave in St Lucy, perched on dramatic cliffs where pools and jagged openings frame breathtaking ocean views.

Barbados is a leader in Caribbean sustainability, with a decades-old eco-policy and a ban on single-use plastics since 2020. In 2026, the recently minted republic celebrates its 60th year of independence, promising an impressive slate of parades, exhibitions and cultural events. Bajans take immense pride in their country and culture. Their slogan promises 'There's never a dull moment', and you can bet on Barbados to deliver.

–Nasha Smith

Clockwise from top left: Limpid waters and white sands at Brownes Beach; Barbados is known for its brilliant bars; Beach cricket at Brownes; Cooking up a seafood storm at Oistins Fish Fry.

TOP PLACES / SOLOMON ISLANDS

SOLOMON ISLANDS

BEST FOR
Island-hopping adventures

Poised to become one of the world's most sought-after surf destinations, the Solomon Islands is shaking off its South Pacific underdog status. Watersports – including snorkeling and diving – may be what puts the country on the tourism map, but travelers who venture away from the coral gardens and white-sand beaches will discover rich biodiversity, incredible hiking and centuries-old cultural traditions.

BEST-KEPT SECRET IN SURFING

Off the coast of the island of Gizo – just a short banana-boat ride from the overwater bungalows of Fatboys Resort – waves crest and plunge toward the shore, creating both left- and right-hand surf breaks. Every weekend, locals gather here for Women Make Waves, a relatively new learn-to-surf program. Most other days, though, breaks are

Left: Head out on the aquamarine ocean in search of the Solomon Islands' rich reefs and superlative surf breaks.

uncrowded – an incredible swell just waiting to be discovered. The same could be said of the rest of the Solomon Islands. Just 26,000 visitors arrive annually, many being WWII history buffs or hardcore birders. But that may change, as surfing is just one of the many outdoor adventures on offer here.

Already considered one of the South Pacific's best diving destinations, the Solomons' reefs cover 2220 sq miles (5750 sq km), and boast the second-highest coral diversity on the planet, with more than 490 known species. Hundreds of WWII ships and aircraft litter the sea floor, creating artificial reefs that teem with life and make it possible to spot sharks, turtles and dugongs. Snorkelers aren't excluded from the action. At Bonegi Beach – a short drive from the country's capital city of Honiara –

TOP PLACES / SOLOMON ISLANDS

wade out to snorkel above the *Kinugawa Maru*, a 442ft-long (135m) Japanese transport ship that was attacked en route to Guadalcanal in November 1942.

A REASON TO LEAVE THE COAST

It's easy to understand why most visitors won't stray far from the crystal-clear waters encircling the country's 992 islands and coral atolls. Still, a journey high into the Solomons' mountainous interiors is worthwhile, revealing rich biodiversity – including 4500 plant species, and 72 endemic bird species like the Makira dwarf kingfisher and the Solomons white-eye – and an even more vibrant cultural past.

The islands were first settled some 4000 years ago by Melanesians. Today, traditions endure, including 63 distinct languages and the trading of shell money. A form of currency made from seashells, it's celebrated annually at the Shell Money Festival on Malaita. Historically, though, these communities weren't built along the coast: prior to the arrival of Christian missionaries in the 19th century, villages were found high in the thick montane rainforest that covers much of islands. There, it was easier to defend against enemy raids. Evidence of the Western Province's ritualistic headhunting past can be seen on a day trip to Skull Island near Munda, where the sun-baked skulls of both conquests and chiefs remain on display.

There's ample opportunity to experience the beauty of the forests. Guests at Imbu Rano on Kolombangara Island – an off-grid lodge favored by visiting scientists – wake to mist drifting across the crater rim of the 5570ft (1698m) Mt Rano. There, they have direct access to hiking trails tackled by fewer than 100 people each year. Local guides are quick

Left to right: Home to nearly 500 coral species, the Solomons' reefs are some of the most biodiverse on Earth; Hike the jungle-swathed interior to secluded waterfalls.

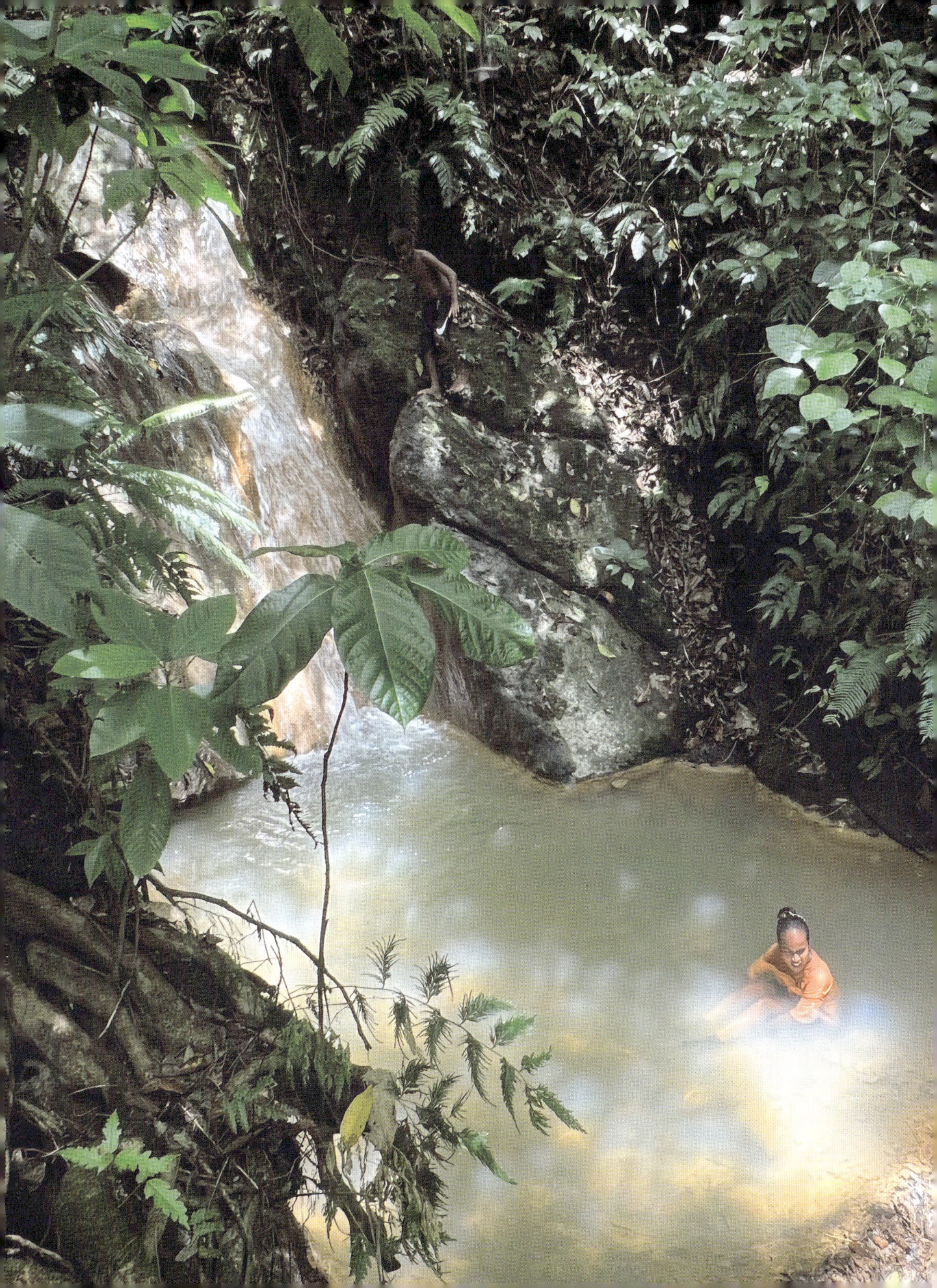

Clockwise from right: The sunken *Kinugawa Maru* is one of many easy-access snorkel sites; Triton's trumpet shell; Savo Island cultural performances offer a window into local traditions; The day's catch of rainbow-hued reef fish.

DON'T LEAVE WITHOUT…

Watching a cultural performance in Kuila village on Savo Island, just off the coast of Honiara. In this traditional village of roughly 200, residents speak the endangered Savosavo language, one of over 60 languages spoken in the Solomon Islands. Ask the experts at nearby Savo Sunset Lodge to help you plan a visit

74 / BEST IN TRAVEL 2026

TOP PLACES / SOLOMON ISLANDS

to point out evidence of ancient villages along the way to waterfalls hidden deep in the bush. Closer to Honiara, a journey into Savo Island's interior rewards hikers with a dip in a sacred, steaming-hot waterfall, warmed by an active volcano.

ACCESSIBLE, UNTOUCHED ADVENTURE

Comparisons between the Solomons and neighboring Fiji and Vanuatu are easy to draw. And sure, if you want to flop down on a beach with a cocktail, you can do that here, too. The beaches even come in two shades: stunning white and volcanic black. But make no mistake: you're not going to find all-inclusive resorts in the Solomons, and connectivity is still a work in progress. Starlink high-speed satellite internet has provided great improvements, but it remains limited.

If you like your beach holidays with a solid side of adventure, you'll find that the Solomons are a surprisingly easy and safe place to travel – you can island-hop by banana boat, ferry or small plane (Solomons Airlines regularly service 23 domestic destinations). It feels a world away, but getting here is easy, too – it's a three-hour direct flight from Brisbane, Australia, or six hours from Auckland, New Zealand. English is widely spoken and Solomons Pijin is easy to understand. And perhaps most importantly, helping one another is considered *kastom* (custom) here. In the Solomon Islands, hospitality isn't just an act of customer service – it's deeply embedded in the culture.
–*Jessica Lockhart*

BEST IN TRAVEL 2026 / 75

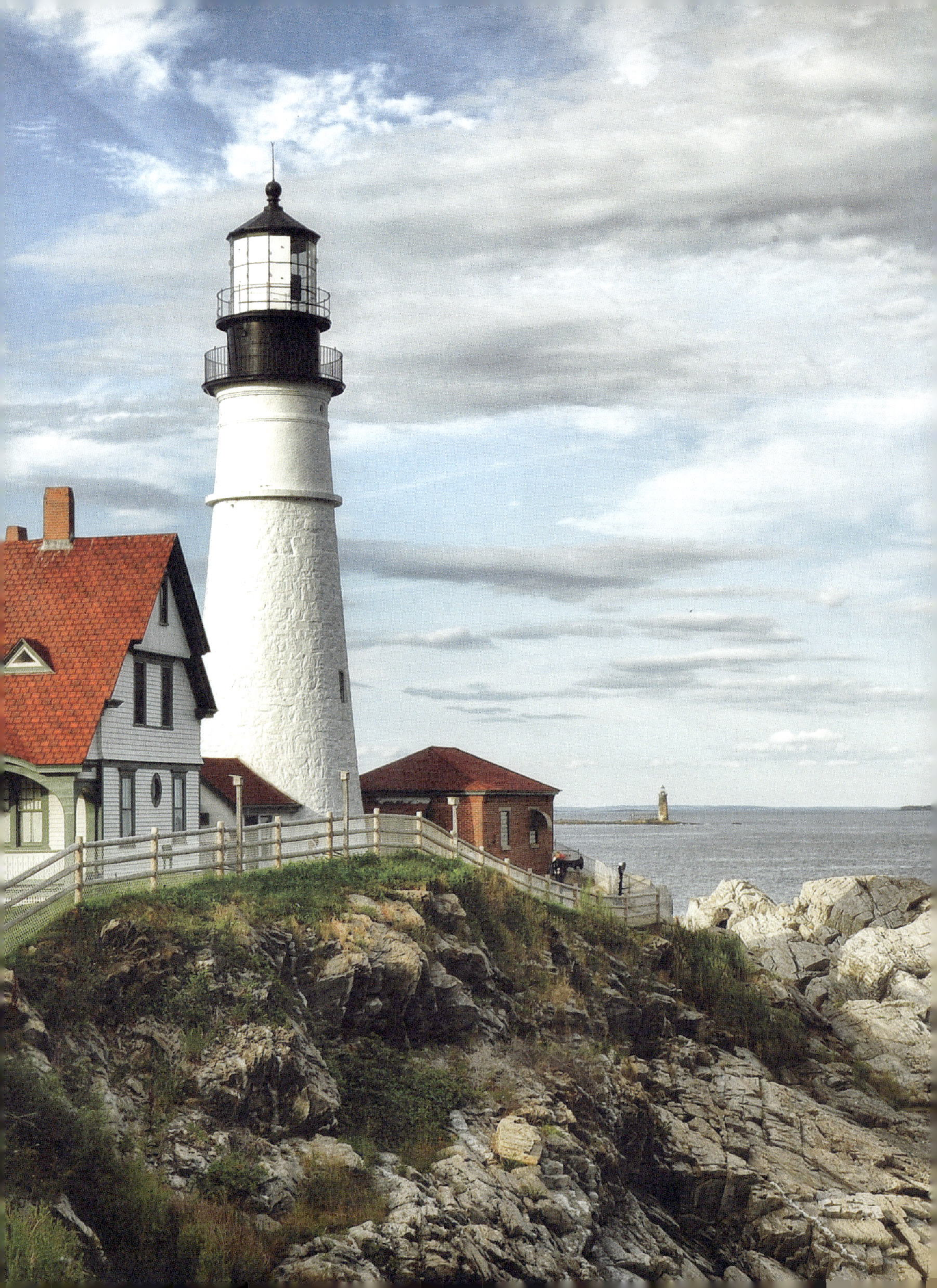

TOP PLACES / MAINE

MAINE

USA

Left to right: Portland Head Light in Cape Elizabeth, one of many historic lighthouses along Maine's coast; Heading out on an Atlantic Ocean boat trip.

BEST FOR
Dreamy and delicious New England summers

It's hard to explain to Mainers that their state is suddenly trendy. They'll let out a sardonic laugh or roll their eyes, or both – expressions that have a particularly salty kind of New England ethos. And to be fair, Mainers are known for practicality and tradition more than an adherence to the latest trends.

COASTING ALONG

Maine's classics, of course, still deliver. The coastal treks here come in two flavors – refined and rollicking. For the former, head to Ogunquit, Bar Harbor and the Kennebunks (Kennebunk and Kennebunkport). These are the places where you'll find grand seaside hotels, dramatic ocean views and visitors sipping rum punch on brightly painted Adirondack chairs. If you're traveling with kids or are just looking for a scrappier, less lofty getaway, try York, Ocean Park or Old Orchard Beach. Maine's summer playgrounds, they're replete with rollercoasters, drippy ice-cream cones and broad stretches of soft sand. There is also, of course, Acadia National Park, Maine's scenic crown jewel, with its emerald offshore islands and wave-pounded cliffs.

BEST IN TRAVEL 2026 / 77

DON'T LEAVE WITHOUT...

Taking a forest hike in the springtime (May to early June) to see Maine in bloom and at its most serene. One remarkable exception: the clattering, activity-filled rookeries of Maine's famous blue herons. Heron colonies can support up to 500 birds, and the sight of the gawky, hungry chicks in their nests is unforgettable.

78 / BEST IN TRAVEL 2026

TOP PLACES / MAINE

EATING YOUR WAY INLAND

The first place in the continental US to see the sunrise, New England feels like it's been renewed. Seaside Portland, its largest city, has become the state hotspot for new restaurant and bakery openings, particularly for chefs who have big-city training and cred but shun the price of entry in Boston or New York. The results are James Beard awards and nominations on nearly every downtown corner. Recent honorees include Norimoto Bakery, which infuses European-style Danishes and meringues with yuzu, red bean and 'Japanese sensibility'; and ZU Bakery, where handmade bread is king.

Or, break with the coast and venture inland, perhaps to Oxford's Oxbow Beer Garden, which is built into a 200-year-old red barn. At the Lost Kitchen, in Freedom, chef Erin French only accepts reservations by postcard. And at Puzzle Mountain Bakery pie stand in Newry – fashioned after many a roadside stall in Maine – you pay by the honor system.

ART, ARCHITECTURE AND AN ACTIVE LIGHTHOUSE

Beyond the food, there are other new sides to this vacation classic. The town of Rockland has led the way with the Center for Maine Contemporary Art, housed in a gleaming glass building by architect Toshiko Mori. It's a dramatic contrast to the Farnsworth Art Museum just around the corner, home to canvases by Andrew Wyeth, who spent his summers here. In neighboring Thomaston, an outpost of Karma Gallery shows cutting-edge work in a deconsecrated Catholic church. On your way, stop at Owl's Head Light, one of many lighthouses in Maine that continue to blink along the coast despite the advent of modern navigation technology. No one, not even the most cynical Mainer, will roll their eyes at that.

–Laura Motta

Clockwise from top left: Danforth, on Maine's Eastern Grand Lake; Historic Moulton St in downtown Portland; Farnsworth Art Museum; Pastries at Portland's celebrated Norimoto Bakery.

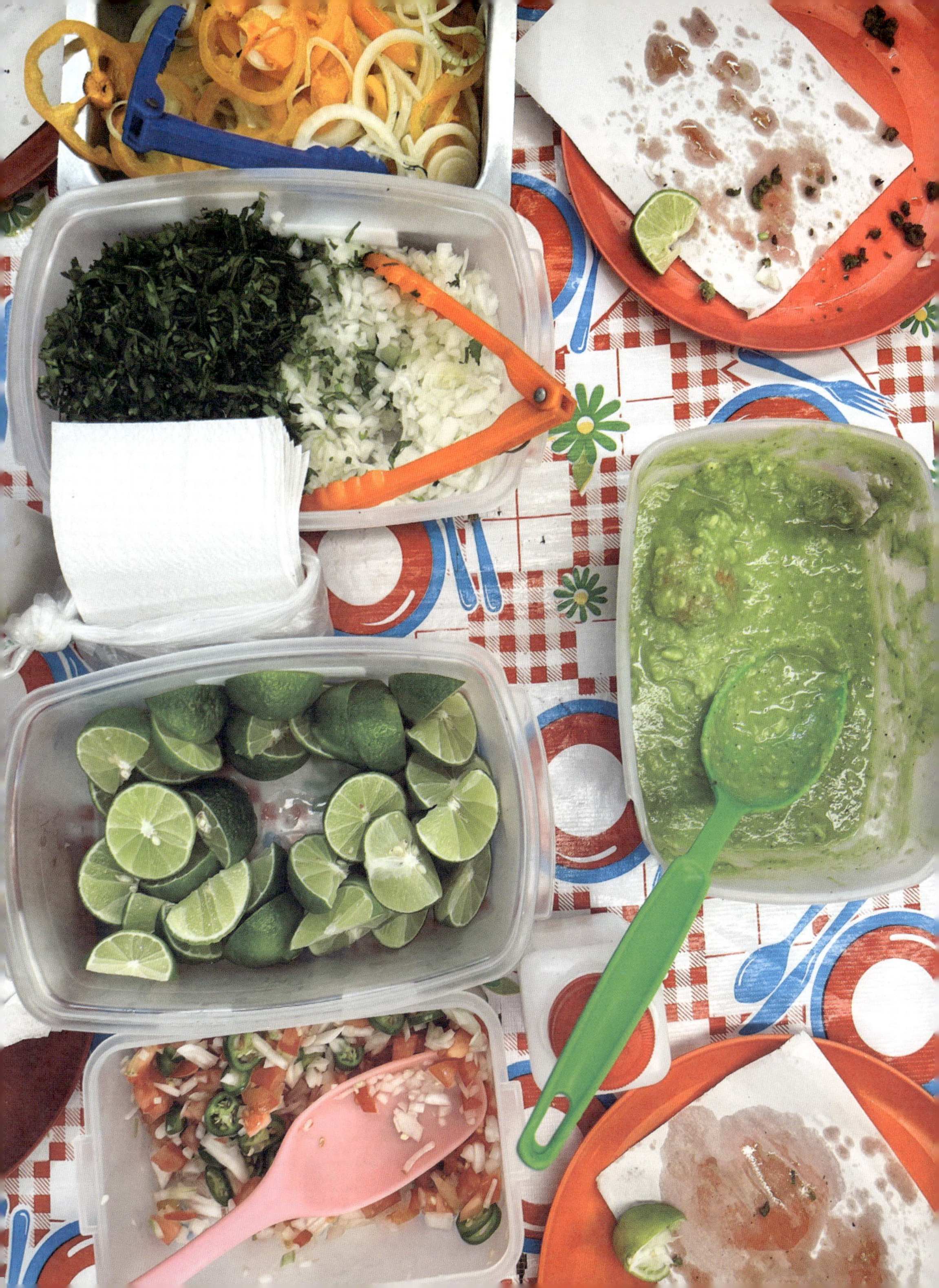

TOP PLACES / MEXICO CITY

MEXICO CITY

MEXICO

Left to right: All the flavorful fixings at a Mexico City street-food stall; Urban style in the city's La Condesa neighborhood.

BEST FOR
A tapestry of creative energy

Mexico City is a tapestry of pre-Hispanic traditions, storybook murals and sizzling hotplates around every corner. Frida Kahlo's museum-house might draw the crowds, but it's the bougainvillea-wrapped neighborhoods of Coyoacán, La Roma and La Condesa – and the city's irrepressible creative energy – that will compel you to extend your stay.

ENVELOP YOURSELF IN THE SIGHTS AND SOUNDS THE CITY

Sit for a moment at a shady plaza in Coyoacán, Frida Kahlo's neighborhood, and you'll hear a carousel of emblematic jingles that define Mexico City: the squeal of a tortilla conveyor belt; a shoe-shiner singing out to couples holding guava ice creams; metal ladles tinkling inside clay pots of meaty stew for *tacos de guisado*.

These traces of village life remain in the capital in a jumble of hand-painted signs for everything from shoe-repair workshops to designer stores.

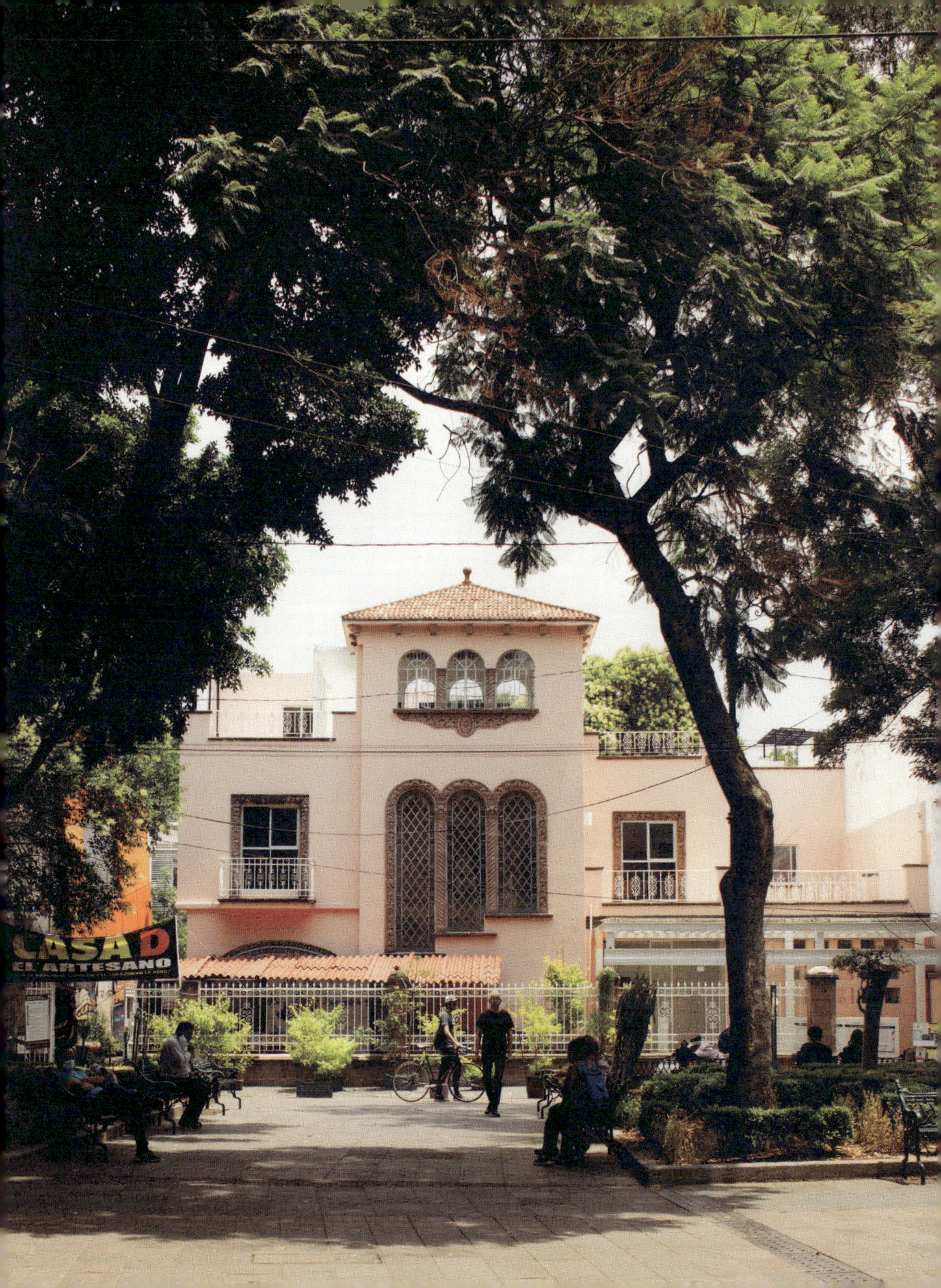
CASA D
EL ARTESANO

Family recipes imported from Oaxaca or the Yucatán are fashioned into the dishes of the country's most esteemed chefs in the Polanco district, or distilled into the sizzle of a street-food hotplate around the corner, where the staff eat.

SOAK IN A WIDE SWATH OF HISTORY AND CULTURE

Vivacious parades, as seen on the Día de los Muertos (Day of the Dead), celebrate life. This is where you can squint up at the sparkling ceiling of the mighty Catedral Metropolitana, and then venture beneath the building to witness the foundations of Aztec-built Templo Mayor. Here, at the center of present-day Mexico City, Aztecs witnessed a vision come true: an eagle perched on a cactus with a serpent in its beak (still visible on the Mexican flag of today). It was a mandate from the gods to build their city, Tenochtitlán, here on the islands of Lake Texcoco in around 1325 CE. In under 200 years, the settlement turned into the thriving capital of the Aztec Empire and then the center of religion and economy in the Valley of Mexico.

Before the Spanish seized control, Tenochtitlán was one of the wealthiest and largest cities in the world, with gleaming red and blue pyramids and an advanced system of four canals within the island-city's four precincts. Causeways also connected it to towns sitting across other interconnected lakes in the Valley of Mexico (traces of which remain in Xochimilco, once a separate city). The Spanish colonizers looted and burned down Tenochtitlán and constructed Mexico City over it, sometimes – as with the cathedral – literally building atop Aztec temples. Yet today, those Aztec temples and traditions refuse to stay buried:

Far left to right:
Catching some shade in a Coyoacán plaza; A traditional *charro* (cowboy) street performer entertains in Coyoacán.

Clockwise from right: The foundations of Templo Mayor, in Mexico City's Centro Histórico; Coyoacán's Casa Azul, now the Museo Frida Kahlo; Cooking up local cuisine; Art nouveau architecture in the city's La Roma district.

MOST MEMORABLE MOMENT

Step into Mercado Medellín and sniff out the whole of Mexico City in one market: pungent cempasúchil (marigolds) around the Day of the Dead, alongside musky guava, smoky sacks of dried chilis and spice-laced mole pastes. Sheets of chicharrón (pork crackling) glow under hot lamps, while perming lotions waft from nearby beauty salons and incense drifts from Santa Muerte effigies.

TOP PLACES / MEXICO CITY

the ruins of Templo Mayor can still be visited. The artifact-stuffed Museo Nacional de Antropología, one of the world's most spectacular museums, takes you through centuries of cultures, and includes insights into the pyramids of Teotihuacán, just outside Mexico City and an easy day trip away.

MAKE EVERY WALK AN ART WALK

Experiencing Mexico City is all cinema. In the plush green park of upmarket Condesa, street sellers lay out a spread of cacti across the roof of a car, while dog walkers march an army of mismatched pups. Next door in bohemian Roma, designer boutiques and jewel-like cafes inlaid into stone mansions are shrouded in a cathedral of trees. Take in the street spectacle with a crackling churro or fresh tuna tostada from its many leafy restaurants. It's hardly surprising that these neighborhoods have become dynamic hubs for digital creatives from around the world, taking advantage of direct flights from the US and Europe and 180-day visitor visas on arrival.

Mexico City was the homebase of Frida Kahlo and Diego Rivera, and artistic smarts are sewn into its very fabric. World-class museums cover every era of Mexico's cultural history. But it's the murals, ingrained into the walls of public buildings, that are a picture-book of the peoples' past, from Aztec times to colonial-era struggles. History is potent here, and yet Mexico City has all the modern comforts you could wish for, from cheap rideshares to cocktail bars.

–Phillip Tang

BEST IN TRAVEL 2026 / 85

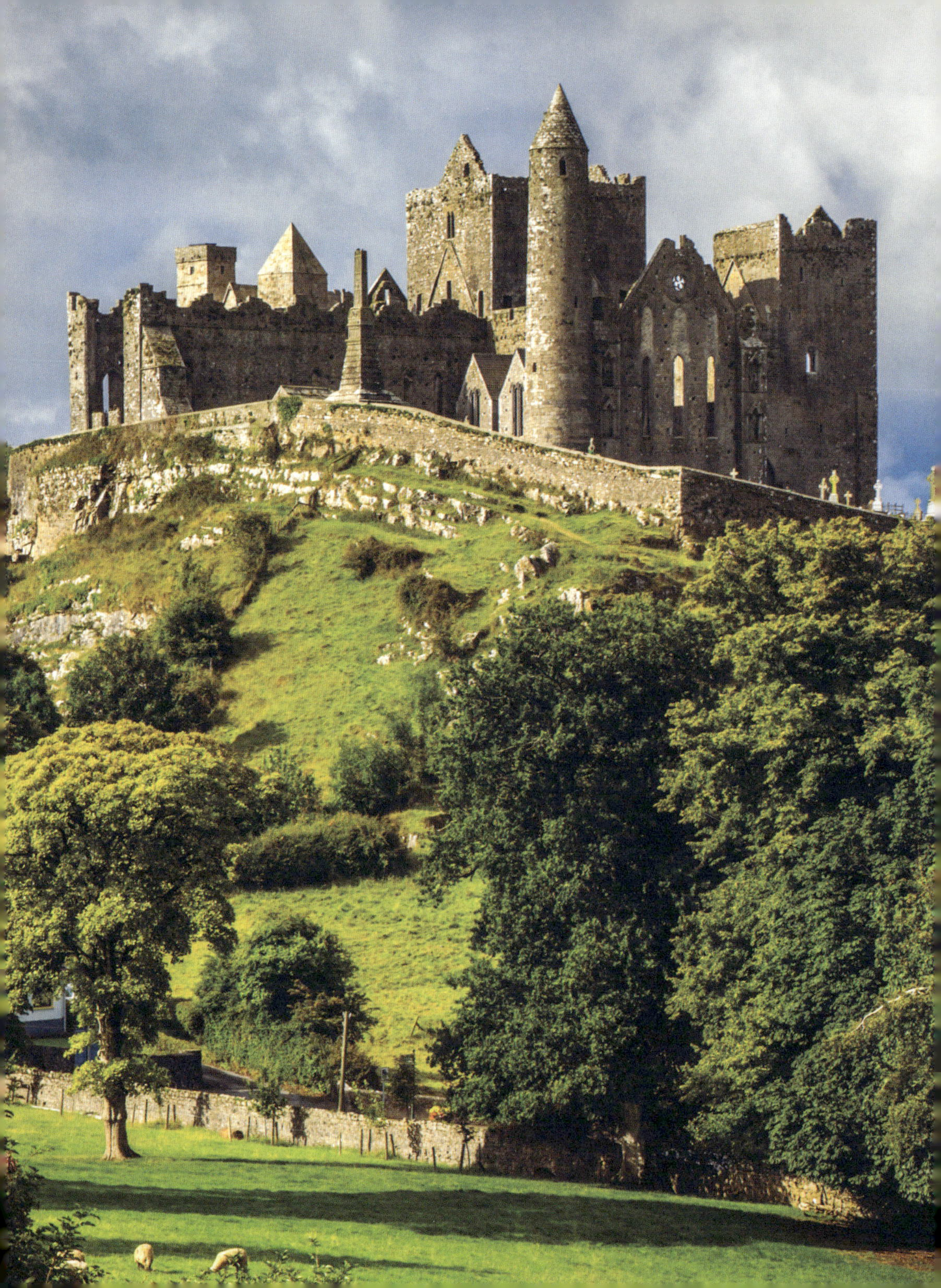

TOP PLACES / TIPPERARY

TIPPERARY

IRELAND

*BEST FOR
Hiking, history and fine food*

In Tipperary, the food is remarkable, the landscapes are generous, and the castles are so casually scattered across the county that you'll probably stumble across one on your way to dinner. This is the Ireland of postcards, yes, but it's also a place with a few surprises.

WHAT IRISH DREAMS ARE MADE OF

In the heart of Ireland's Golden Vale, County Tipperary stretches between the Galtee Mountains and the River Shannon. Just two hours from Dublin, it's the largest inland county in Ireland, where landscapes shift from dramatic mountain ranges to quiet valleys. It's a place where family farms supply artisan cheese to Michelin-starred kitchens, hiking trails weave past medieval ruins, and tiny villages hide pubs where traditional music sessions bring people together from all over the country.

Food heritage runs deep here, especially in the region's apple orchards. Tipperary is famous for producing the crisp, juicy variety that makes its way into exceptional tarts at local farmers markets, and into even better cider. At the Apple Farm in Cahir, pick fruit straight from the trees and camp under them. Or, visit the Bulmers Factory in Clonmel for a sip of Ireland's most famous cider (known as Magners

Left to right: The stunning Rock of Cashel castle, perched on its emerald throne; Chefs at glorious gastropub Mikey Ryan's in Cashel.

BEST IN TRAVEL 2026 / 87

TOP PLACES / TIPPERARY

worldwide). Then there's the cheese – specifically Cashel Blue, Ireland's answer to Roquefort, made by the Grubb family; it is creamy, tangy and nutty, a cheese with a reputation that stretches well beyond Tipperary's borders. Somehow, though, it tastes even better here.

DAILY BREAD, DAILY CONSTITUTION
These ingredients shine in kitchens across the county: Bishop's Buttery, tucked away in the vaults of Cashel Palace Hotel (just a short drive from Cashel Farmhouse Cheese), delivers classically French dishes that showcase the best of Ireland's produce, from East Cork crab to Irish Sea scallops. The nearby gastropub Mikey Ryan's has mastered the art of elevated comfort food, their locally reared lamb and aged steaks drawing diners from across the country. On the south shore of Lough Derg in Garrykennedy, you can retreat after a day spent on the lake to whitewashed, red-trimmed Larkins, for the pub's famous beef-and-Guinness stew and live-music sessions.

Between meals, Tipperary's walking trails help work up an appetite. Follow the mountain path to Silvermines Ridge for views that sweep from Lough Derg's silvery expanse to Kerry's distant peaks. In the Glen of Aherlow, lake-dotted valleys unfurl beneath the great frowning folds of the Galtee Mountains, Ireland's highest inland range. The Suir Blueway offers gentler strolls along trails that weave through moss-draped trees – you're more likely to encounter a heron taking flight from the River Shannon than another human being. Go quieter still with a stroll along the newly opened Littleton Peatway, a disused

Left to right: Hiking the mountain trail to Silverman's Ridge and its sweeping vistas; The 13th-century stronghold of Cahir Castle has since starred in TV shows and movies.

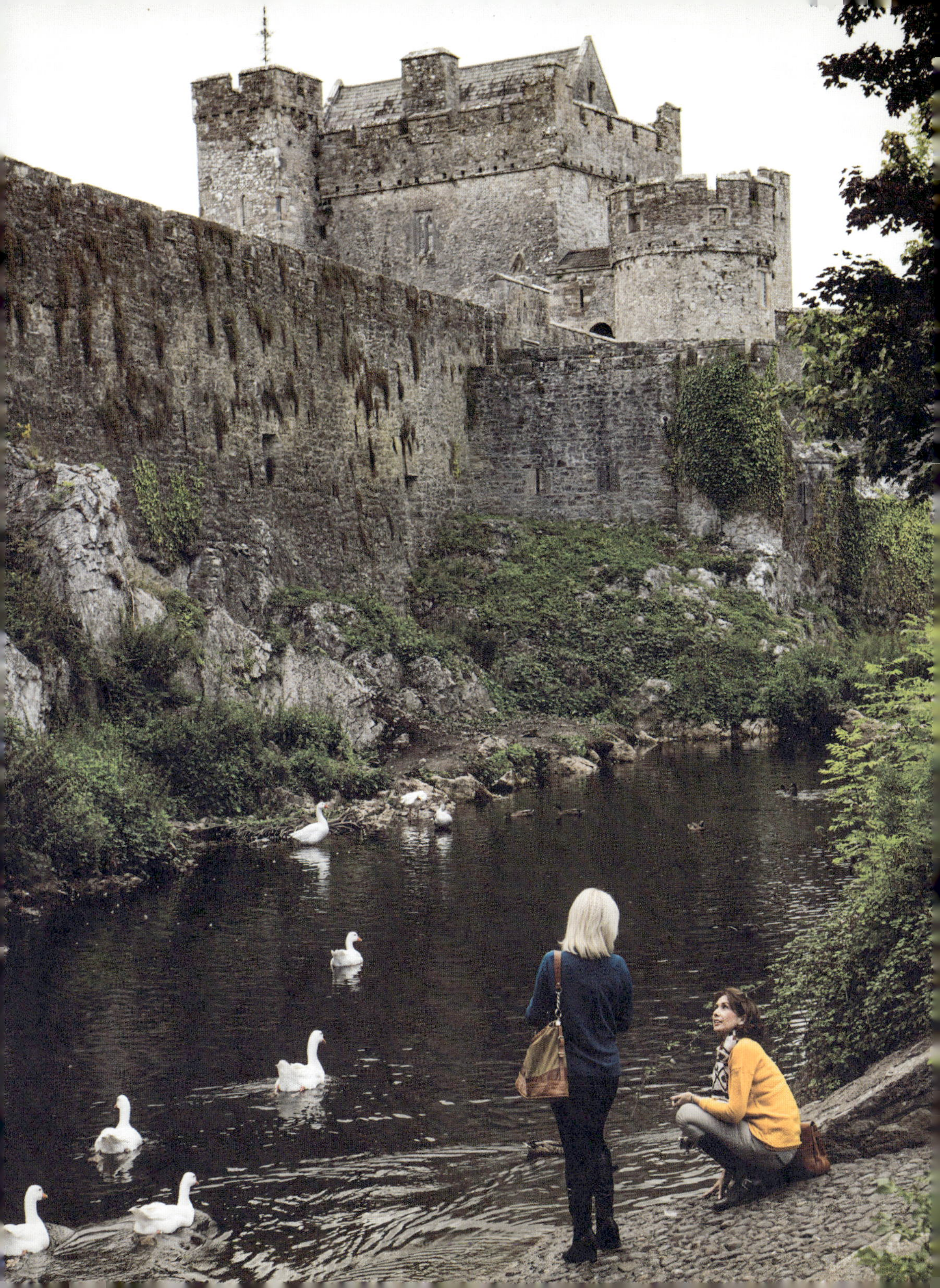

MOST MEMORABLE MOMENT

Take a drive along the Vee, a v-shaped stretch of road in the Knockmealdown Mountains that's considered one of Ireland's most scenic routes. It's beautiful at any time, but especially in early summer, when the landscape is a riot of rhododendron and heather blanketing rocky headlands.

TOP PLACES / TIPPERARY

rail line turned walking trail that slices straight through the stillness of ancient bogland.

CASTLES, AND MORE CASTLES

Of course, this is castle country too. The Rock of Cashel is the showstopper, its 12th-century tower looming dramatically over the town – a silhouette that's instantly recognizable from films like Stanley Kubrick's *Barry Lyndon* and Ridley Scott's *The Last Duel*. Nearby Cahir Castle is no less cinematic, an Elizabethan relic that remains one of Ireland's largest and best-preserved bastions, while Ormond Castle in Carrick-on-Suir is a Tudor masterpiece famous for its decorative rooms.

But ask anyone what draws them back to Tipperary, and they'll likely tell you about an evening spent in one of its pubs. Jim o' the Mills, hidden in the mountains outside Thurles, opens only on Thursdays. It's less bar, more family living room, where musicians come from all over Ireland and beyond to play, filling the space with traditional tunes and a camaraderie that can't be manufactured. In Cloneen, the Thatch has been owned by the same family for seven generations, its decor unchanged since the 19th century. Ask about its role during the Great Famine in the 1840s, and the decades that followed, and the owner might pull out a dusty ledger from the late 1800s, still filled with customers' names and the items bartered. These pages show how local families survived by coming together, a spirit of community that still defines Tipperary today – in its family-run farms, its easygoing restaurants and especially in its pubs, where every visitor is treated like a regular.
–Sasha Brady

Clockwise from top left: Along the Vee's scenic serpentine; Glen of Aherlow's Rock an Thorabh Loop trail; Larkins pub, Garrykennedy; Tipperary cheesemakers include Cooleeney Farm.

BEST IN TRAVEL 2026 / 91

2008
1980
Jesus
Cristo
y
Vive
Reina
ympre
ra
1901
Dios
hombie

TOP PLACES / QUETZALTENANGO

QUETZALTENANGO (XELA)

GUATEMALA

Most visitors to Guatemala zip straight to Antigua or Lago Atitlán, but go just a bit further west to Quetzaltenango (also known as Xela) to discover a rich, fascinating city that has only the paltriest of crowds, despite its stately squares, inviting alleys and quiet cafes and bars. In Xela, foodies will find everything from fancy fine dining to grab-n-gobble street eats.

BEST FOR Culture without the crowds

ONE CITY, TWO IDENTITIES

That this city has two names often confuses people; don't think they're two different places. The reason for the schism goes back to the days of the Spanish conquistadors, who called this place Quetzaltenango, the Nahuatl-language name for the city used by the Aztec allies who helped them conquer here. Xelajú (shortened to Xela) is the original Maya name; both are now used interchangeably.

This duality is more than just a metaphor. It's part of what makes the city so special, and it can be seen throughout: ancient and modern architecture sit side by side here, with Spanish-era cathedrals overlooking Maya monuments. This juxtaposition is part of the fabric of Xela.

Gourmands will find great eats around every corner. Choose from tasty avocado-smash toasts with excellent cafe latte (or other espresso drinks) at Xelapan, a bakery near the Parque Centro America. Or splurge at

Left to right: The colorful church at San Andrés Xecul; Laguna de Chicabal crater lake near San Martín Sacatepéquez, Quetzaltenango Region.

Clockwise from right: Lava erupts from Volcán Santa María, Quetzaltenango region; Xela's Iglesia del Espíritu cathedral; Bakers at work in Quetzaltenango; The rotunda in the city's Parque Centro America.

DON'T LEAVE WITHOUT…

Making time for people-watching at Xela's Parque Centro America, with its beautiful columned rotunda dedicated to Rafael Álvarez Ovalle, composer of Guatemala's national anthem. Women wearing traditional handmade *traje* clothing wait to braid customers' hair, while children play with balloons snapped up from street vendors. At night, couples dip into the park to hold hands on benches.

TOP PLACES / QUETZALTENANGO

Restaurante Tertulianos, where Italian-meets-Guatemaltecan cuisine is served in a beautiful historic building. Try the house special, *pata negra*, made with Ibérico ham that's been cured for 36 months; or one of the specialty fondues, dipping in with everything from shrimp and chipotle peppers to sirloin and cremini mushrooms.

LAUNCH BEYOND XELA

The city makes a great stepping stone for wider Guatemala exploration, with easy day trips to many quirky marvels. A curious bright-yellow church in San Andrés Xecul looks like a child made it out of Play-Doh. Make the scramble up craggy Volcán de Cerro Quemado to where church congregations gather on the rocks, strewing colorful offerings of flowers and listening to sermons on loudspeakers. That the Christian religion is blended into Indigenous beliefs may seem a contradiction, but it makes perfect sense in a region that has been a melting pot for so long.

Those visiting during the Christmas-to-New-Year holiday will want to keep an eye out for the Festival de Venado, a wildly photogenic tradition. During this Maya festival, masked dancers dressed as monkeys or deer parade in the streets, while choosing specific bystanders in the crowd to dance for.

Afterwards, revelers carrying a heavy figure of Christ fill the streets, followed by a marching band. The sights, sounds and costumes make it one of the city's highlight festivals.
–Ray Bartlett

BEST IN TRAVEL 2026 / 95

TOP PLACES / JAFFNA

JAFFNA

SRI LANKA

Perhaps one of Sri Lanka's last remaining stretches untouched by mass tourism, Jaffna – with its easy-access countryside, marshy lagoons and remote islands – is reviving itself as a prominent cultural destination. Come for multi-day Hindu festivals, Portuguese-built seaside forts and delectable spreads of seafood – paired with a dose of unparalleled hospitality.

BEST FOR
Culture, cuisine and island adventures

AN AUTHENTIC CULTURAL CONNECTION

The historical, religious and political core of the country's Tamil community, Jaffna's center is a hubbub of activity. Stalls are neatly stacked with displays of juicy local mangoes, or laden with bottles of sweet syrup and deep-brown molasses made with flowers of the palmyrah (a fan palm that grows abundantly in the region). In the outskirts, sarong-clad uncles and saree-wearing women cycle palmyrah-fringed country roads where deep wells water fields planted with tobacco, chili peppers and spring onions. Along the asphalted highways, boiled paddy lies drying in the sun.

Only a smattering of the nearly two million tourists who travel to Sri Lanka each year visit the country's north; those that do tend to have an intrepid bent or an eye for history and vibrant culture. But as the Tamil diaspora from across the world – alongside ambitious locals – invest in their motherland, this once war-torn city is buzzing with life and anticipating a tourism revival.

Left to right, from above: City streets in central Jaffna; Explore the region's backroads to discover stunning Hindu temples like Maviddapuram's Nallur Kandaswamy Kovil.

96 / BEST IN TRAVEL 2026

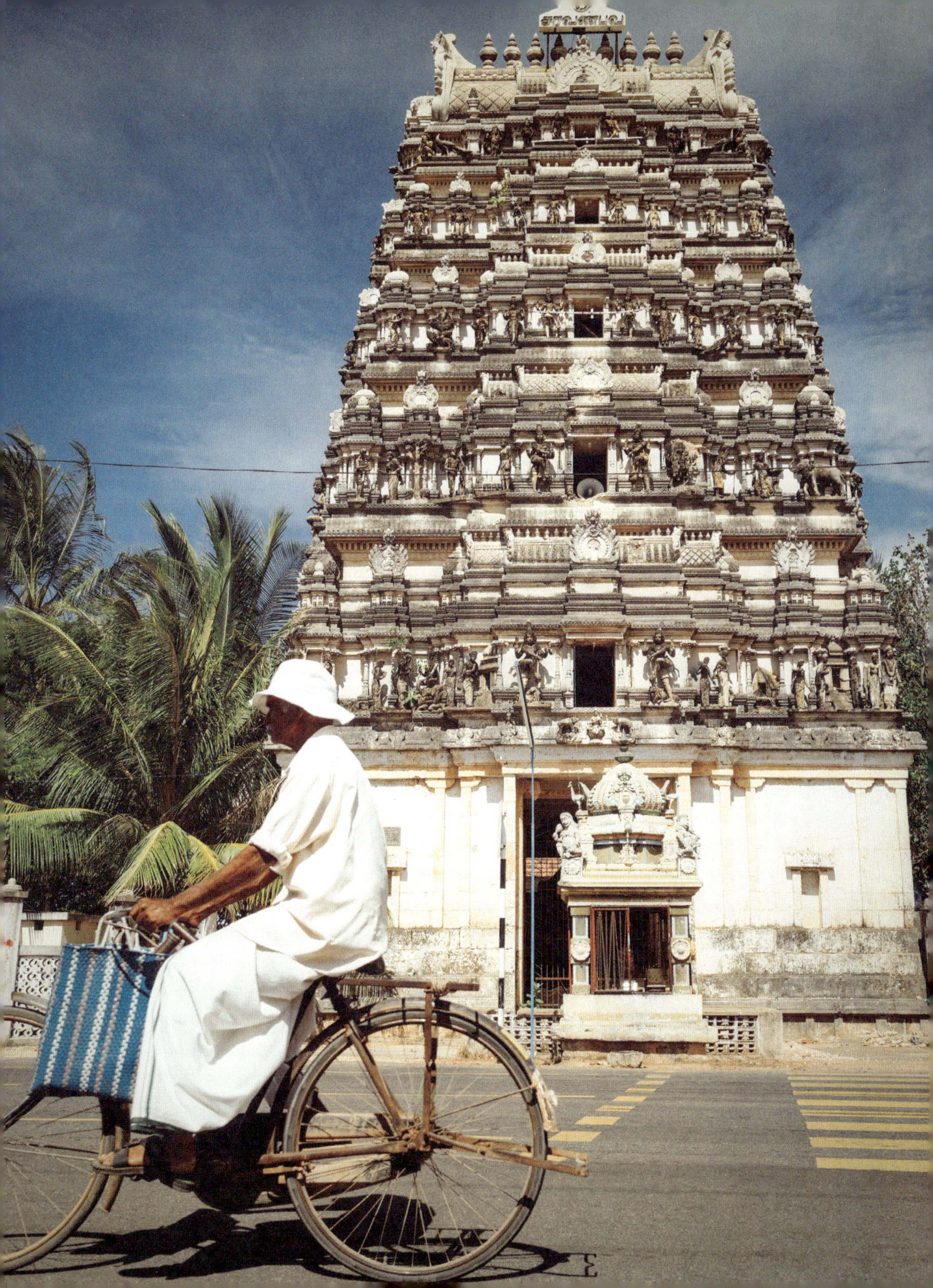

TOP PLACES / JAFFNA

Jaffna is a far cry from the Sri Lanka's tourist-centered, resort-speckled south coast, frequented by honeymooners and vacationers looking for idyllic stays and fine-dining restaurants. But if you're looking to feel connected to the country's way of life and enjoy local hospitality with delicious, home-cooked meals, you'll find that in Jaffna. Of course, you'll still have comfortable, design-led accommodations like Fox Jaffna, where two onsite museums are housed in Civil War–era bunkers.

Faith intertwines Jaffna life. The city streets are studded with Catholic churches; suburban Nallur is home to the Nallur Kandaswamy Kovil. A Hindu temple with decorative brasswork and a massive gilded entrance column, it attracts thousands of pilgrims from across the world to its 25-day annual festival, in which colorful chariots parade the streets carrying statues of Hindu gods. A short tuk-tuk ride away in Keerimalai, men and women take holy dips in separate aquamarine natural springs.

A LIVING HISTORY LESSON

Tamil dynasties ruled over Jaffna for centuries, but the Portuguese invaded in 1560, destroying the region's Hindu temples in their mission to spread Christianity. In 1619, they built the Jaffna Fort, which was later captured by the Dutch and expanded into today's pentagonal shape. Battled over for decades by the Sri Lankan army and the militant LTTE (Liberation Tigers of Tamil Eelam), who fought for a separate Tamil state, the fort's ramparts are now where locals and tourists come to enjoy the sunset over flatwater lagoons teeming with birdlife.

Today, guests are warmly welcomed by local families such as those who run the Malabar Homestay, a well-kept ancestral

Left to right:
Nagadeepa Purana Viharaya, Nainativu Island's Buddhist shrine; Looking down on perfectly pentagonal Jaffna Fort, now a popular place to watch the sun sink into the sea.

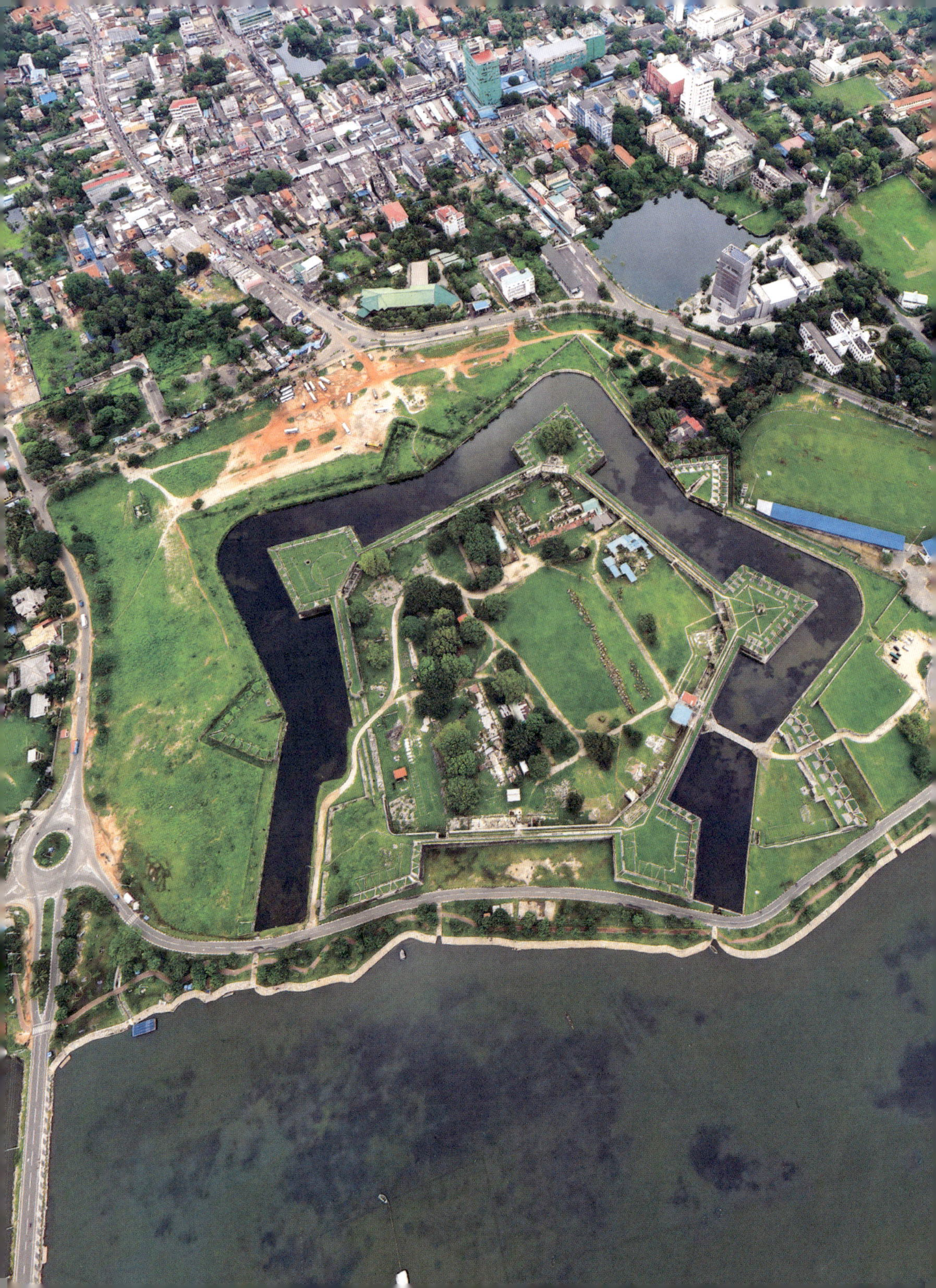

DON'T LEAVE WITHOUT...

Taking the public ferry to Nainativu Island, home to two temples: the Hindu Nagapooshani Amman Kovil, and the Buddhist shrine of Nagadeepa Purana Viharaya. According to legend, Buddha arrived here during his second visit to Sri Lanka, and the temple is a place of pilgrimage. Nainativu's name alludes to its folkloric connection with Sri Lanka's mythical Naga people.

TOP PLACES / JAFFNA

home where hosts prepare fiery crab curry, washed down with water from coconuts grown in the backyard. The remnants of the three-decade-long war, though, are still evident in parts, like the rebuilt Jaffna Public Library. Before Sinhalese mobs set fire to it in 1981, the library was one of the largest in South Asia and housed important Tamil palm-leaf literature.

Out across the Palk Strait, far-flung Delft Island – an hour-long ferry ride from Jaffna – is nonetheless a close cousin to the rest of the region. Local homes here are separated from each other by fences made of coral and palmyrah fronds. Now and then, a handful of curious day-visitors cycle around the island, and even fewer overnight at the simple but homely thatch-roof tents at Delft Village Stay. On most days, though, the island remains quiet, with women tending their herds of goats against the backdrop of the ebbing and flowing ocean as it gently laps the shallow surrounding reef. A diminishing poulation of wild horses – some now domesticated – graze the island's rainfed grass.

Jaffna is located on a mostly flat, sparsely populated peninsula. Getting around is a breeze, with ample buses, tuk-tuks and ferries (the region's countryside is also great for cycling). Getting here is relatively easy, too, as trains and air-conditioned buses connect Jaffna with Sri Lankan capital Colombo; hour-long direct flights from Chennai have resumed, alongside ferries from South India. Tamil is the region's native language, but English is widely spoken. And as elsewhere in Sri Lanka, a smile goes a long way – you may even get invited into local homes for a hearty meal, washed down with cups of frothy, milky tea.

–Zinara Rathnayake

Clockwise from top left: Local produce in Jaffna Market; Delft Island's wild horses; Jaffna Public Library; Rice and curry, Sri Lanka's delectable national dish.

BEST IN TRAVEL 2026 / 101

TOP PLACES / PHUKET

PHUKET

THAILAND

With its expansive white sands, verdant jungles and increasingly vibrant communities stacked with trendy social hangouts galore, Phuket is steadily becoming Southeast Asia's most fabulous work-and-travel spot. Throw in Thailand's digital nomad visas and it's easy to see why young professionals are flocking to the island. This is easy, breezy coastal living spiked with urban adventure.

Photographs by Lauren Ishak; Text by Barbara Woolsey

TOP PLACES / PHUKET

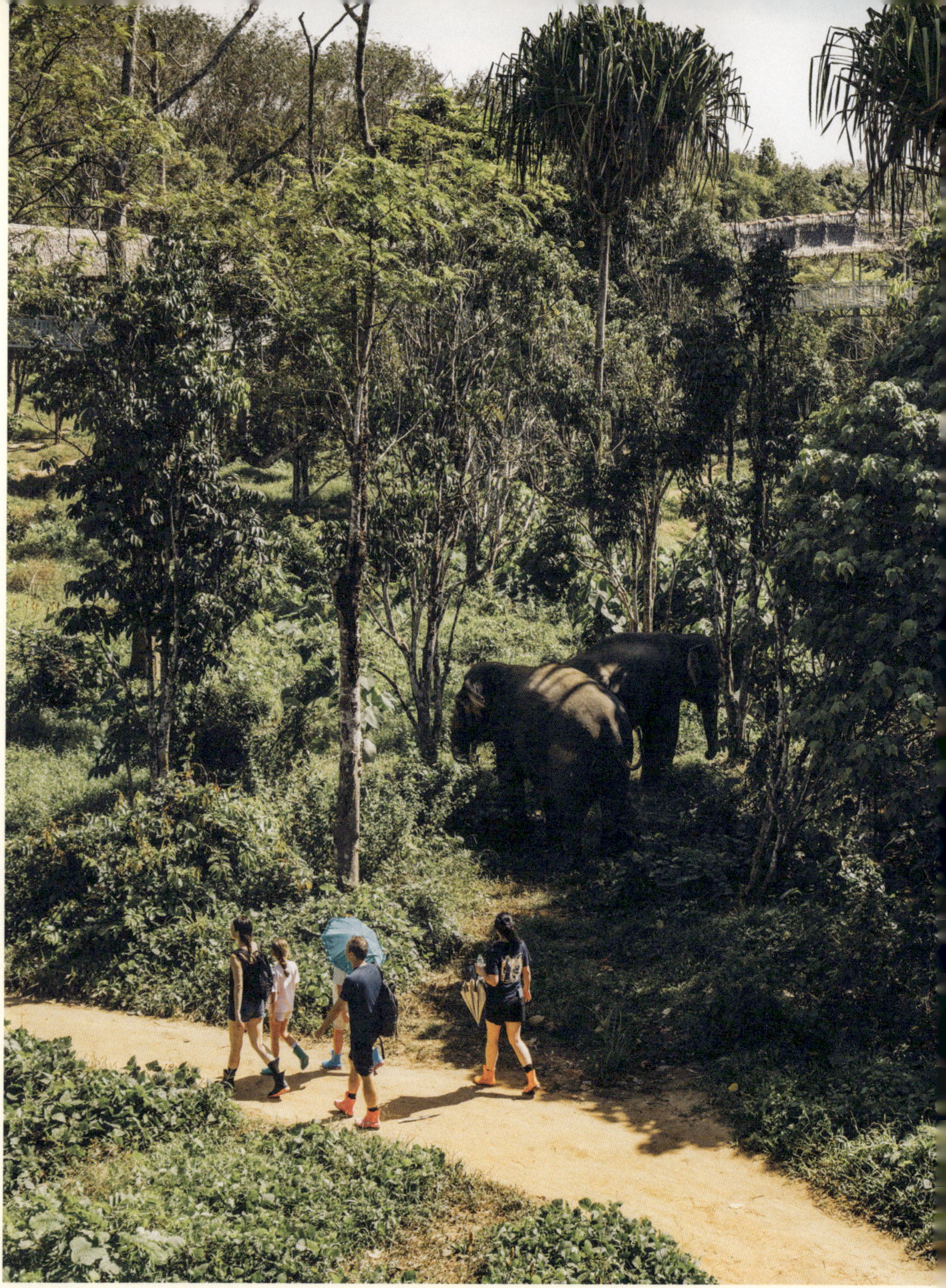

TOP PLACES / PHUKET

Previous spread:- Phuket's coastline is home to more than 30 golden beaches, which range from flashy watersports hotspots to luscious, low-key spots like Hat Layan. And in Phuket's largest bay, Chalong Pier unlocks sailing journeys to uninhabited isles sculpted with towering limestone cliffs and powdery sands, or deep-sea dives throughout the famous Andaman Sea.

This spread: Winding jungle-covered peaks and valleys add rocky, untamed perspectives. Hidden beneath forest canopies are some of Thailand's most respected animal sanctuaries, offering travelers a chance to support conservation and encounter wildlife in an ethical way.

Spend a morning at the Gibbon Rehabilitation Project, tucked into Phuket's last remaining rainforest, learning to decipher loud songs and calls with a gibbon specialist. Nearby, the Phuket Elephant Sanctuary lodges rescued pachyderms taken care of by volunteers.

BEST IN TRAVEL 2026 / 105

TOP PLACES / PHUKET

Many Bangkokians moved to Phuket during the pandemic and stayed on, impressed by its tropical freedom and sense of community. In historic Phuket Town, Chinese- and European-influenced heritage architecture surround many friendly, colorful night markets (Sunday's Lard Yai Market is a favorite for street-food feasts).

Kamala Beach and Bang Tao Beach also feel increasingly like cozy neighborhoods rather than resort areas, thanks to new cafés and restaurants. Karon Beach, known for its big resorts, has added charming hangouts like A Blanket & A Pillow for cliffside cocktail-sipping, and chic live-music haven the Commune.

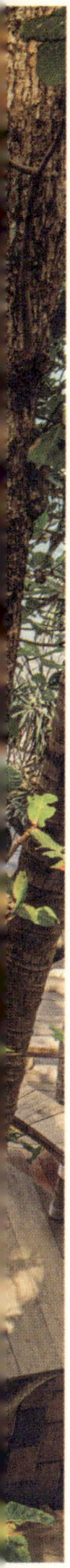

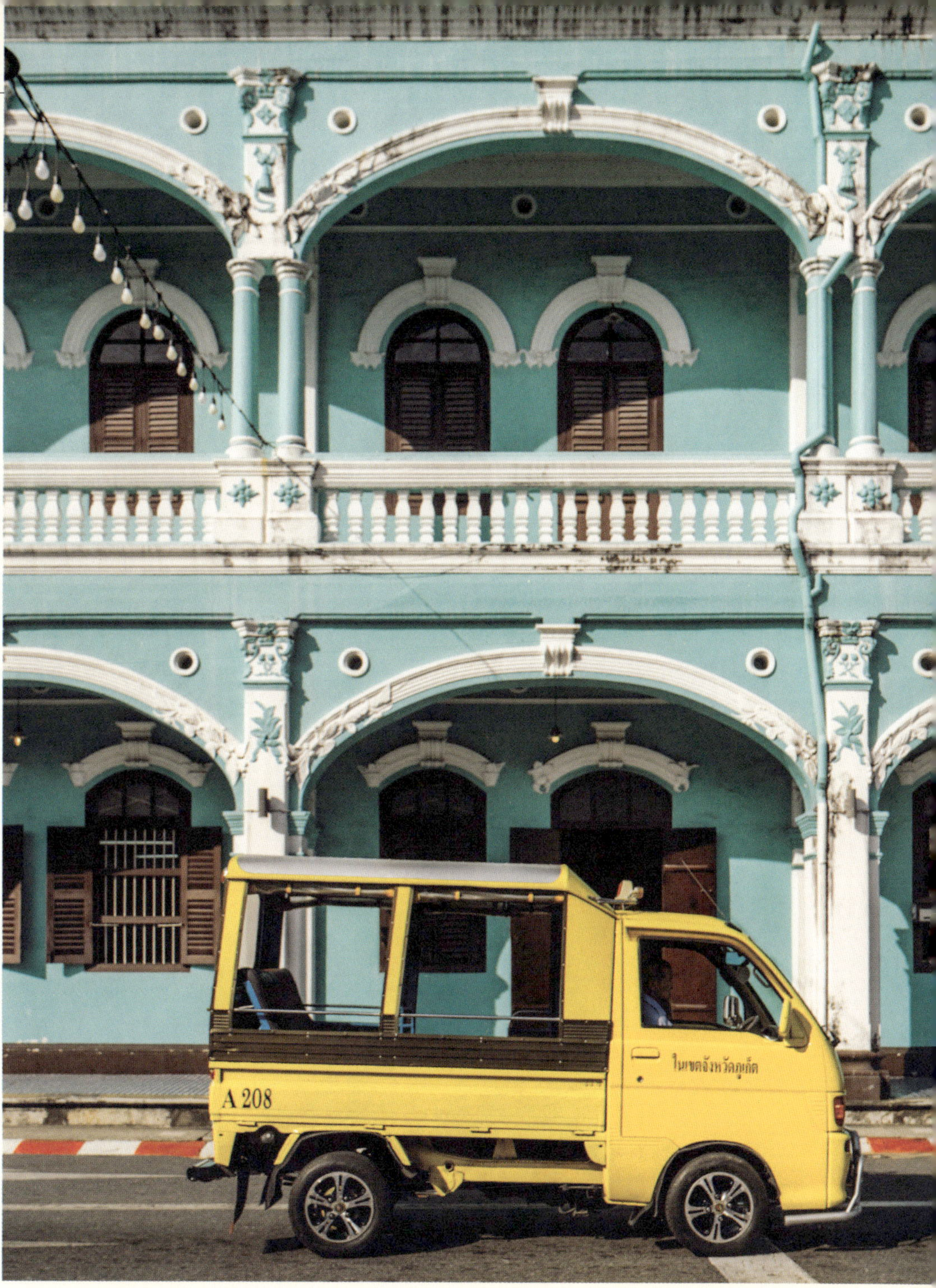
A 208
ในเขตจังหวัดภูเก็ต

TOP PLACES / PHUKET

108 / BEST IN TRAVEL 2026

Soak up the sights in Phuket Town: Wat Mongkhon Nimit, one of the island's most revered temples, sits just beyond the northern end of photogenic Soi Romanee, with its gorgeously revamped Sino-Portuguese architecture.

Multicultural and sustainable gastronomy is on the rise, with many excellent expat-run restaurants, from Turkish to Moroccan. Sample Chinese-style noodles at hole-in-the-wall Somchit, or splurge at PRU, the island's only Michelin-starred restaurant.

Dive into the island's coffee culture at Phuket Town's Graph, where local-grown beans are roasted on site; or head to beachfront bistro Hern in Patong Beach, for decadent slow-drip coffee and croissant sandwiches.

TOP PLACES / UTRECHT

UTRECHT

NETHERLANDS

The most baffling thing about Utrecht is that it hasn't already become the European city break everyone insists you take. Yes, there are tourists here, but it's rarely overcrowded or complicated. Just a short train ride from Amsterdam, it offers plenty: a medieval center laced with canals; gabled houses that belong in a Vermeer; and a bounty of bookshops, restaurants and museums.

BEST FOR
A cultured European city break

EXPECT UNEXPECTED DISCOVERIES

Exploring Utrecht is blissfully simple. Start with the canals, which are two-tiered. Above, cyclists bump along cobbled streets and neat stone bridges while below, tree-lined paths skirt the water, flanked by wharves that form an entirely separate canal-level street. These wharves were once loading bays for merchants, but now their 13th-century cellars are reimagined as workshops hosting artists and small creative businesses, as well as minimalist guesthouses and low-lit bars.

The city's history is just as layered. At its heart is the Domtoren, the tallest spire in the Netherlands, which locals will talk about with justifiable pride. Climb 465 steps to the top for views that, on a clear day, stretch all the way to Amsterdam, some 26 miles (42km) away. Or, go underground and explore the companion museum DOMonder, where you can play amateur archaeologist, armed with a flashlight as you explore 2000 years of Utrecht's history.

Left to right, from above: Dating from 1925, the Rietveld-Schröderhuis is a shining example of Dutch De Stijl architecture; Canalside color in Utrecht's medieval-era core.

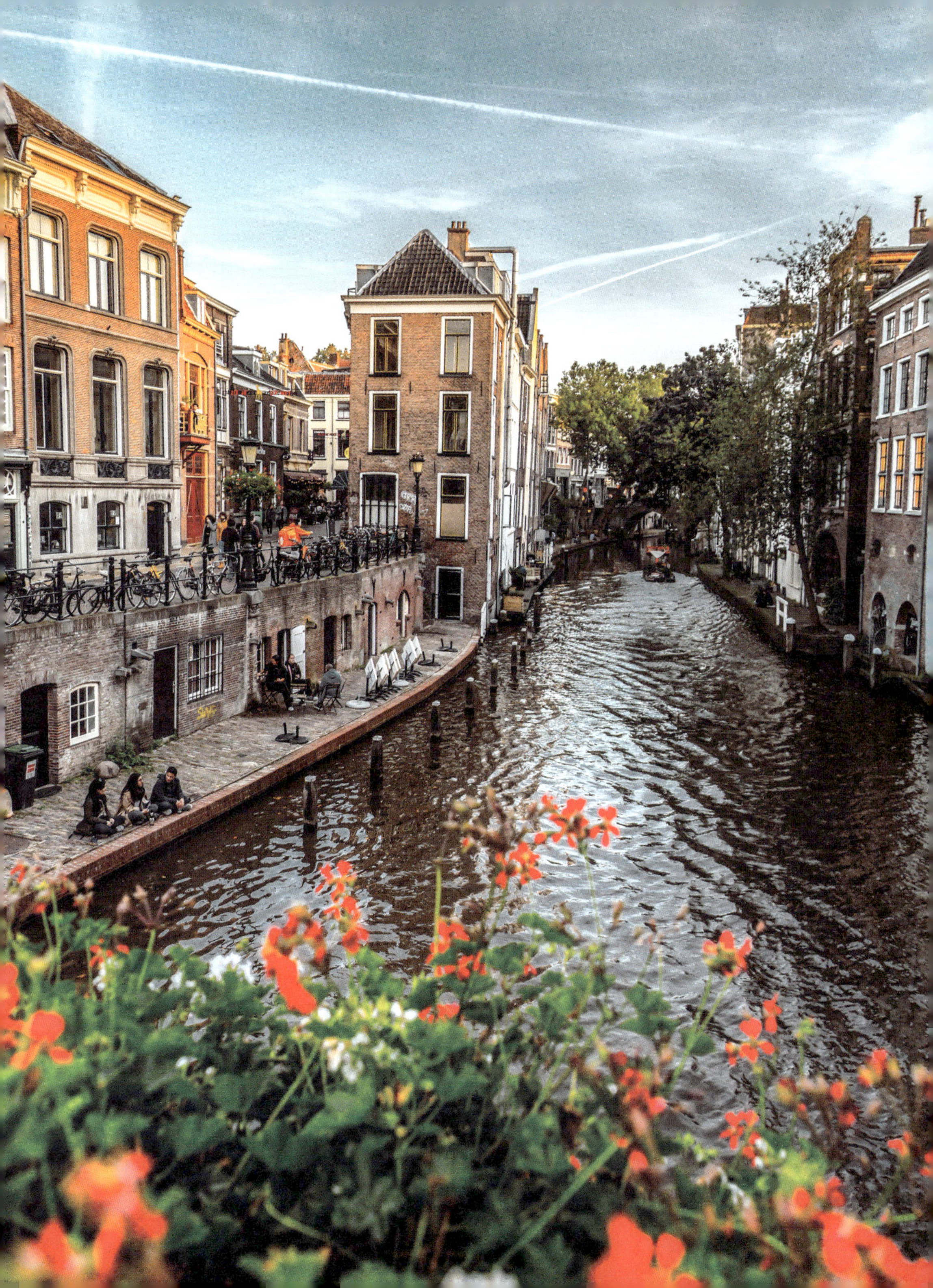

DON'T LEAVE WITHOUT…

Visiting Boekhandel Den Boer, an old wood-paneled bookshop where the shelves threaten to collapse under an eclectic mix of titles. The decor in this art nouveau building may not have changed since 1887, but the selection of books is constantly updated.

112 / BEST IN TRAVEL 2026

TOP PLACES / UTRECHT

No matter where you end up in the city, you'll find unexpected displays of creativity. At Museum Speelklok, an eccentric collection of self-playing instruments takes center stage. Nearby, at the Centraal Museum, you'll see Pyke Koch's magical realist art alongside Viktor&Rolf's experimental fashion. As you wander, keep an eye out for Miffy, Dick Bruna's famous picture-book bunny, whose iconic silhouette pops up everywhere. Look down, too: *De Letters van Utrecht*, a 'Poem for the Future', is etched into the canal stones, one letter at a time every Saturday; it's a project that will linger on, long after we're gone.

LEAN INTO THE EASY (AND JOYFUL) ENERGY

True to Dutch form, Utrecht is a bike-first city with a goal to double cycle commutes by 2030. It's hard not to be impressed by the efficiency of it all. Hop on two wheels and the city opens up effortlessly. A short ride out of the center takes you to the Gothic sprawl of Kasteel de Haar, the largest castle in the Netherlands; or the UNESCO-listed Rietveld-Schröderhuis – this radical 1925 masterpiece of the Dutch De Stijl architectural movement feels way ahead of its time, even now.

Utrecht doesn't have to try too hard. It's simply an easy and excellent place to be. Maybe it's how the streets feel designed for people rather than cars, with bike paths and tram lines that make every corner feel within reach. Or perhaps it's the pace. Despite it being a university city, it feels delightfully calm. You see it in how life unspools gently by the canals, with locals lingering over a coffee and a book, as though they have all the time in the world. Utrecht is a city that's hard to shake off and, before you've even left, you'll find yourself plotting your return.
–*Sasha Brady*

Clockwise from top left: Period model chairs at Rietveld-Schröderhuis; Bike out to Kasteel de Haar; Utrecht cafe culture; Browsing the shelves at historic Boekhandel Den Boer.

BEST IN TRAVEL 2026 / 113

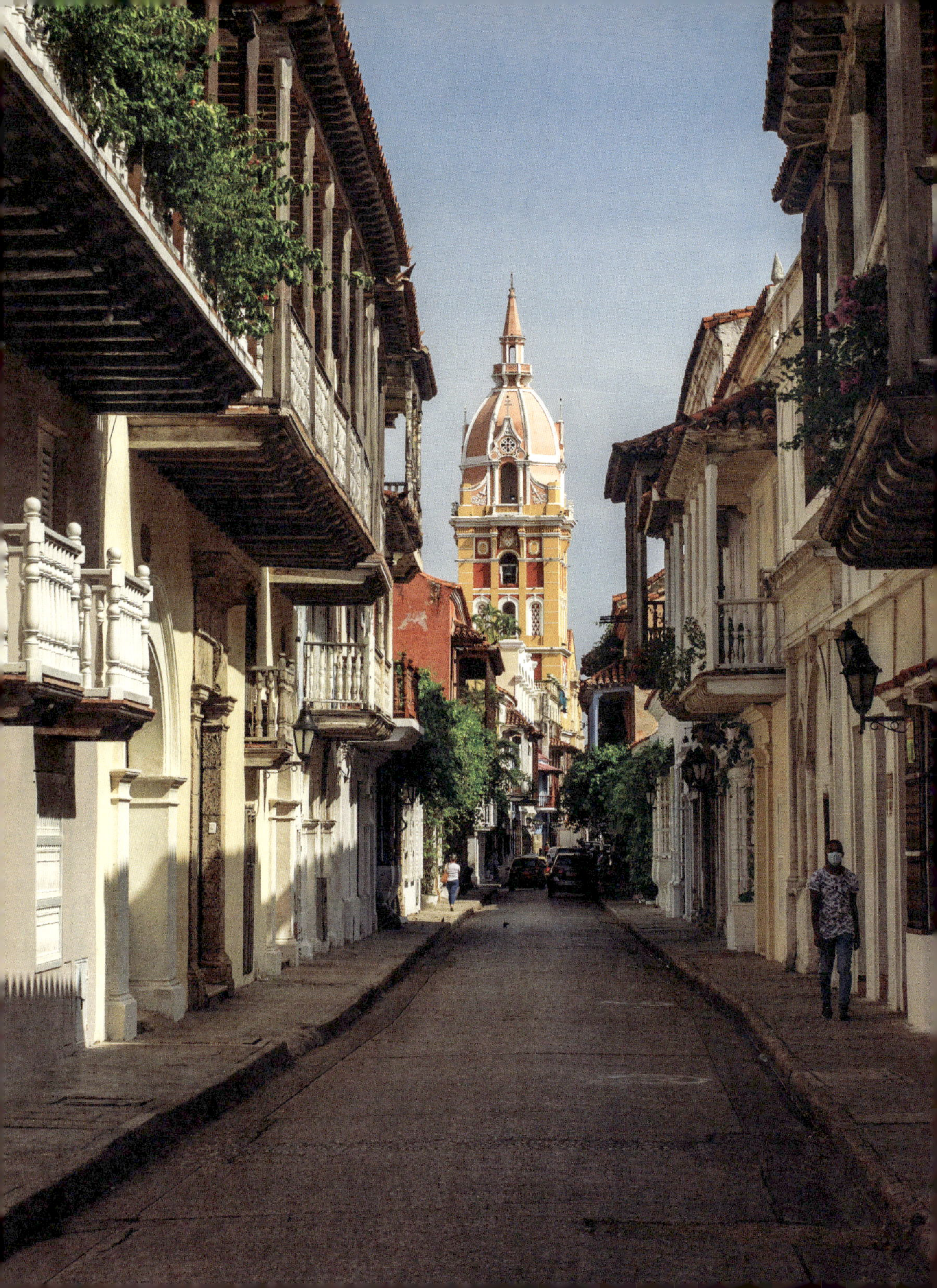

TOP PLACES / CARTAGENA

CARTAGENA

BEST FOR
Vibrant nightlife and history

COLOMBIA

To really know Cartagena, look beyond the photogenic street scenes and step into its soul – found in the lively plazas where locals gather, in the infectious beats of champeta, and in the rich aromas of sizzling street food. In Cartagena's hidden courtyards and bustling markets, past and present blend into an experience as vibrant as it is unforgettable.

DROP INTO THE CITY'S STORYBOOK CHARM

While modern Cartagena stretches along the coast and inland, the city's Old Town fiercely preserves its antique essence. Surrounded by stone walls, its collection of Spanish-built plazas, palaces and mansions comprises one of the best-preserved historic districts in all of the Americas.

Wander the labyrinthine streets, where ornamental flowers drape over the second-floor balconies of pastel-hued buildings, giving the city its signature postcard-perfect aesthetic. Street vendors crack open coconuts with a swift chop, and the clip-clop of horses' hooves mingles with the melodies of street musicians strumming guitars in the shade of historic churches.

Mansions that belonged to merchant mariners, military officers and members of high society during the 16th and 17th centuries are now filled with stylish shops, luxury boutique hotels, chic cocktail bars and candlelit restaurants.

Left to right:
Looking toward the Basilica Santa Catalina de Alejandria, in Cartagena's photogenic Old Town; Awash with color in the cultural canvas of Getsemani.

BEST IN TRAVEL 2026 / 115

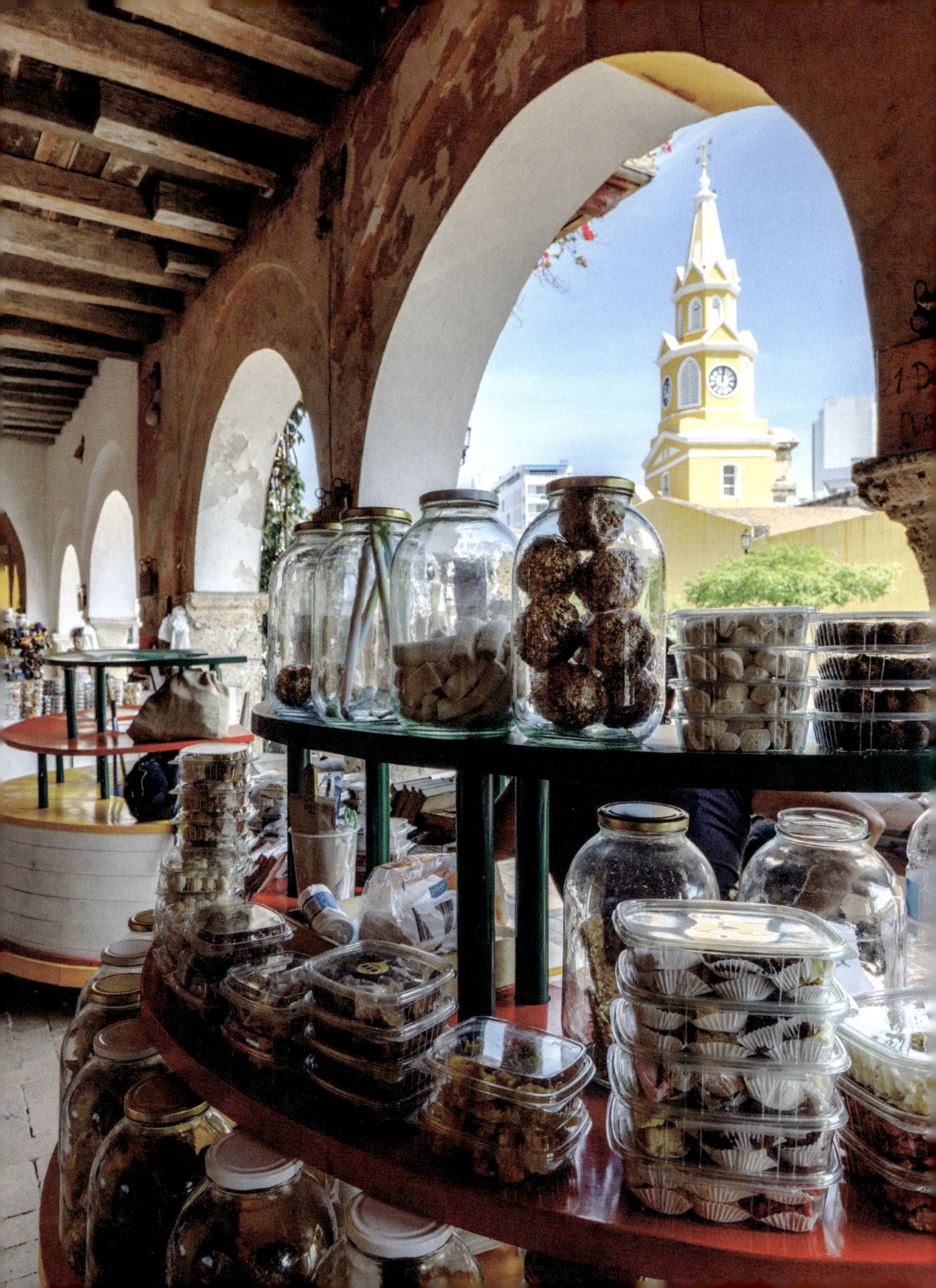

HONOR A COMPLEX HISTORY

But beyond the Old Town's picturesque facade lies Cartagena's complex history of conquest, colonization and resistance. The city's museums are worth visiting to better understand the events that shaped its identity.

Start with the Museo del Oro Zenú, home to exquisite gold artifacts crafted by the Zenú people, who lived along the Caribbean coast before the Spanish conquest of Colombia. Their ancestors, who continue to fight for cultural preservation, are famous for the *sombrero vueltiao*, a woven hat with geometric designs created using *caña flecha*, or palm fibers. The hats are a symbol of Colombian national identity and are often sold in Cartagena's markets.

Across the Parque de Bolívar, the Museo Histórico de Cartagena explores the brutal legacy of the Spanish Inquisition and the transatlantic trade of enslaved Africans. Nearby, the Sanctuario San Pedro de Claver honors the Jesuit priest who championed the dignity of enslaved people.

EXPLORE CARTAGENA'S CULTURE VIA COLORFUL MARKETS

Cartagena's Afro-Colombian legacy lives on through its people and culture. In the Old Town, *palenqueras* sell sweets under the Portal de los Dulces – once a market for buying and selling enslaved people. Others work the streets balancing fruit baskets on their heads, posing for pictures in front of the reclining statue by Colombian artist Fernando Botero in the Plaza Santo Domingo. Try their sweet treats known as *alegrías* (meaning 'happiness') – a nod to their intense pride and joy in the face of adversity.

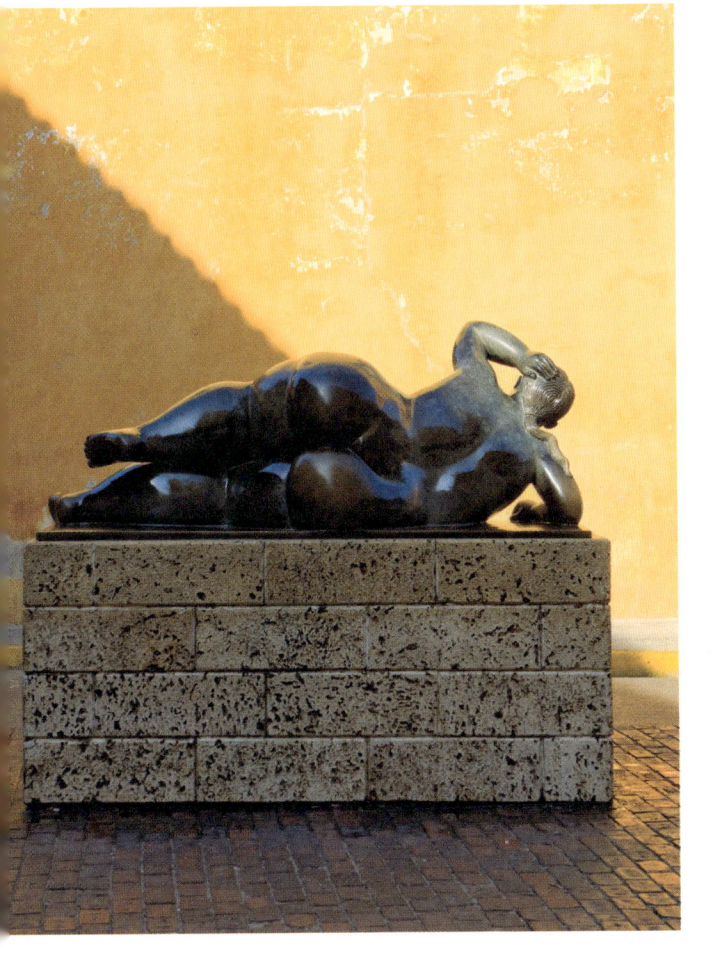

Far left to right: Traditional treats for sale in the Portal de los Dulces; Fernando Botero's reclining La Gorda Gertrudis *statue in the Plaza Santo Domingo.*

DON'T LEAVE WITHOUT…

Taking a boat trip to the Islas de Rosario. Diving Planet's snorkel tour includes two excursions in the crystal-clear water. You may spot an octopus hunting the reef's bounty or harmless jellyfish bouncing off your body as you drift by. Afterwards, take a dip in the pool and eat lunch at Hotel Cocoliso on Isla Grande.

TOP PLACES / CARTAGENA

These vendors are the descendants of those who established the first free towns for self-emancipated formerly enslaved people, outside the grip of Spanish authority.

GO WHERE EVERY STREET IS A MOSAIC OF MUSIC, ART AND FLAVOR

The vibrant spirit of Cartagena extends beyond the Old Town and into the streets of neighboring Getsemaní. Once a refuge for African and working-class communities, this enclave has blossomed into a cultural canvas where street art adorns crumbling walls, and colorful flags, umbrellas and lanterns add Instagram-worthy appeal to its already dynamic streetscape.

The Plaza de la Trinidad is the community's hub, where people from all walks of life gather – especially after dark, when food vendors entice passersby with the aroma of sizzling chorizo and deep-fried empanadas. The cloud of fragrant smoke swirling under the warm glow of streetlights creates the perfect stage for impromptu street performers moving to Cartagena's soulful beats.

Locals and travelers come together to dance the night away at Club de los Carpinteros, celebrated for its warm, laid-back atmosphere. Here, everyone surrenders to the movement and the music, and becomes part of the multicultural tapestry that makes Cartagena unforgettable.
–Laura Watilo Blake

Clockwise from top left: Neighborhood bar in Getsemaní; Vintage wheels and a classic Old Town facade; Cooling off at Cartagena's Playa Marbella; Sea turtles offshore of Islas de Rosario.

BEST IN TRAVEL 2026 / 119

TOP PLACES / FINLAND

FINLAND

Finland flies under the radar in terms of Nordic travel, but this wondrously eccentric land deserves to be better feted. Whether you're hanging out in happy Helsinki, with its Baltic light and cultural riches, or tripping the Northern Lights fantastic in the reindeer-bobbled winter wonderland of the frosty Arctic north, this country feels touched by a kind of magic.

BEST FOR
Finding happiness in wild places

COME ON, GET HAPPY

Year after year, Finland tops the charts in the UN's World Happiness Report, despite stiff competition from its Scandi neighbors. Perhaps that's because it dares to be different; you can't help but smile when you're in the world's happiest country.

The Finns prize *sisu*, an untranslatable quality comprising ideals of freedom, courage and inner strength. *Sisu* is expressed in wife-carrying world championships, and in roasting naked in a sauna – of which there are three million for a population of 5.5 million – before whipping your sweaty self with birch branches. *Sisu* is diving into an *avanto* (icehole) for a heart-stoppingly cold swim for the hell of it, or wading through mosquito-infested Arctic swamps for miles to pick summer cloudberries when you could just flop on a beach. Eccentric? Yes – but happy.

DROP INTO STORYBOOK LANDSCAPES

Finland is the quirky sister of the Nordic nations, with an elfin-esque language that inspired Tolkien

Left to right, from above: Foraging wild cloudberries is a Finnish summertime tradition; Taking a reindeer-powered sleigh safari through the snowscape.

120 / BEST IN TRAVEL 2026

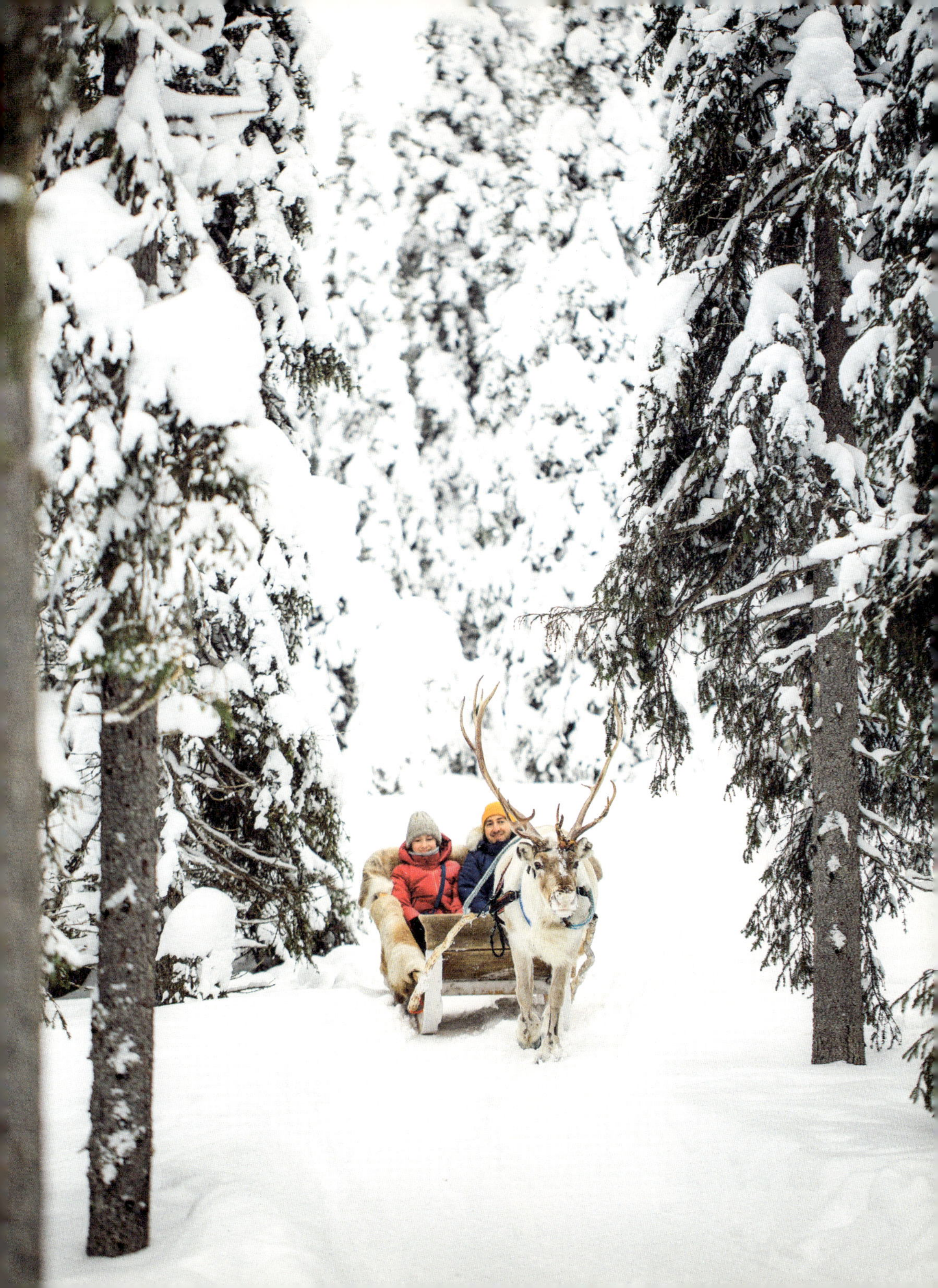

Clockwise from right: See the Northern Lights from your bed with stays at Finland's aurora-viewing domes; Fresh fish on the menu at a Finnish festival; Sea, sky and spires in Helsinki; The sinuous home of Helsinki's Central Library Oodi.

DON'T LEAVE WITHOUT...

Embracing Sámi culture in Lapland. Give Santa the slip and head to Inari or, further north still, Utsjoki, for reindeer-driven sleigh rides, and joik (rhythmic poems) sung around a flickering campfire in a simple lavvu tent. Go the whole Arctic shebang with husky mushing, snowshoeing and ice fishing, then hole up in a log cabin, igloo or aurora-gazing dome to watch the flakes silently fall or the Northern Lights erupt.

TOP PLACES / FINLAND

and landscapes seemingly sprinkled with fairy dust. In the Arctic north, Lapland fulfills childhood fantasies with snow-blanketed fells straight out of Narnia, flashing Northern Lights, and Santa's year-round HQ, Rovaniemi. This is a country at the final frontier of the imagination: here reindeer fly and Moomins get their own island, Muumimaailma. The never-dying summer light of the midnight sun and the eternal darkness of winter has a profound effect on the national psyche.

EMBRACE AN OUTDOOR PLAYGROUND

With its Baltic breezes and easygoing air, Helsinki is an enticing springboard, with upbeat food, art and design scenes. Don't miss the laid-back beat in towns and cities such as island-skipping, castle-topped Turku; cultured, lakeside Tampere; and riverside Oulu with its lively market square, Kauppatori. But these are just the prelude for Finland's truly great outdoors. The idiom *'Metsä kuuntelee silloin kun kukaan muu ei'* ('The forest listens when no one else does') speaks volumes about what Finns hold dear. And whether you are paddling through Finnish Lakeland to your cottage in the golden light of a midsummer evening, feeling the heartbeat of Sámi reindeer-herding culture in Inari, embracing the bitter cold and echoing silence of Northern Lapland dog-sledding or snow-shoeing as the aurora comes out to play, you will quickly realize that Finnish happiness is tuning into nature and being in touch with your inner child.
–*Kerry Walker*

BEST IN TRAVEL 2026 / 123

TOP PLACES / QUY NHƠN

QUY NHƠN

VIETNAM

BEST FOR Coastal adventures and seafood delights

Tucked between the mountains of Vietnam's south-central coast, Quy Nhơn is a beach city that masterfully blends tradition with modern flair. Its fishing villages preserve a timeless charm, while a growing skyline signals a city on the rise. With all the perks of an urban hub but none of the crowds, Quy Nhơn maintains a laid-back, unpolished vibe. It's a well-kept secret among domestic travelers, to which the rest of the world hasn't quite caught up.

AN UNFUSSY AND BELOVED BEACH TOWN

At its heart, Quy Nhơn's beachfront stretches along golden sands, lined by a well-kept promenade ideal for sunset strolls. As night falls, the city shifts gears, revealing a nightlife scene that's both relaxed and full of character. While it may not match Nha Trang's buzz, Quy Nhơn has its own mix of stylish cocktail lounges, lively sports bars

Left: Enjoy sunrise over Quy Nhơn from the peaks behind the city.

and beachside hangouts where comfy beanbags invite you to linger a little longer.

Quy Nhơn's culinary scene is equally enticing. Along Xuân Diệu St, seafood lovers can pick their feast straight from tanks, while Ngô Văn Sở St is the place to sample local specialities like *nem nướng* (grilled-pork rolls) or *bún sứa* (a must-try jellyfish-and-noodle dish).

For a change of pace, venture beyond the city on a motorbike to discover secluded coves and pristine beaches like Kỳ Co, a crescent-shaped bay of soft white sand that is especially popular in the summer months. Or, make your way to Bãi Xếp, a peaceful retreat where the beach transforms into an open-air dining spot at night, where fresh seafood is served in a casual yet lively atmosphere

DON'T LEAVE WITHOUT...

Making a spiritual detour to Ông Núi Temple, just north of Quy Nhơn, where a 600-step climb rewards you with one of Southeast Asia's largest seated Buddha statues, watching over the region's rugged coastline. The statue sits atop a circular temple, with thousands of smaller gilded Buddhas placed in niches recessed into the walls.

126 / BEST IN TRAVEL 2026

TOP PLACES / QUY NHƠN

under the stars. There are also a couple of lovely hotels and homestays – if time allows, spend at least one night here to truly experience Quy Nhơn's laid-back charm.

VIBRANT FISHING COMMUNITIES AND HISTORY COLLIDE

The region's soul is perhaps best found in its fishing communities. In Nhơn Hải, narrow alleyways hum with life and the smell of sizzling *bánh xèo mực* (crispy squid pancakes) draws you in. If you visit in June, paddle above shimmering fields of cultivated seaweed, which turn the water into a patchwork of gold and green. Just south of Quy Nhơn, the sleepy village of Xuân Hải springs to life at dawn. A flurry of activity unfolds as fishing boats roll in, unloading hundreds of buckets brimming with freshly caught fish. Walk through the scene as crashing waves, shouted bargains and the unmistakable scent of the morning catch fill the air.

Beyond the beaches, Quy Nhơn unveils another layer of its charm – its rich history. The region is dotted with ancient Cham ruins, their weathered red-brick structures quietly standing as reminders of a civilization long past. Among these, the Tháp Đôi Cham towers, located in the heart of the city, are the most accessible. Venture a little further and you'll find the larger Cham towers of Bánh Ít, perched high on a hill with panoramic views of the surrounding province. For a deeper dive into Quy Nhơn's past, visit the city's Bình Định Museum, where an impressive collection of Champa artifacts and sculpture shares the space with fascinating Vietnamese opera masks and costumes.

–Karla Foronda

Clockwise from top left: Quy Nhơn's Eo Gió coast, near Kỳ Co; Buying the catch of the day in Nhơn Lý.; Lovely Từ Nham, to the south of Quy Nhơn in Phú Yên; The supersized seated Buddha atop Ông Núi Temple.

BEST IN TRAVEL 2026 / 127

TOP PLACES / BRITISH COLUMBIA

BRITISH COLUMBIA

CANADA

BEST FOR
Embracing Mother Nature

TOP PLACES / BRITISH COLUMBIA

Larger than any US state outside Alaska and almost four times the size of the UK, British Columbia is a geographical giant. Crisscrossed by mountains and indented with deep fjords, this is the region that gave the world heli-skiing, Greenpeace, Nanaimo bars and the 2010 Winter Olympics. Continuing the tradition, hub city Vancouver will co-host the 2026 FIFA World Cup.

WANDER THE WILDERNESS

Mossy forests, saw-toothed mountains, whitewater rivers and wildlife-rich ecosystems: British Columbia (BC) is the kind of place that makes you want to dash out of your hotel room and energetically embrace the natural elements. There's plenty to get the pulse racing. Topped by 15,300ft (4663m) Mt Fairweather, the nation's second-largest province is a burly piece of Canadian real estate where the local culture revolves around hiking, biking, skiing and kayaking. Navigating your way around is your first big adventure: welcome to a land of grizzly bears, crevasse-ridden glaciers, uninhabited islands and whole parks that are off the road grid.

DIP INTO BC'S MELTING POT

Beyond the wilderness, more human elements beckon. Multiculturalism is an increasingly important part of BC's fabric. Not only is the province the ancestral home of 204 First Nations, whose heritage is visible in everything from totem poles to ceremonial masks, but its largest city, Vancouver, has developed into a complex melting pot of international food and culture. Drop by the Lower Mainland cities of Richmond and Surrey to enjoy some of the most creative Asian food outside Asia: novel local

Left: Ocean-fringed Vancouver is BC's buzzing hub, its metro lure backdropped by the trail-laced woodlands of Stanley Park.

BEST IN TRAVEL 2026 / 129

inventions like salmon-and-cucumber BC sushi rolls or butter-chicken pizza.

The diversity also extends to the landscape. The arid interior around the town of Osoyoos shelters Canada's only true desert, while cocooned in the east, the ginormous Columbia Icefield covers an area the size of metro Vancouver. Suspended somewhere in between, the lake-filled Okanagan region is a powerhouse of fruit-growing and viticulture. Its wine industry has exploded in recent years, with the number of wineries in the region tripling between 2004 and 2024. The vineyards extend well beyond the Okanagan, too: the Cowichan Valley on Vancouver Island is a west-coast outlier, where grapes are grown alongside peaches, apples and even tea.

EMBRACE WINTER

World Cup football might be a primary reason to visit in 2026, but with Whistler just north of Vancouver, BC has long been a fantastic skiing destination. North America's largest ski resort is an attractive Alpine-style village sitting handsomely at the north end of the Sea-to-Sky Corridor. Its 200 runs are spread across two mountains and joined by one of the world's longest free-span gondolas. In February 2025, Whistler (along with Vancouver) hosted the inaugural winter Invictus Games, nurturing an international pedigree first cemented during the 2010 Winter Olympics.

If you can't handle Whistler's crowds, there are plenty of alternatives, with more than 30 other ski resorts scattered around the province. This is a great place to try heli-skiing, a sport first conceived of in the Bugaboo

Left to right: Rocky Mountain–ringed Emerald Lake, the picture-perfect poster child of BC's Yoho National Park; Carving pristine powder in the Whistler backcountry.

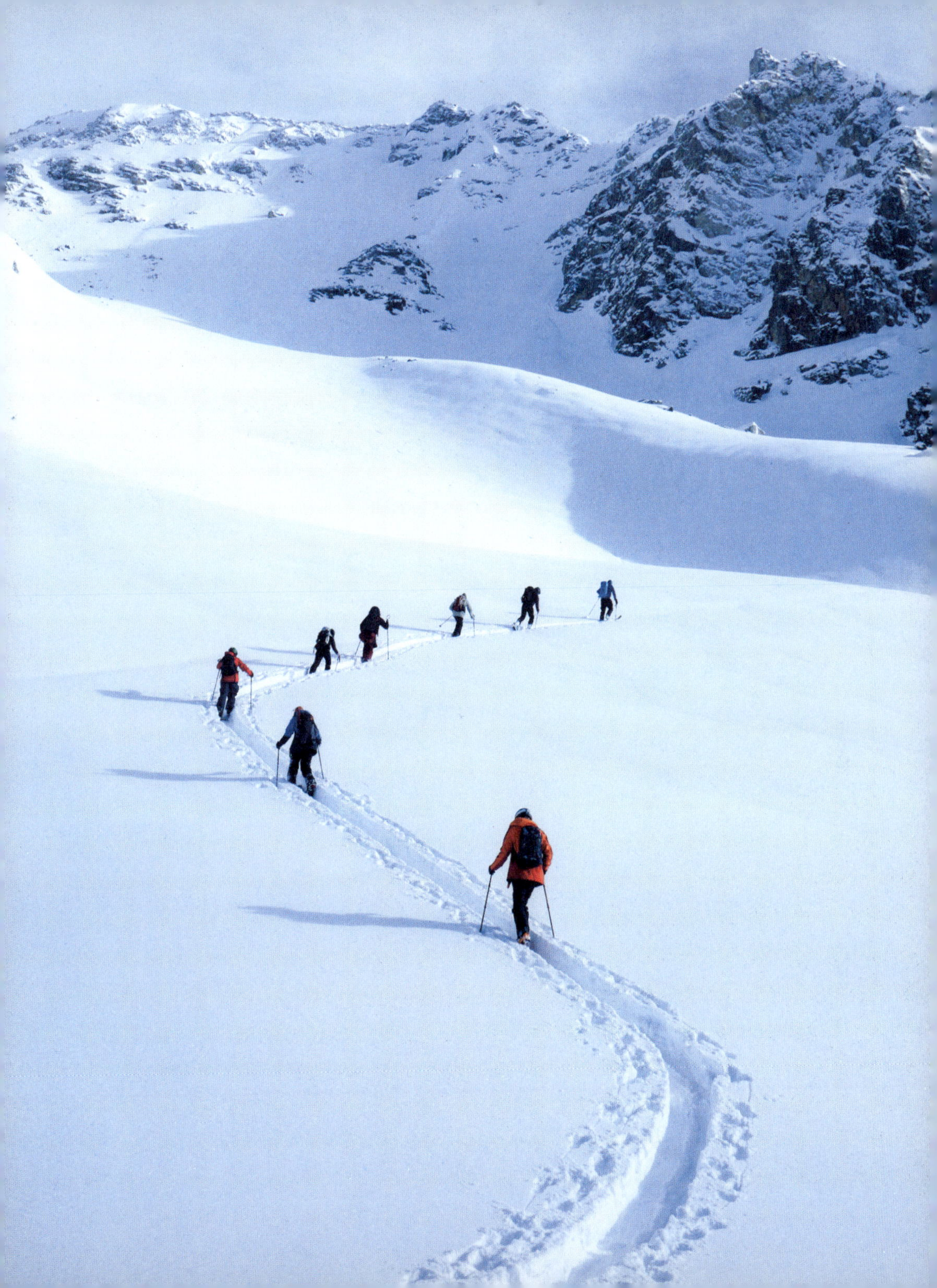

Clockwise from right: Waterside bolthole on Emerald Lake, Yoho NP; Totem pole at SGang Gwaay (Ninstints) village in Gwaii Haanas NP; Vancouver's Nitobe Memorial Garden; Lakeside Osoyoos, in the Okanagan Valley.

DON'T LEAVE WITHOUT...

Hiking the North Shore Mountains. Flush against the northern suburbs of Vancouver lies a mini-Switzerland of craggy peaks, narrow ridges and swimmable lakes, accessible via a well-marked network of trails. Within a couple of hours, you can be transported from the salubrious streets of North Van into a vast primordial backcountry, with only bears and eagles for company.

TOP PLACES / BRITISH COLUMBIA

Mountains (a subrange of the Purcells) during the 1960s. Golden is the hub town and adventure nexus, where recent developments – including a bungee-like canyon swing, an axe-throwing range and Canada's highest suspension bridge – have made it a Rocky Mountain rival to Whistler.

GET OUTSIDE

With only 5.5 million inhabitants, BC has plenty of open space to roam and explore. Herein lie seven national parks, more than any other Canadian province, with an eighth – the South Okanagan–Similkameen – currently in the planning phase. Yoho and Glacier in the Canadian Rockies are two of the oldest national parks in the world, founded in 1886 when environmentalism was still in its infancy. Subsequent BC parks include Mt Revelstoke, an early pioneer in ski-jumping; Gwaii Haanas, protecting the remnants of a Haida Indigenous village; and Pacific Rim, a surfing paradise known for its stormy, untamed beaches. The province's newest protected area is Howe Sound, a spectacular fjord north of Vancouver, established as a UNESCO Biosphere Region in 2021. It has become the latest green initiative in a province that generates over 98% of its electricity from renewable sources.
–Brendan Sainsbury

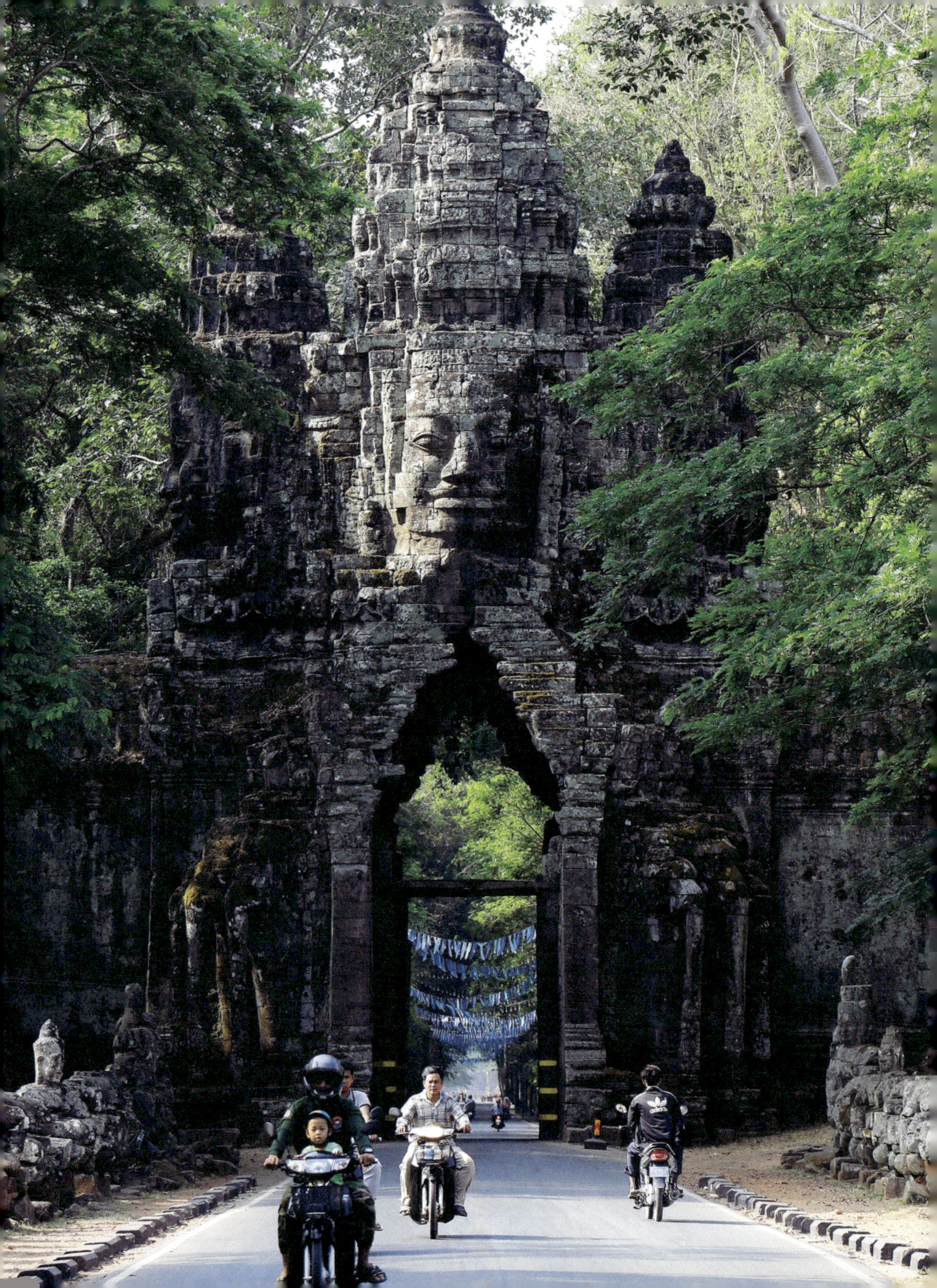

TOP PLACES / SIEM REAP

SIEM REAP

CAMBODIA

Left to right: Speeding through the ornate North Gate of Angkor Thom, part of the Angkor Wat complex; Pub St is party central in Siem Reap.

BEST FOR
Spiritual days and spirited nights

Gateway to the temples of Angkor, Siem Reap has emerged as a leading light in its own right thanks to affordable gastronomy, vibrant nightlife, adrenaline-fuelled activities, otherworldly floating villages and a host of lifestyle experiences beyond. And, sure, it might just help that the eighth wonder of the world, Angkor Wat, is right on the doorstep.

DISCOVER A TERRIFIC TEMPLE-TOURING BASE
Following two decades of uninterrupted expansion, boom turned to bust in Siem Reap in 2020 as the Covid pandemic locked the world down – but that offered some breathing space from overtourism and the chance to hit the reset button. Siem Reap remains one of the best-value destinations in an already absurdly affordable region; and in Angkor Wat, the world's largest religious building, it has an iconic attraction that puts all others in the shade. The new Siem Reap–Angkor International Airport has connections throughout the region; Mekong River cruises offer a slower, sublime alternative route to Ho Chi Minh City (Saigon); and there are bus services to all major cities in Cambodia. An easy-to-arrange e-visa (US$30) and the all-inclusive

BEST IN TRAVEL 2026 / 135

TOP PLACES / SIEM REAP

temple pass (currently US$37/62/72 for one, three or seven days) are the big-ticket budget items, but after that it is US$5 massages or US$1 beers all the way to Pub St.

Siem Reap is northwest Cambodia's gateway to the majestic temples of Angkor – a UNESCO World Heritage site that tops the historic bucket list for many travelers to the Mekong region. A first glimpse of Angkor Wat is matched by only a few select sites on Earth, perhaps Machu Picchu or Petra.

This vast complex has the epic proportions of the Great Wall of China, the detail and intricacy of the Taj Mahal and the symbolism and symmetry of the Great Pyramid all rolled into one.

The ancient Khmer kings of old packed the equivalent of all Europe's great cathedrals into an area the size of Los Angeles, making the fabled structures of Angkor a veritable 'Templeland' for archaeology enthusiasts. And beyond the main Angkor site awaits an incredible diversity of other temples that would be the envy of any country in the region: the enigmatic faces of the Bayon, the so-called *Tomb Raider* temple of Ta Prohm and the exquisite carvings of Banteay Srei, all remarkable in their own right.

FLOATING VILLAGES, ZIPLINES AND A TRIP TO THE CIRCUS

Siem Reap is so much more than its fabled temples. It's located just down the road (and river) from Tonlé Sap, the largest lake in Southeast Asia, home to several floating villages and soaring stilt-house communities. The most atmospheric are the large stilted villages of Kompong Pluk and Kompong Khleang. And, if it floats your boat, try a wet-season kayaking trip through the flooded forests of Me Chrey.

Left to right: Sunrise over Angkor Wat, the moat-ringed temple complex that put Siem Reap on the map; Embraced by ever-encroaching forest, Ta Prohm is Angkor's most atmospheric site.

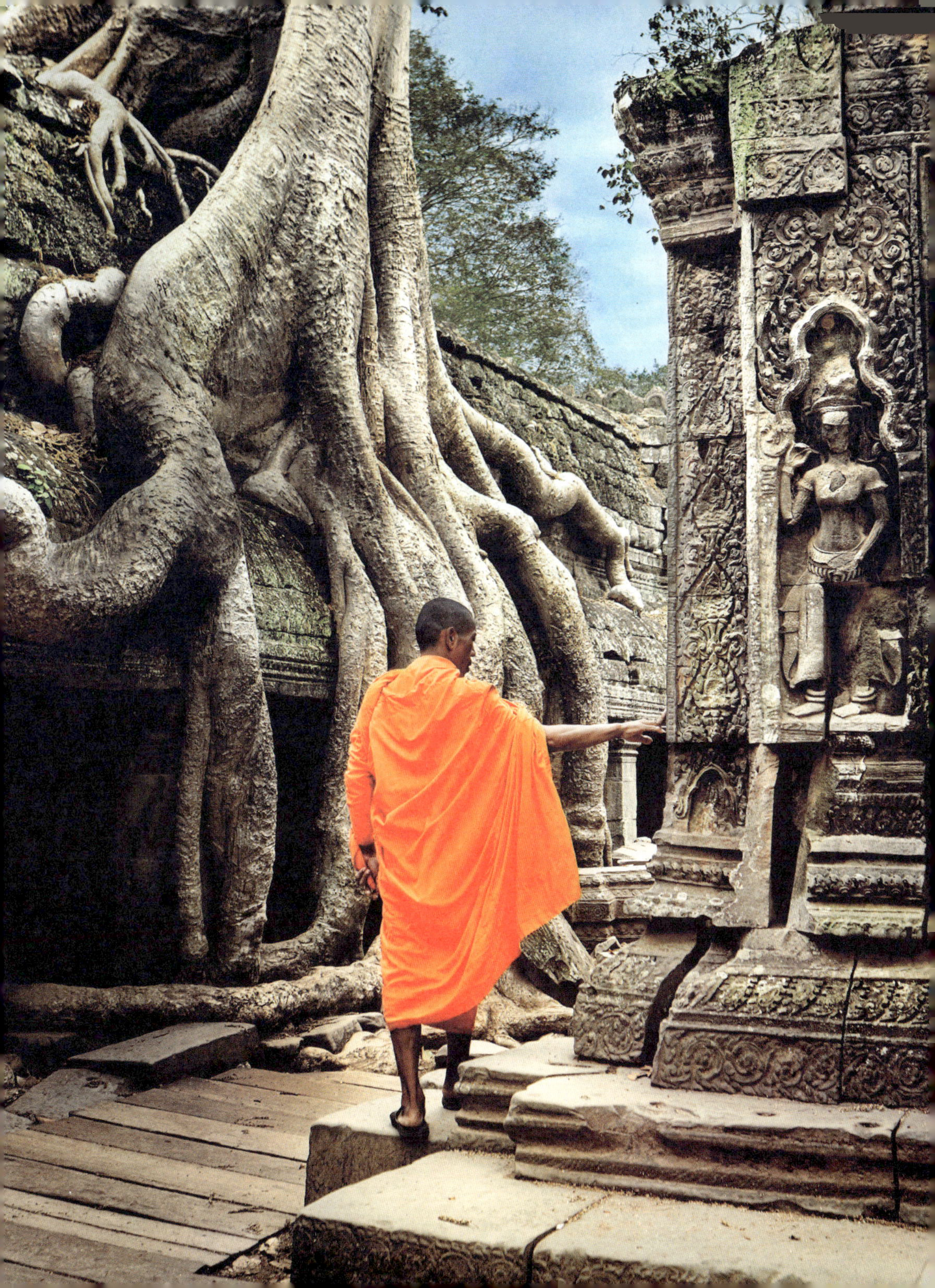

Clockwise from right: Siem Reap's cityscape at sunset; Khmer-style *amok* fish curry is a highlight of Cambodian cuisine; Finely carved temple walls inside Angkor Wat; Paddling Tonlé Sap mangroves near the floating village of Kompong Pluk.

MOST MEMORABLE MOMENT

The cycling track connecting Siem Reap to the Angkor area follows jungle paths long used by locals to move between village and temple. Ride the ancient walls of Angkor Thom, linking the Gate of the Dead (East) with the South Gate and passing the vast moat, whose dimensions would make a European castle blush. Up among the jungle treetops, birds dart about, and you may even spot a gibbon or otter.

TOP PLACES / SIEM REAP

But if you prefer the rush, there are adrenaline activities aplenty. The Angkor Zipline is a treetop web of cables that whizzes through the forest home of a resident family of funky gibbons. For a more extensive walk on the wild side, head to Kulen Elephant Forest, where a herd of peaceful pachyderms roam in retirement. Cometh the night, there is no better date than the brilliant bunch of clowns at Phare the Cambodian Circus, a homegrown social enterprise shining a light on the complexities of Khmer culture.

At the infamous Pub St in Siem Reap, the volume is permanently turned up to 11, but there are also mellower boltholes to experience the legendary nightlife of 'Temple Town'. The Boho neighborhood is an enticing option, home to Miss Wong, a throwback to 1920s Shanghai that serves some of the best cocktails in town; or Laundry Bar, a late-night haunt with pool tables and ambient tunes.

Angkor is the diva to lure you in and Siem Reap provides the script for your stay, with its hip hostels and boutique hotels – but the soul of the region lies in the Cambodian people. Their warmth and welcome is legendary and their spirit will leave an indelible mark on your soul.
–Nick Ray

BEST IN TRAVEL 2026 / 139

TOP PLACES / NORTH ISLAND

NORTH ISLAND

BEST FOR
Cultural tourism that gives back

NEW ZEALAND/AOTEAROA

No trip to New Zealand is complete without learning about Māori culture, with most visitors eager to watch a kapa haka *(traditional song and dance)* performance or take part in a hāngī *(earth-cooked meal)*. But on the country's North Island, its Indigenous tourism experiences are about far more than just a dinner and a show.

TRAVEL AND PAY IT FORWARD
As concerns about the negative effects of mass tourism intensify – including environmental and cultural degradation – destinations are increasingly turning to 'regenerative tourism' as the answer. It's frequently defined as 'leaving a place better than you found it', but the practice requires an entire mindset change – one in which

Left: Dramatic Cape Reinga headland at the top of the North Island, where the Tasman Sea meets the Pacific Ocean.

the needs of communities are put before those of tourists.

Still not sure exactly what it looks like? Then a trip to New Zealand's North Island might be in order. Aotearoa (NZ's Māori-language name) has emerged as a world leader in regenerative tourism, with the federal government embedding regenerative principles throughout its tourism strategy. This is in no small part due to 'te ao Māori' (the Māori worldview), which emphasizes concepts like *kaitiakitanga* (guardianship and protection of the environment) and *manaakitanga* (caring for others and showing kindness) while also focusing on interconnectedness and relationships – including those between ancestors and future generations.

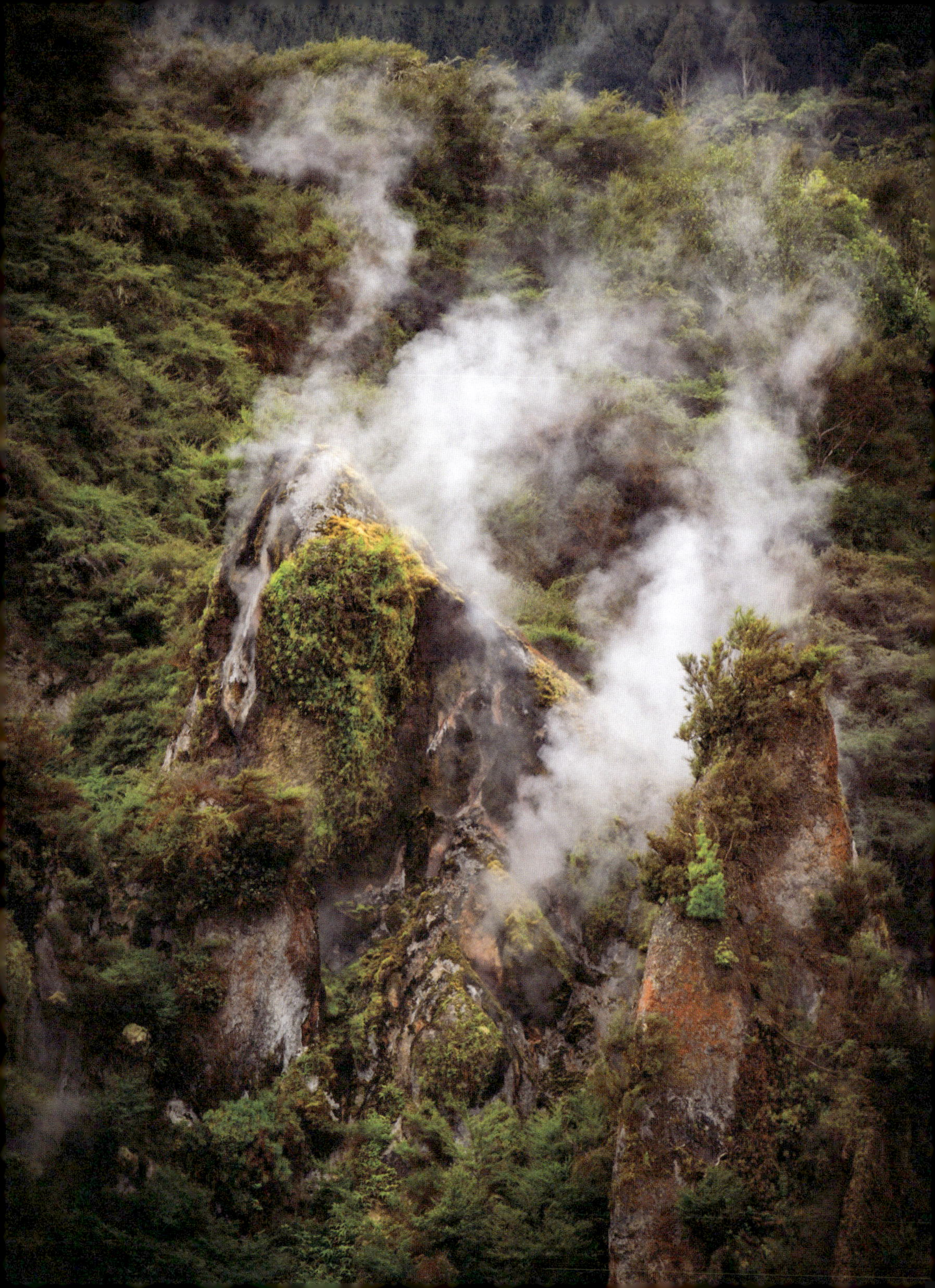

UNDERSTAND THE BACKSTORY

Simply put, Māori-led tourism is regenerative tourism. Its roots date back to the mid-19th century, when wealthy Europeans first traveled to the Antipodes to see the 'Eighth Wonder of the World': Rotorua's Pink and White Terraces. They were destroyed by Mt Tarawera's 1886 eruption, but the tradition continues today throughout the Bay of Plenty region. Rotorua is still the spot to visit *marae* (meeting grounds), watch skilled *kapa haka* performers and indulge in a *hāngī* cooked in the bubbling-hot geothermal pools. But these attractions aren't purely performative. Rather, Māori tour operators dedicated to uplifting their communities are emerging across Te Ika-a-Māui (the North Island).

One example is Kohutapu Lodge in Murupara, about 45 minutes from Rotorua. This family-owned business was developed to create economic opportunity and help youth develop pride in their culture. It was needed in one of the country's most socially and economically disadvantaged areas, where substance abuse and gang violence have taken root. Visitors can learn to do the *haka*, fish for *tuna* (eel) or take a guided walking tour to ancient rock carvings. And by bringing tourists into a town that most visitors would otherwise bypass, Kohutapu has been able to invest back into the community.

Further afield in Te Tai Tokerau (Northland), you'll find Manea Footprints of Kupe, an immersive cultural experience that shares the story of Polynesian explorer Kupe's arrival in NZ. When it opened in 2021, it became the region's third-largest employer, hiring many local youth in an area with high unemployment

Far left to right: Steamy Waimangu Volcanic Valley lies just south of Rotorua; Experience Te Tai Tokerau (Northland) culture at Rotorua Māori settlements like Ōhinemutu Village.

Clockwise from right: See Kiwi chicks at the National Kiwi Hatchery Aotearoa in Rotorua; Towering kauri trees hold special significance in Māori culture; Sheep graze the vineyards in Hawke's Bay wine country; Soak in the hot springs of Wai Ariki and enjoy views of Lake Rotorua.

DON'T LEAVE WITHOUT…

Taking a dip in geothermally heated waters at Wai Ariki, the area's first and only spa and wellness center to be developed, owned and run by Māori. At this luxurious new hot springs and spa on the shores of Lake Rotorua, you can experience the centuries-old practices of local iwi *(tribe) Ngāti Whakaue.*

TOP PLACES / NORTH ISLAND

rates. As a charitable enterprise, all of Manea's profits go directly back into the community.

BUILD COMMUNITY, SAVE THE PLANET, DRINK WINE
Across the North Island, you'll meet tour operators who are protecting native birdlife and the country's biodiversity through eradicating invasive predators. North of Wellington, Māori-owned Kapiti Island Nature Tours act as *kaitiaki* (guardians) of the predator-free island, where it's possible to spot endemic birds including kākā, takahē and kākāriki (red-crowned parakeets). Stay the night in one of the glamping tents and you may even encounter one of the island's population of little spotted kiwi, now extinct on the mainland.

This care for the land and its people isn't restricted to ecotourism. In Hawke's Bay – a wine-producing region known for its food festivals and award-winning restaurants – viticulturalists no longer rely on the French term *terroir* to describe provenance. Instead, they're increasingly using *tūrangawaewae*. It roughly translates to 'a place to stand', but the term embodies more than just the soil in which the grapes were grown – it also refers to a multigenerational connection to the land. Learn more about this ethos at Smith & Sheth's Heretaunga Wine Studio, a powerful wine-tasting experience.

For centuries, the North Island has been renowned for its geothermal wonders and rich cultural experiences – and these local businesses are ensuring this will be true for centuries to come.
–*Jessica Lockhart*

BEST IN TRAVEL 2026 / 145

BEST EXPER

151 *Hike and wildcamp:* Tajikistan

154 *Go on a cultural food tour:* Old Dubai, United Arab Emirates

161 *Stay in a train carriage:* Kruger National Park, South Africa

164 *Visit Eileen Gray's house:* Southern France

168 *Spend the night in a ryokan:* Japan

175 *Track desert elephants:* Namibia

178 *Look for jaguars in the wetlands:* Iberá, Argentina

182 *Watch a Flying Cholitas match:* Bolivia

191 *Rapid-raft the Colorado River:* Grand Canyon, USA

195 *Explore the Bathing Trail:* Victoria, Australia

198 *Cruise the Mekong River:* Vietnam & Cambodia

204 *Ride horses in the Andes Mountains:* Ecuador

209 *Take a Creole trail ride:* Louisiana, USA

214 *Go on a culinary tour:* Kerala, India

IENCES

219 *Attend a Premier League game:* England

225 *Visit Willamette Wine Country:* Oregon, USA

228 *Savor the exciting food scene:* Melbourne, Australia

233 *Become a citizen scientist:* The Amazon, Peru

238 *Party in the Caribbean:* Grenada

247 *See the sights by bike:* Batanes Islands, Philippines

250 *Experience the legendary nightlife scene:* Belgrade, Serbia

257 *Stay at Hawai'i's Volcano House:* Volcanoes National Park, USA

261 *Go whale-watching:* Azores, Portugal

265 *Deep-dive into street art:* Bristol, England

269 *Go stargazing:* Wairarapa, New Zealand/Aotearoa

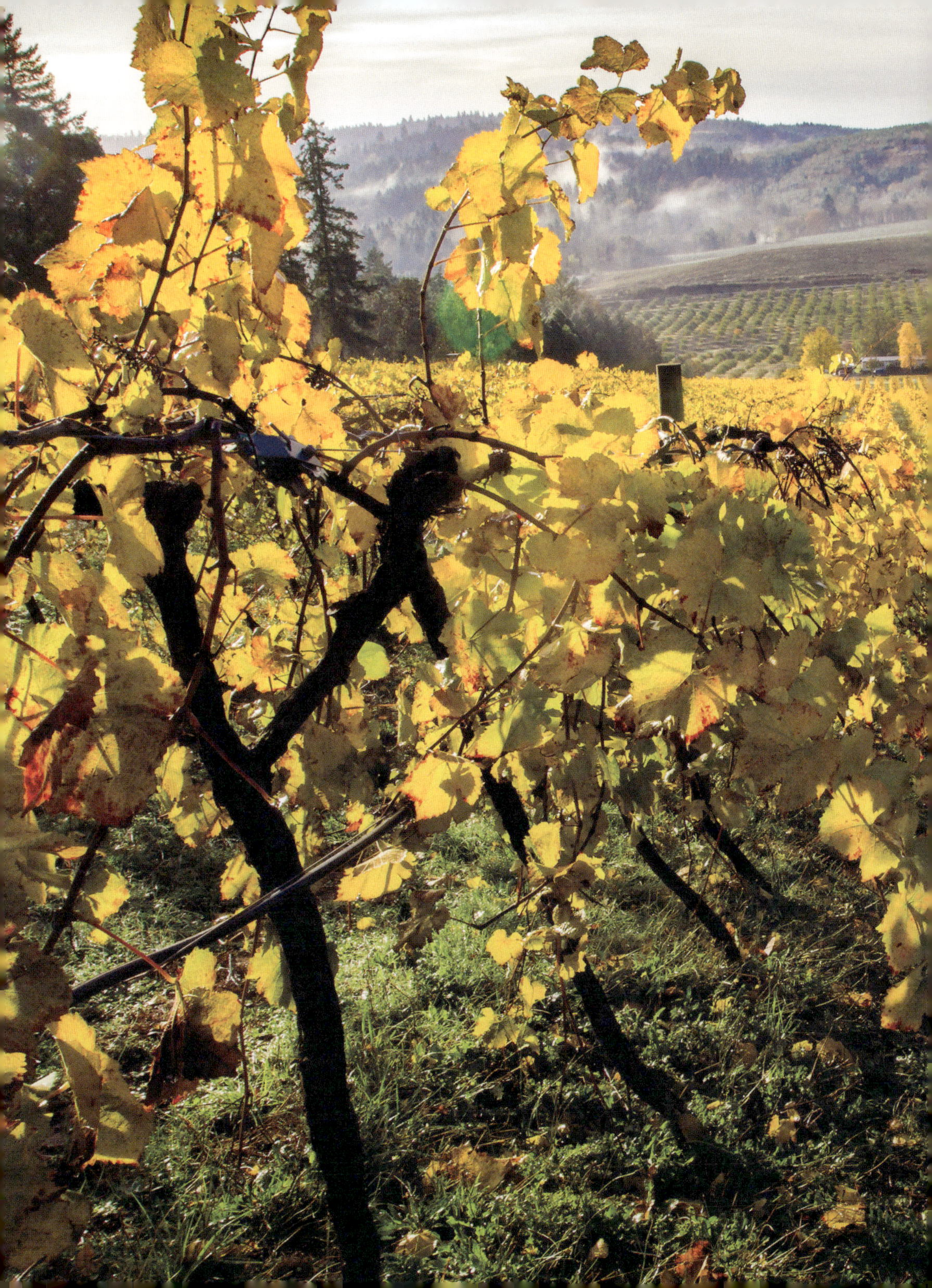

Fall colors flood the vineyards of Oregon's Willamette Valley (p225).

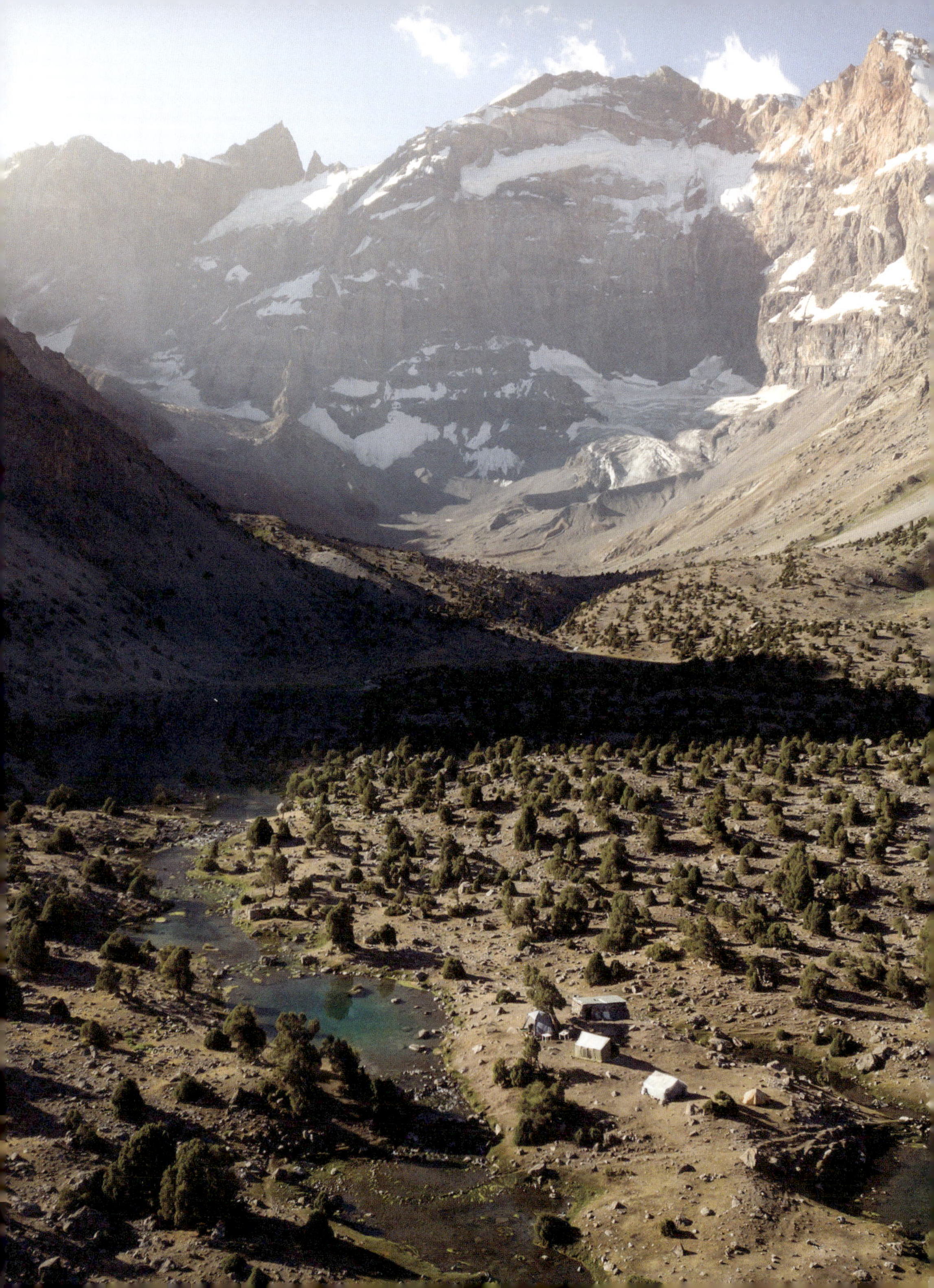

TOP EXPERIENCES / TAJIKISTAN

Hike and wildcamp
TAJIKISTAN

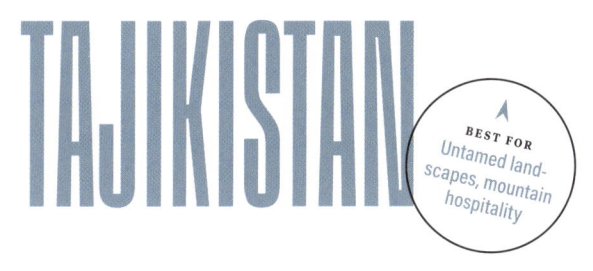

BEST FOR
Untamed landscapes, mountain hospitality

Tajikistan's saw-toothed skyline and glacier-carved valleys are phenomenal. But perplexingly, this Central Asian nation's affordable, unsupported treks remain relatively unsung. With cinematic lakes and snow-speckled peaks seconds from your sleeping bag, the Fan Mountains furnish a life-affirming wildcamping adventure.

A TRIP TO THE UNPARALLELED AND UNSUNG

With a topography that's 93% mountainous, Tajikistan and trekking should be synonymous. Outlandish jagged scenes unfurl as you schlep through saddles between the summits; stories of the Silk Road and Sogdia's ancient Iranian civilization whisper on the eagle-swooped breeze; and pure glacial lakes mirror snow-pinnacled massifs. Few countries roll out a wildcamping carpet like this, yet the nation's invitation to intrepid wayfarers is largely overlooked.

Unzipping your tent to frame any of the country's preposterously pretty panoramas is indelible. But you'll find the (subjectively) most spectacular sweep of swoonworthy vistas in Sughd Province, where the Fan Mountains (Fannsky Gory) will forever burn into your mind.

Folded among the Fan's soaring, snow-sheathed peaks are camping-ripe verdant valleys and a succession of ice-clear lakes

Left to right: A jaw-dropping campsite setting in the Fan Mountains' Kulikalon Basin; The tent-flap view at Alovaddin Lakes.

BEST IN TRAVEL 2026 / 151

MOST MEMORABLE MOMENT

Tajik hospitality is endless. Even out here, you'll likely stumble upon a spontaneous invite. Be it sharing a shepherd's fire-cooked oshi palav *(pilaf) and a starlit vodka swig, an unprompted offer of donkey support to ascend a pass, or helping a fisher reel in their lake catch – perhaps rewarded by a camp-stove feast – the kindhearted, impromptu encounters are unforgettable.*

TOP EXPERIENCES / TAJIKISTAN

scintillating in shades of cerulean, cyan, teal and psychedelic green. In pictures or in person, it appears practically photoshopped.

For an easygoing introduction, head to Haft-Kul. Translated as Seven Lakes, the route traverses a string of pristine pools and stone-built hamlets. Spend a night in a homestay, slumbering on stacked *kurpatchas* (thick carpets), and you'll experience Tajikistan's legendary hospitality as you break (Tajik's circular flat) bread with your kindhearted hosts. Then, venture towards towering, craggy Mt Chimtarga for the Lakes Loop, a rewarding multi-day trek bypassing the most challenging pass.

A TREK WORTH THE EXTRA CARGO AND MILES

Camping waterside at Alovaddin Lakes and in the fertile Kulikalon Basin, roamed by shepherds and their sheep in summer, it's hard not to feel a sense of backpacking bliss: you're humbled, ecstatic, serene and vivaciously alive – even after lugging your load up the sometimes strenuous gravel saddles.

For the most part, society is welcomingly scarce up here. Infrequent tent *chaikhanas* (tea houses, selling dried fruits, nuts, tea and beer) provide the only sustenance you haven't hauled in. Otherwise, encounters are exclusively the occasional fellow rambler, ranger or mountain resident, often as you pause for chai.

If going it alone sounds daunting, contact Zerafshan Tourism Development Association (ZTDA), which arranges supported tours during the May to September trekking season. Either way, come prepared. Once you've marveled at the Milky Way from your 'front door' and sipped your first camp-stove coffee while surveying a shimmering sunrise, you'll be elated that you've heeded Tajikistan's invitation.

–Daniel James Clarke

Clockwise from top left: Nomadic shepherds graze flocks across Tajikistan's steppes; A frigid snowmelt pool in the Fan; Crossing the Alovaddin Pass; Cooking *oshi palav* (pilaf) trailside.

TOP EXPERIENCES / OLD DUBAI

Go on a cultural food tour
OLD DUBAI

UNITED ARAB EMIRATES

BEST FOR
Food-loving culture vultures

TOP EXPERIENCES / OLD DUBAI

Ask a Dubai old-timer and they'll confess their love for a side of the city that few tourists experience. Beyond posh luxury hotels and gargantuan shopping malls, the atmospheric souks and backstreets of Dubai's oldest neighborhoods invite culturally curious visitors to hole-in-the-wall cafeterias and family-run restaurants to savor a taste of the simpler life.

A HISTORIC, SECRET SIDE TO DUBAI

With its majestic minarets, vibrant souks and heady experiences, Old Dubai harks back to a bygone era, in a striking contrast to the modern city's shimmering skyscrapers and contemporary attractions. In the 1950s, when Dubai's population numbered just 20,000, this was the center of the city. It includes the working-class neighborhoods of Bur Dubai, Deira and Shindagha, sprawling around Dubai Creek – the beating heart of Old Dubai.

An ancient pearl-diving site with a history spanning thousands of years, this natural creek formed Dubai's first port. Before oil was discovered in the 1960s, ships arrived here from East Africa, Iran and India to trade gold, textiles and spices in Old Dubai's souks. The culinary influence of these imports, along with the food of the city's first immigrants (from Iran and the Indian subcontinent), significantly impacted Emirati cuisine and the city's overall food culture. A walking foodie tour of Old Dubai reveals the rich tapestry of flavors shaping the diverse cuisine scene that defines the city today.

Left: Emirati breakfast spreads at Old Dubai's Arabian Tea House include delicious *balaleet* (omelet-topped vermicelli) and *chebab* (pancakes).

TAKE A DIY WALKING (AND EATING) TOUR

Start with a stroll through the narrow alleyways of the Al Fahidi Historical Neighborhood, where over 50 19th-century houses sit on the banks of Dubai Creek. Once

BEST IN TRAVEL 2026 / 155

TOP EXPERIENCES / OLD DUBAI

the residences of wealthy traders, their restored sand-hued walls and leafy courtyards house restaurants, boutique hotels and museums. You can't miss the houses' most distinctive feature: the *barjeel*. Built from sandstone, teak, gypsum and wood, these wind towers kept them cool on hot summer days.

Begin at the Arabian Tea House, which serves hearty Emirati dishes prepared from the founder's family recipes. Sit in the courtyard on blue benches, or indoors, where black-and-white photographs of Dubai line the walls. The Emirati breakfast tray includes favorites like *balaleet* (omelet-topped vermicelli) and *chebab* (pancakes). For lunch, order the *machboos* (spiced rice with meat or fish) or *saloona* (a vegetable and meat stew).

A few doors down, stop at the Bayt Al Khanyar Museum to admire rare Emirati daggers and old photographs of former sheikhs wearing these decorative blades. Nearby, the Sheikh Mohammed Centre for Cultural Understanding offers guided tours, authentic Emirati meals, and insights into traditions like Arabic calligraphy and *gahwa* (Arabic coffee). To dive deeper into Dubai's culinary subcultures, go on a curated food walk with local expert Frying Pan Adventures.

From there, it's a brisk 10-minute walk past the 1787 Al Fahidi Fort (Dubai's oldest building) to Bur Dubai Souq, where it's hard not to find yourself longing for exquisite pashmina shawls, colorful handmade pottery, Persian rugs and beautiful custom-made sand art.

Continue until you emerge on the waterfront at Bur Dubai Abra Station. Take an *abra* (water taxi) across the creek and disembark at the Deira Old Souq Abra Station. Head to Jafer Biman Ali Cafeteria; this tiny spot has stood

Left to right: Relax Emirati-style in the comfortable courtyard at Arabian Tea House; Taste traditional dishes prepared from beloved family recipes at the Tea House's shaded streetside tables.

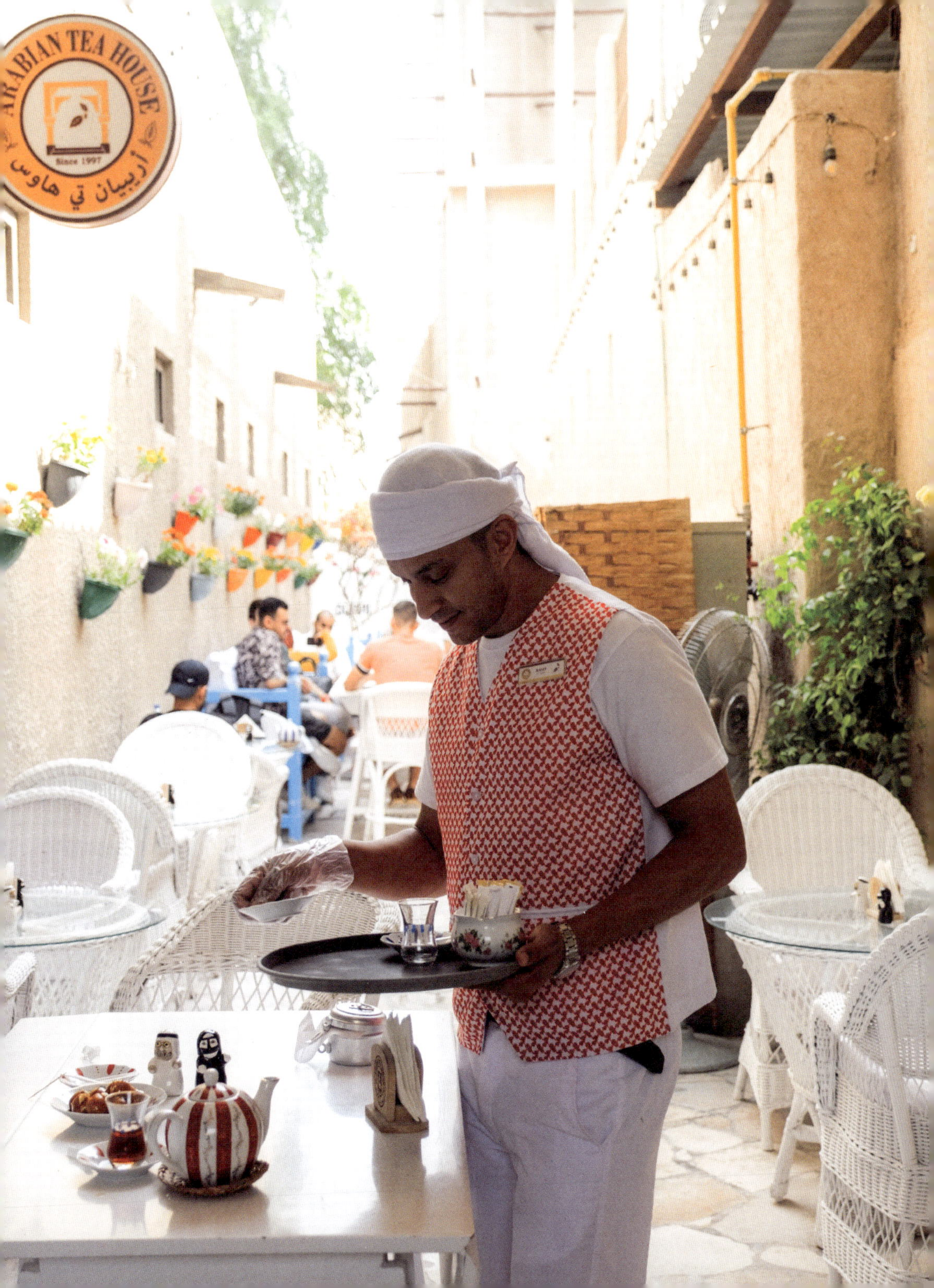
ARABIAN TEA HOUSE
Since 1997
أريبيان تي هاوس

Clockwise from right: Board an *abra* to cross the storied Dubai Creek; Atmospheric Al Fahidi Historical Neighborhood; *Gahwa* (Arabic coffee) at the Sheikh Mohammed Centre for Cultural Understanding; Spices for sale at Bur Dubai Souq.

MOST MEMORABLE MOMENT

Watching yellow-beaked seagulls spread their slender wings over *abras crossing the Dubai Creek. Passengers put their phones away to appreciate views of colorful wooden dhows, minarets, heritage architecture, busy souks and the city's first skyscrapers. At this seawater inlet between Bur Dubai and Deira, time seems to stand still in a city that changes so frequently.*

TOP EXPERIENCES / OLD DUBAI

in this historic marketplace since the 1950s and is a classic example of Dubai's humble cafeterias. Started by the city's earliest immigrants, these became go-to spots for working class locals to grab a meal or snack at any time of day. Get a refreshing rose-and-lime-syrup-doused Iranian *faloodeh* (frozen vermicelli dessert) and continue towards the Spice Souq. Sacks of saffron, turmeric, cinnamon, rose petals and tea line the streets, their aromas mingling with burning frankincense.

WINDOW-SHOPPING WITH ALL FIVE SENSES

Stroll through the Gold Souq, where windows showcase tiered gold necklaces, diamond bracelets and wedding jewellery. Walk on through the Perfume Souq to reach Shiraz Nights for delicious *shawarma* sandwiches – thin *saj* bread stuffed with freshly shaved meat and garlic sauce, believed to have arrived from Türkiye in the 20th century and now the city's favorite street food.

From Al Sabkha Marine Transport Station, take a five-minute *abra* ride to Al Fahidi Marine Transport Station and walk to Al Ustad Special Kabab. At this no-frills, family-run institution, the walls proudly show off photographs of famous customers – from Bollywood celebrities and international footballers to members of Dubai's royal family. After just one bite of their yogurt-marinated *kabab khas*, saffron-flavored *joojeh kabab*, creamy hummus and butter-drenched rice, their iconic status will begin to make sense.

–Natasha Amar

BEST IN TRAVEL 2026 / 159

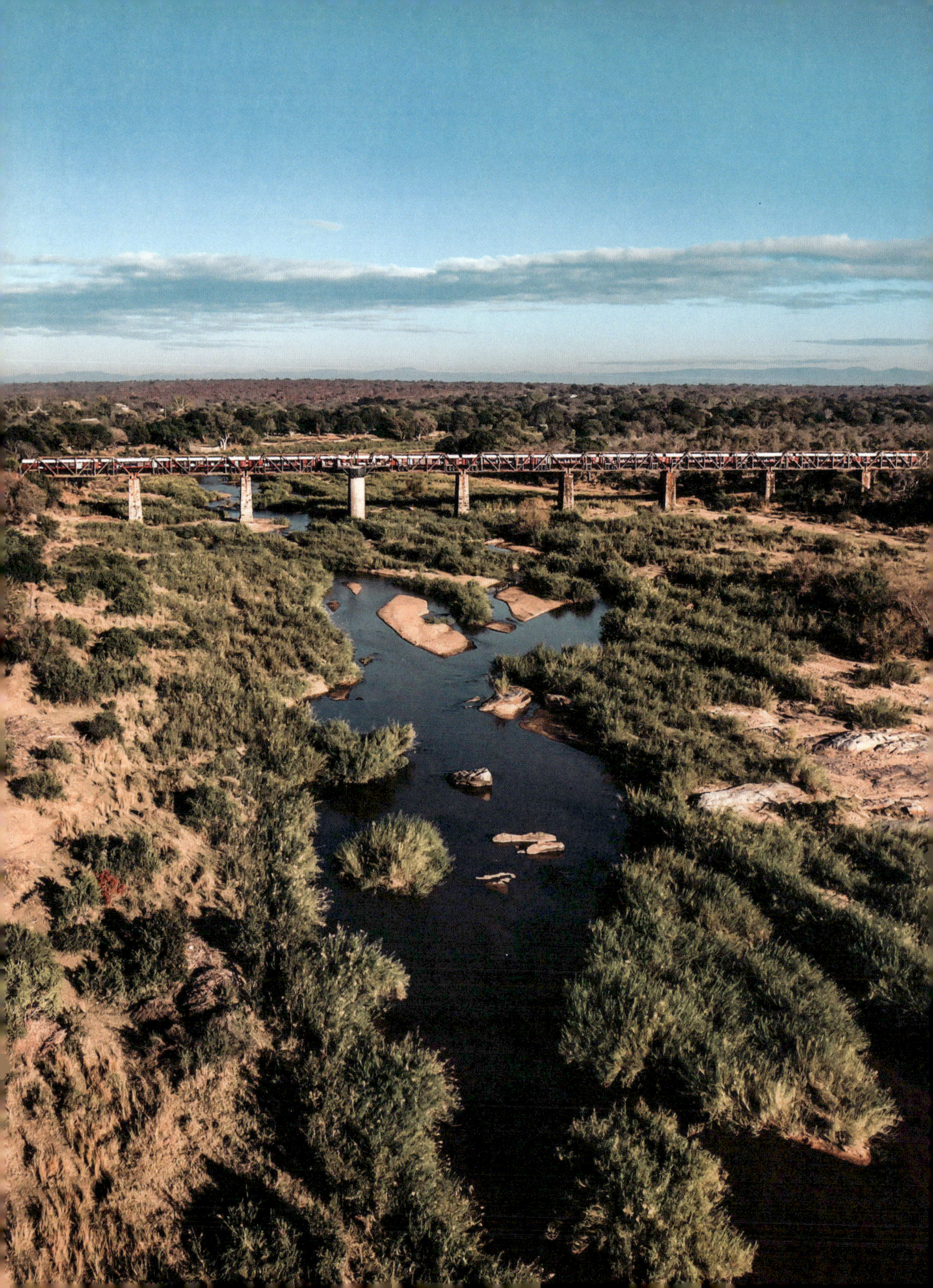

TOP EXPERIENCES / KRUGER NP

Stay in a train carriage
KRUGER NATIONAL PARK

BEST FOR A unique safari rethink

SOUTH AFRICA

Nature and history converge in the glass-walled carriages of the Kruger Shalati. Suspended high above the Sabie River on a century-old railway bridge, this vintage train – sensitively converted into a luxe hotel and positioned in this picture-perfect spot – offers a unique setting from which to watch the park's wonderful wildlife.

LOOK OUT BELOW
The origins of the railway that once ran through Kruger National Park date back to 1893, when construction of tracks through the Selati Basin began. Disrupted by the South African War, the Selati Line began carrying passengers in 1912; by 1923, it was ferrying fortune-seekers and early safari-goers on the 'Round in Nine' route, which included an overnight stop on the Selati Bridge. Accompanied by campfire dinners and bush walks, the Selati experience became legendary, and helped spark the tourism boom that would see Kruger declared a national park in 1926. The train line ceased operation in the 1970s, but vintage carriages were carefully restored by the Motsamayi Tourism Group and transformed into today's train hotel. With glass-walled carriage suites and an infinity pool set over 900ft (275m) above the river, this is arguably the country's best vantage point from which to gaze out at wildlife.

Left to right: Rooms in the Kruger Shalati 'Train on the Bridge' enjoy a panoramic perch above the wildlife-rich Sabie River; Spotting hyenas on a safari excursion.

BEST IN TRAVEL 2026 / 161

MOST MEMORABLE MOMENT

As dusk begins to fall, make your way to the restored carriage bar and order a vintage-themed cocktail or a glass of South African Pinotage. Claim a corner of the infinity pool – your own 'watering hole' above the Sabie – while elephants gather below at theirs.

TOP EXPERIENCES / KRUGER NP

The setting alone is pure magic. Beneath the Selati Bridge, the Sabie carves its way through the bushveld. Crocodiles glide just below the river's surface, their presence betrayed only by the faint ripple of water. Pods of hippos laze in the shallows, their grunts the soundtrack to many an evening sundowner. Beyond the river, the acacia-dotted plains of Kruger stretch endlessly.

A COCKTAIL IN THE CARRIAGE BAR

Many come to Kruger for the wildlife: the promise of leopards draped over trees, blood-red sunsets and early morning game drives to spot a pride of lions. Kruger Shalati delivers on all of these. But the true magic of the Train on the Bridge is how it encourages you to linger. Guests often forgo a game drive or two for lounging in the infinity pool with a cocktail from the carriage bar, or to pick out the shape of springbok from the comfort of their bed at dawn, as the sky slowly lightens against the bushveld.

The Kruger Shalati's decor honors local craftsmanship without resorting to safari clichés. Seanamarena blankets – traditional Basotho wool designs known for their rich patterns and cultural symbolism – lie draped over king-sized beds, their bold motifs blending with the rusty reds, ochres and soft creams of the carriages. Handwoven screens filter golden light from floor-to-ceiling windows, local art adorns the carriage walls, and handmade robes hang for guests to slip into after a soak in the rooms' enormous tubs. And unlike many all-inclusive hotels, the Kruger Shalati's culinary offering steers well clear of bland internationalism. With dishes like venison bobotie croquettes or delicate ostrich carpaccio, alongside a curated wine list of more than 100 options, local flavors take center stage.

–Sophie Baker

Clockwise from top left: A sunset view aboard the Kruger Shalati; Wildlife sightings might include lions and their cubs; The train in situ on the Selati Bridge; Elephants in Kruger National Park.

BEST IN TRAVEL 2026 / 163

TOP EXPERIENCES / FRANCE

Visit Eileen Gray's house

SOUTHERN FRANCE

BEST FOR
Architecture and design buffs

Tucked into the cliffs of Roquebrune-Cap-Martin in the Côte d'Azur, Villa E-1027 is a prime example of modernist architecture and design. Completed in 1929 by architects Eileen Gray and Jean Badovici, the villa emphasises functional beauty, clean lines and clever furniture, plus sweeping views of the Mediterranean. Its history, character and location make it an unexpected delight.

DISCOVER EILEEN GRAY'S VISION

Just a few bays over from Monaco, perched on the rocky cliffs of Roquebrune-Cap-Martin and overlooking the Mediterranean Sea, is Villa E-1027. Though accessible only by foot, a well-worn path (once patrolled by customs officers watching out for smugglers) winds along the sea and the train line, continuing for a few hundred meters to a rather

Left: With an enviable cliffside location in the storied Côte d'Azur, Eileen Gray's pioneering Villa E-1027 is a masterpiece of modernist design.

nondescript gate that opens to a tiny staircase down toward the Med. The walk is well-rewarded: the descent opens up to rows of prettily manicured citrus trees, while bright bougainvillea petals spill onto the ground, even in winter. The breathtaking view of the sea alone is worth the short trek.

Villa E-1027 – so enigmatically named after the architect, Eileen Gray, and fellow architect Jean Badovici, with whom she designed the building ('10' for 'J', '2' for 'B' and '7' for 'G') – was completed in 1929. It's an example of functional design and clean lines, with an emphasis on practicality and a seamless connection with nature – this at a time when lavishly decorated, ornate design dominated. Upon entry, heavily stenciled text on the walls and furniture – some obvious labels, others wickedly funny

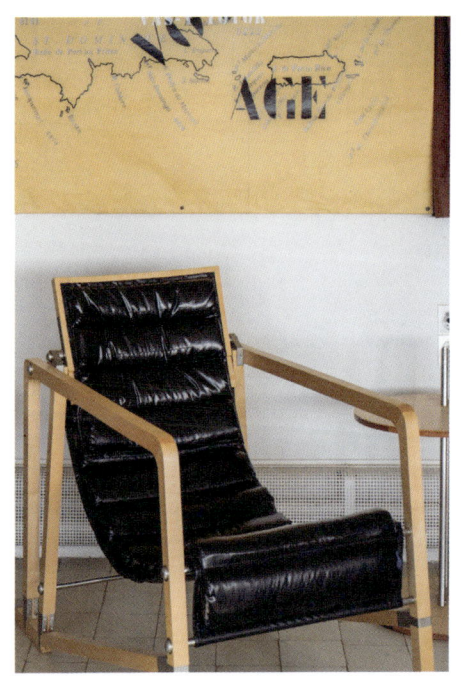

MOST MEMORABLE MOMENT

Gazing from the villa's sun-drenched gardens, you'll understand why Gray's design is considered a love letter to the coast. Nestled within the lush Mediterranean landscape, E-1027's design deliberately blurs indoor and outdoor living, emphasising a harmony with nature that was perhaps inspired by Gray's Japanese apprenticeship.

166 / BEST IN TRAVEL 2026

TOP EXPERIENCES / FRANCE

puns, all in French – bring you into Gray's modernist world, where she focused on designs that adapted to her guests, from adjustable tables to accordion-style glass doors opening onto a terrace to showcase the jewel colors of the Mediterranean landscape.

ENCOUNTER A MONUMENTAL HISTORY
Villa E-1027 was the first major architectural project for Eileen Gray, who was something of a visionary. Irish by birth, she studied fine art in London and Paris before an apprenticeship under Japanese sculptor and lacquer master, Seizo Sugawara. Initially, she was celebrated for her interiors and furniture designs (Elsa Schiaparelli and James Joyce were fans), but a growing interest in architecture led to this monumental project along the French Riviera. Gray's minimalist, human-centered approach was a departure from the mainstream, and today, she is recognised as a pioneer of the modernist architecture movement.

The villa is only open via guided tours, and that's a good thing: the small details – from the alfresco kitchen to the tiny, austere maid's quarters with convertible bed-table – are best appreciated with the insights of an expert.

Though many visit the villa for Gray, others come for its history: once Gray had sold it to Badovici, their friend and fellow groundbreaking architect Le Corbusier painted a colorful (and still-intact) mural in the entryway that Gray considered to be an act of vandalism. During WWII, E-1027 was occupied by Nazis, who stripped it of furniture. It fell into disrepair after decades of neglect before being bought by conservationists, who rescued and restored the site. It is now a part of Cap Moderne, recognized as one of France's national historic monuments.
– Chloé Braithwaite

Clockwise from top left: E-1027's windows frame Med views; The villa's design emphasizes a seamless connection to its setting; Le Corbusier's entryway mural; An Eileen Gray chair.

BEST IN TRAVEL 2026 / 167

TOP EXPERIENCES / JAPAN

Spend the night in a ryokan

JAPAN

BEST FOR Mindful retreats and hot-spring bathing

Japan's ryokan – travel inns – offer a glimpse of traditional Japanese interiors, gourmet cuisine and hot-spring culture. They are built for relaxation, harkening back to a slower, more analog time: spend your visit strolling in the gardens, savoring multi-course kaiseki *meals, or reading a book over a pot of green tea.*

SURRENDER TO THE SLOW-DOWN

The pace is downright languid: a kimono-clad attendant glides down a hallway before disappearing behind a sliding paper door; the murmur of conversation drifts from a dining room; a soothing susurrus of bamboo and maple leaves whispers in from the garden.

Don't come to a ryokan when you're looking for large-screen televisions, a business center to take conference calls or an espresso bar to fuel your packed itinerary. The tempo is a lot slower here.

DIP INTO HOT SPRINGS

Traveling to hot-spring towns to bathe in therapeutic waters has long been a tradition in Japan, dating to ancient times – it's even mentioned in the *Nihon Shoki*, a historical chronicle published around 720 CE – though this kind of travel was out of reach for normal people and limited to the upper class. Travelers' inns proliferated 400 years ago in Japan during the Edo period, when the booming capital of Edo – now Tokyo – was linked by five major

Left to right, from above: Ryokan originated as travelers' inns along pilgrimage routes like the scenic Kumano Kodō; The traditional Motoyu Ishiya ryokan and onsen in Kanazawa.

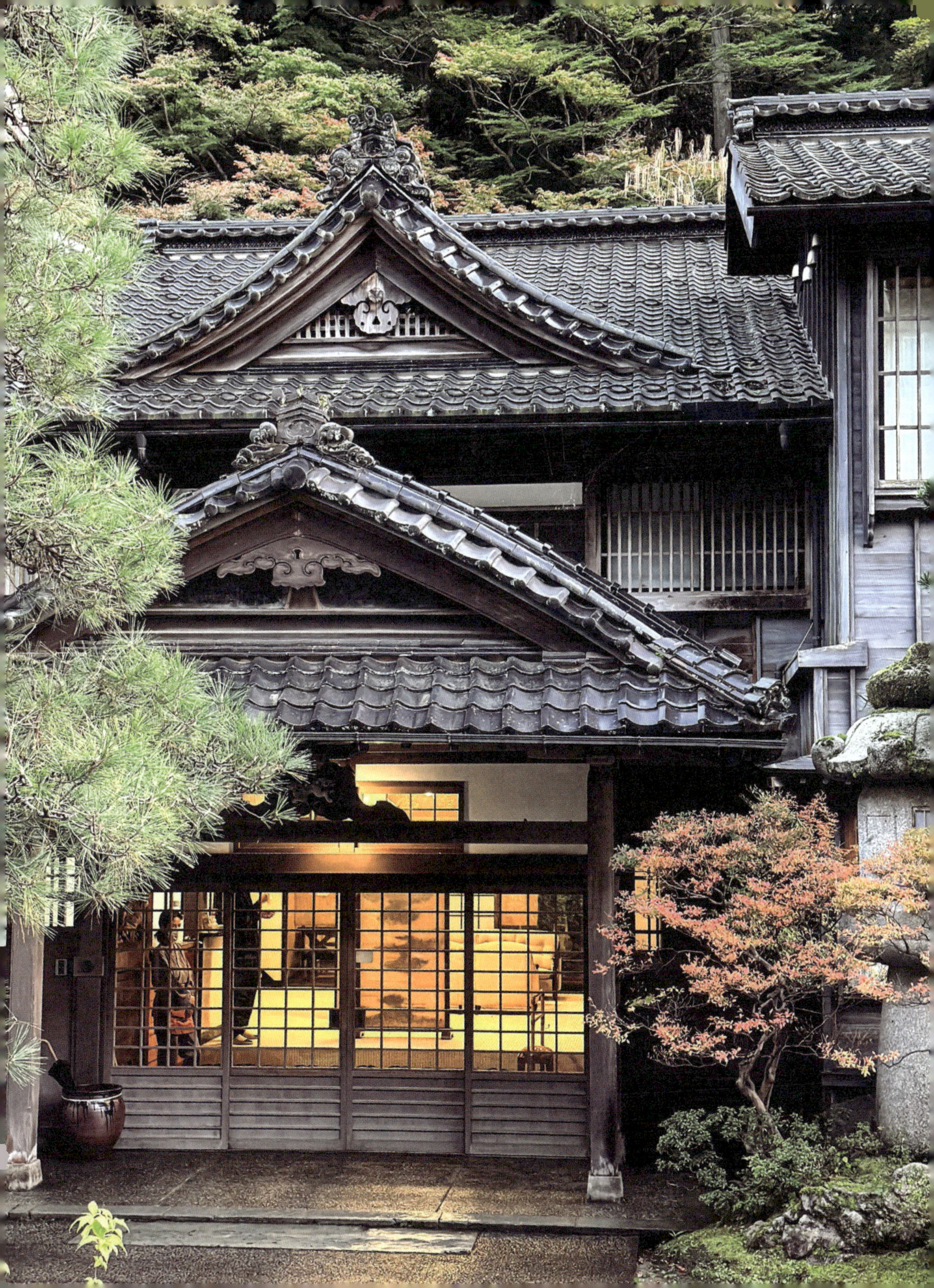

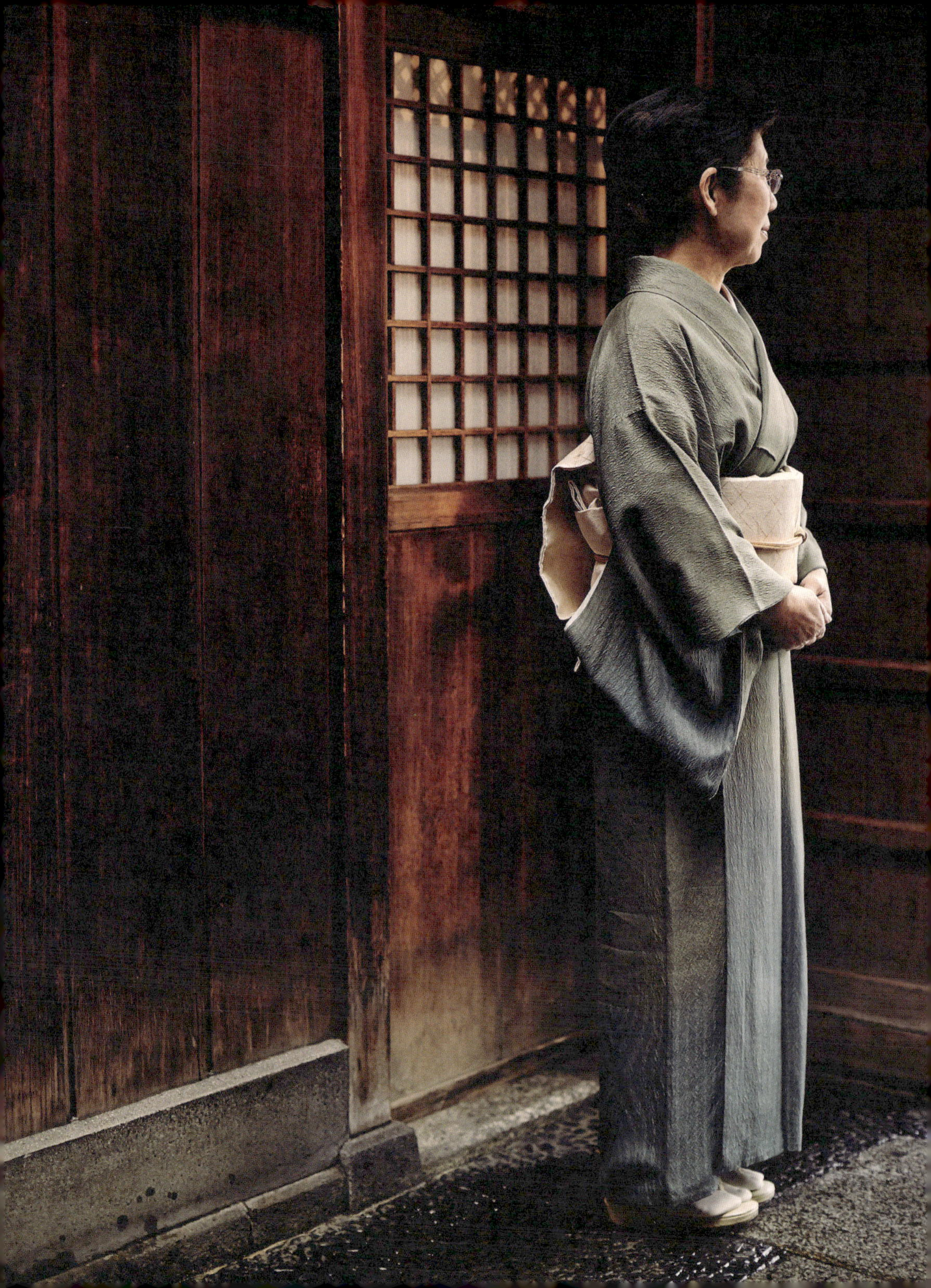

TOP EXPERIENCES / JAPAN

roads to outer regions under control of the military government. It was the construction of these roads that made travel for leisure alone far more accessible to the wider population.

Today, ryokan are distinct from other kinds of lodgings in that they are, by law, classified as Japanese-style, and hew most closely to those lodgings of old. Expect tatami mats, shoes off and elaborate set meals, plus large, communal (sex-segregated) bathing facilities and futon bedding.

To slip into a hot spring is to commune with the Earth's molten core: heated by magma, elementally nourished. To that end, the ideal form of ryokan is the onsen ryokan: an inn that includes natural hot-spring baths, often open-air, like the multiple onsen offered at Ginzanso in Yamagata Prefecture.

Bathing areas are usually sex-segregated but shared, and guests scrub well in a separate shower area before entering the large baths. Toilets may also be in shared areas, though many inns have ensuite facilities as well. Some, like Ohnuma Ryokan in Miyagi Prefecture, have onsen available by reservation for private use, and you'll probably see guests in provided *yukata* (cotton kimonos) shuffling between rooms and baths.

EXPECT UNMATCHED HOSPITALITY

The standard stay at a ryokan comes with two meals (dinner and breakfast), either served in your room or in a dining room on site. In some of the higher-end ryokan, such as Asaba Ryokan in Shizuoka Prefecture, you'll have not only the *okami-san* – the female inn manager – but also a *nakai*, a room attendant. These professionals practice the art of *omotenashi*, Japanese

*Far left to right:
Higher-end ryokan are presided over by okami-san (female inn managers); Soothing Japanese-style gardens surround ryokan buildings.*

BEST IN TRAVEL 2026 / 171

Clockwise from right: Dusk at Asaba Ryokan; Wintertime onsen baths in steaming thermal waters are a special delight; Cherry blossom in bloom at Asaba; Refreshing green tea and a sweet treat.

MOST MEMORABLE MOMENT

Dressed only in a thin robe and wooden sandals, pick your way around the milky blue hot-spring pools on a winter visit to Tamagoyu. The frigid air will nip at your skin, raising goosebumps as a creeping sulfurous mist gives the scene a mysterious tinge. Strip off the yukata robe and step into a gloriously toasty pool, as steam rises up and catches in the branches of the vermillion maples in attendance.

TOP EXPERIENCES / JAPAN

hospitality, which is about anticipating what a guest might want, perhaps before they know they want it. Those touches might look like an escort with an umbrella meeting you at your taxi to shield you from rain in the few steps between the car and the entryway; or pairs of slippers neatly laid out at the entrance while your shoes are whisked away – all signaling 'be comforted, be at home'.

The *nakai* is in charge of serving in-room meals. The gourmet set meals at ryokan are highly seasonal and elaborately presented. There's no menu – the inn cooks what's local and fresh – but many ryokan can accommodate dietary needs with advance notice. Sumptuous vegetarian spreads from Tamagoyu in Fukushima Prefecture, for example, might include tempura, sweet potato dumplings, grilled and marinated eggplant, gingko nuts, *sakura mochi* (a rice cake confection) and more.

Each season has its own recommendations. Hot-spring baths are most satisfying spring through fall, with snowflakes dissolving as they meet steam creating a particularly atmospheric scene. In the spring, tender local vegetables star in the cuisine. Summer retreats offer a respite from urban heat, and the blazing colors of autumn foliage make the perfect backdrop for your relaxing idyll.
–Selena Takigawa Hoy

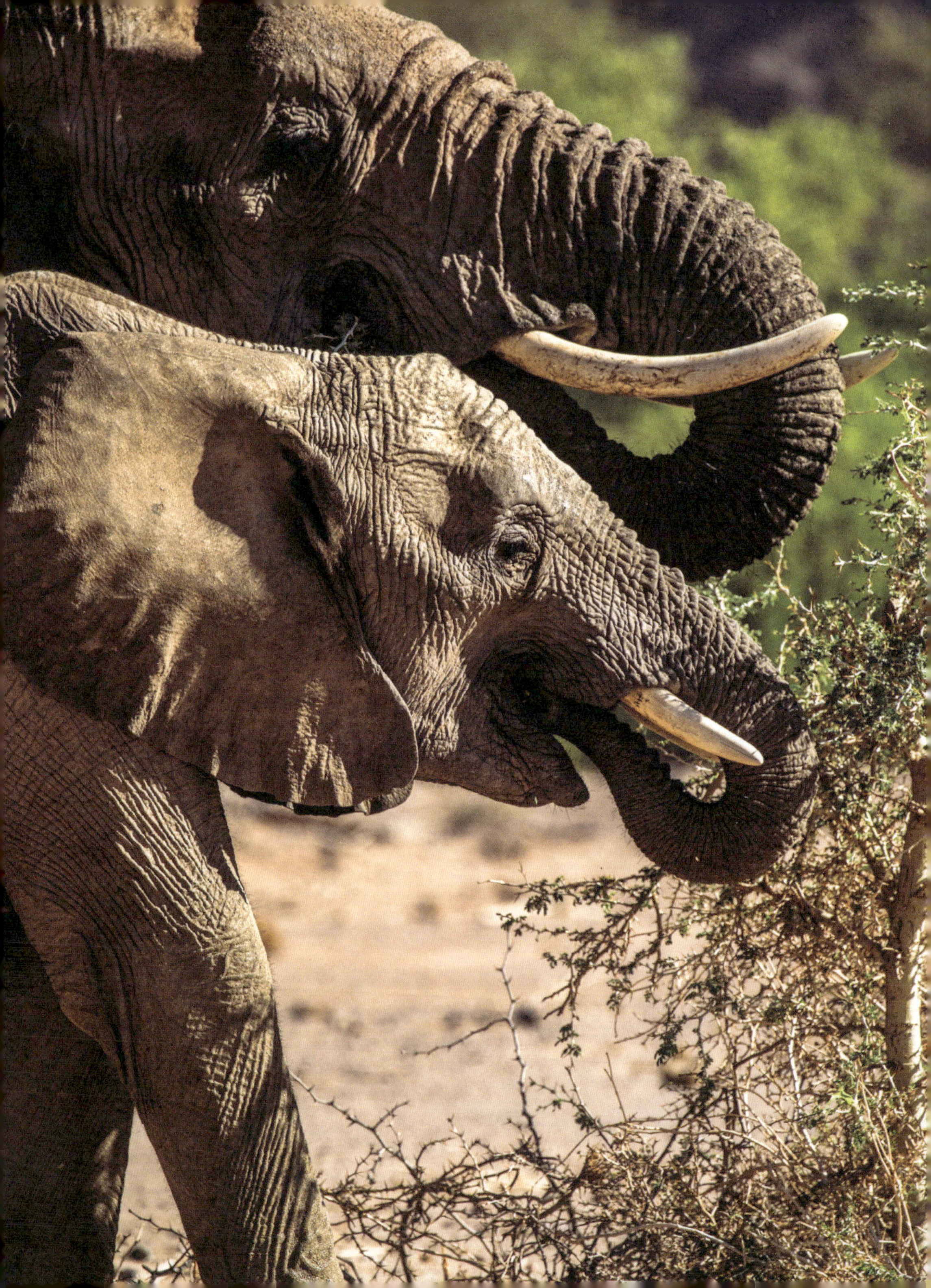

TOP EXPERIENCES / NAMIBIA

Track desert elephants
NAMIBIA

BEST FOR
Pachyderm fanatics and desert devotees

Left to right: Up close with Namibia's desert-dwelling pachyderms; Tracking elephants along the dry Huab rivercourse, Kunene Region.

Marvel at the massive footprints of northwestern Namibia's desert-dwelling pachyderms. Only two populations of elephants live in the planet's deserts (the other is in Mali), and Namibia is an incredible place to see these rare animals amidst a stunning sandscape backdrop.

NAMIBIA'S RARE GIANTS

Desert-dwelling elephants have survived against the odds in northwest Namibia's harsh and stunning desert, near the country's highest peak, Brandberg Mountain. While there were once many more elephants in the Namibian desert, a great number perished due to human–wildlife conflict, and far fewer remain today. These fascinating animals are a group of African savannah or 'bush' elephants that have adapted to the desert conditions. All African savannah elephants are listed as endangered, due to threats like habitat loss and poaching for their ivory.

BEST IN TRAVEL 2026 / 175

MOST MEMORABLE MOMENT

Listening to elephants crunching on leaves and tearing branches from trees, or watching a playful calf twirling its trunk. Feeling the grit of dust in the air, while breathing in the scents of the desert's plants and animals.

TOP EXPERIENCES / NAMIBIA

Guides know where the elephants usually like to spend their time – generally eating at stands of trees and shrubs along dry riverbeds – so they know the best places to spot them. It's an adventure of its own to find the herds, but you'll get great views and likely have opportunities to see other wildlife along the way. If you do spot elephants, guides will drive up close enough to give visitors a good view, but stay at a safe distance while carefully observing the animals' behavior to avoid disturbing them – and beat a hasty retreat if necessary. With such a small number of elephants in the Namibian desert, sightings aren't guaranteed – but the scenery is stunning, and seeing footprints (or even a pile of dung!) is an experience to remember.

SEARCHING FOR DESERT ELEPHANTS
Book a small-group day tour with your accommodation, hire a private guide, or sign up for a multiday (or multi-week) tour that includes desert-elephant tracking, among other experiences. The dry season (May to September) is usually considered the best time to go.

Desert elephants live in northwest Namibia's Erongo and Kunene Regions, in an area once known as Damaraland. This is a remote landscape, but you can maximize your time here by also visiting the Education Centre run by Elephant-Human Relations Aid near the Ugab River Bridge; and the UNESCO-listed Twyfelfontein rock-art site, which has extensive outdoor galleries of ancient rock art, including depictions of elephants and other animals.

Clockwise from top left: Tracks give guides intel on elephant locations; Giraffes in the scrubland of northwest Namibia; Finding food on the Huab riverbed; Twyfelfontein rock-art site.

Bring your binoculars and long camera lenses; if you get lucky with a sighting, you can pick out the individual features on each elephant, from the wrinkles and scars on its body to its eyelashes.
–Kristen Pope

BEST IN TRAVEL 2026 / 177

TOP EXPERIENCES / IBERÁ

Look for jaguars in the wetlands

IBERÁ

ARGENTINA

*BEST FOR
Big cats and big adventure*

The chance to see an apex predator in the wild motivates many wildlife-loving travelers. In northern Argentina, visitors can celebrate the success of a rewilding program during boat, canoe and horseback explorations into the vast Iberá Wetlands, in search of the growing number of wild jaguars that have returned to this landscape, decades after disappearing.

WILDLIFE ADVENTURES IN A UNIQUE PLACE
For nature lovers, seeing a big cat in the wild is an epic experience. The task requires time, patience, persistence and no small amount of luck – but the payoff is spine-tinglingly satisfying. Thanks to local conservation efforts, the odds of seeing a jaguar in the Iberá Wetlands of northern Argentina are now better than ever.

Left: Thanks to the sterling work of Rewilding Argentina, Iberá's jaguar population is on the rise.

Low-slung motor boats push slowly and quietly through the still, dark waterways that crisscross the Iberá Wetlands, a marshy, boggy and remarkably flat landscape – named in honor of the Indigenous Guarani-language word for 'brilliant water' – that sprawls over thousands of square miles. As the boat glides forward, all eyes are trained on the water's edge, scanning for signs of movement.

Horseback explorations on land and through shallow tributaries give an elevated perspective for spotting movement or, perhaps, a flash of spotted fur. Horse-drawn canoe rides through just-wide-enough waterways provide a jaguar's-eye view into the dense, low vegetation that spreads out in every direction. Along the way, sightings of preferred jaguar prey will be frequent.

MOST MEMORABLE MOMENT

Feeling the thrill of sharing an environment with wild jaguars, and the satisfaction of knowing these top predators are returning to their rightful place in the landscape. And even if you don't see a jaguar in Iberá, odds are now pretty good that one will see you.

TOP EXPERIENCES / IBERÁ

Statuesque and skittish red pampas deer graze warily through the grasslands, raising their heads at passersby. Family groups of capybara (the largest rodents in the world) gather in and around the water, where they seem to eat nonstop. Foxes dart about, energized by a heady mixture of curiosity and caution. Birds also flock to this marshy landscape, including vociferous southern lapwings and ostrich-like rheas.

PATIENCE PAYS OFF FOR BIG CATS AND THEIR FANS
More than 70 years ago, habitat loss, hunting and prey depletion contributed to the jaguar's disappearance from this landscape. But after a quarter-century of systematic and intensive preservation and reintroduction efforts, conservationists from Rewilding Argentina – an offshoot of Tompkins Conservation – estimated the wild jaguar population in Iberá totaled 25 animals as of 2024.

While spotting wildlife is never guaranteed, the jaguars are expected to thrive and multiply naturally, making jaguar sightings in Iberá increasingly likely with each passing year.

The remote wetland ecosystem of the Iberá Provincial Reserve – Argentina's largest protected area – is best reached via domestic flight from Buenos Aires to the city of Corrientes, where you can rent a car for the six-hour, 225-mile (362km) drive to the small town of Colonia Carlos Pellegrini.

Your journey into the wetlands from Corrientes begins on a paved road that quickly gives way to red dirt and gravel. Keep binoculars handy during the drive to spot storks, kingfishers, woodpeckers and distinctive roseate spoonbills.
–Karen Catchpole

Clockwise from top left: Iberá offers a habitat for family groups of capybara; Poling through the wetlands on an ecotour; Iberá from above; Palms shimmy over the Iberá marshlands.

BEST IN TRAVEL 2026 / 181

TOP EXPERIENCES / BOLIVIA

Watch a Flying Cholitas match
BOLIVIA

Every Sunday evening, a group of cholitas (indigenous Aymara and Quechua women) gather in the wrestling ring to rise above the oppression that has plagued them and perform alongside their male counterparts as equals. As indigenous women, the cholitas have long been one of Bolivia's most marginalized groups. With limited career opportunities and a need to put food on the table, the women began organizing and advocating for civil rights in the 1960s. As these women gained more power and freedoms, reaching greater equality with their male counterparts, the term 'cholitas' evolved into a symbol of female empowerment. For the cholitas, the ring offers independence – from men, from their responsibilities as wives and mothers, from life as an indigenous woman.

Photographs and text by Luisa Dörr

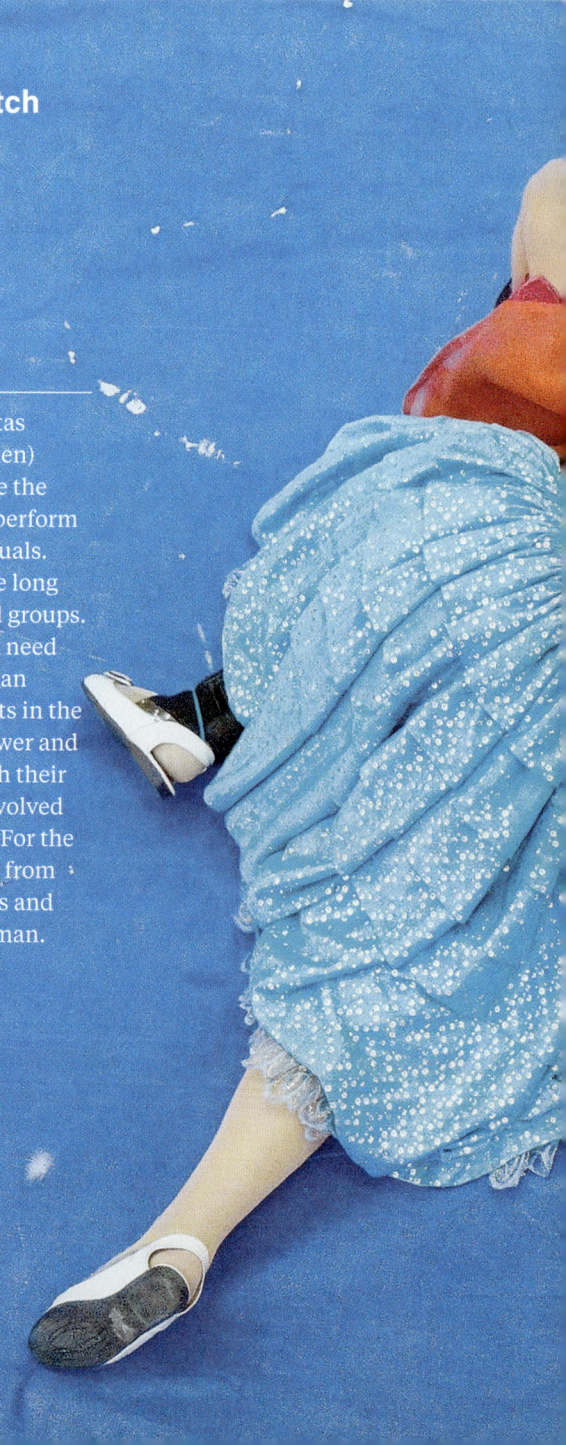

TOP EXPERIENCES / BOLIVIA

184 / BEST IN TRAVEL 2026

TOP EXPERIENCES / BOLIVIA

Previous spread: Wrestling in the *lucha libre* ring at El Alto's Multifuncional Center.

Many years ago in Mexico – the cradle of wrestling – the 'Superbarrio' character, a defender of the poor, was created. Around the same time, the Flying Cholitas were born in El Alto, Bolivia's most creative territory. Known for their wide skirts and tall bowler hats, these women are the heart and soul of El Alto.

On the outskirts of the city, wild llamas roam.

BEST IN TRAVEL 2026 / 185

TOP EXPERIENCES / BOLIVIA

TOP EXPERIENCES / BOLIVIA

When you look at the streets, the schools, the squares and the markets of El Alto, you find traces of calloused hands – the hands of thousands of women who made the construction of this city possible. While the men worked in the neighboring city of La Paz, the women transformed the community spaces in El Alto in exchange for a little rice, wheat, milk powder and other foods. Those behind the businesses of El Alto are the women.

TOP EXPERIENCES / BOLIVIA

Thousands of people head to the Dolores de El Alto Multifuncional Center to cheer, shout, insult, laugh and watch each other fight. It's part acrobatics, part theatrics. In traditional Bolivian dress, the Flying Cholitas launch themselves at each other, executing perfect moves in a disheveled quest to win. They climb the corner ropes above the ring and 'fly' across the stage, like any Hollywood hero endowed with superpowers; hence their nickname. With their heads held high and their tiered skirts spinning, the Flying Cholitas pave the way for the empowered women of Bolivia. Despite how far they've come, they refuse to let up the fight.

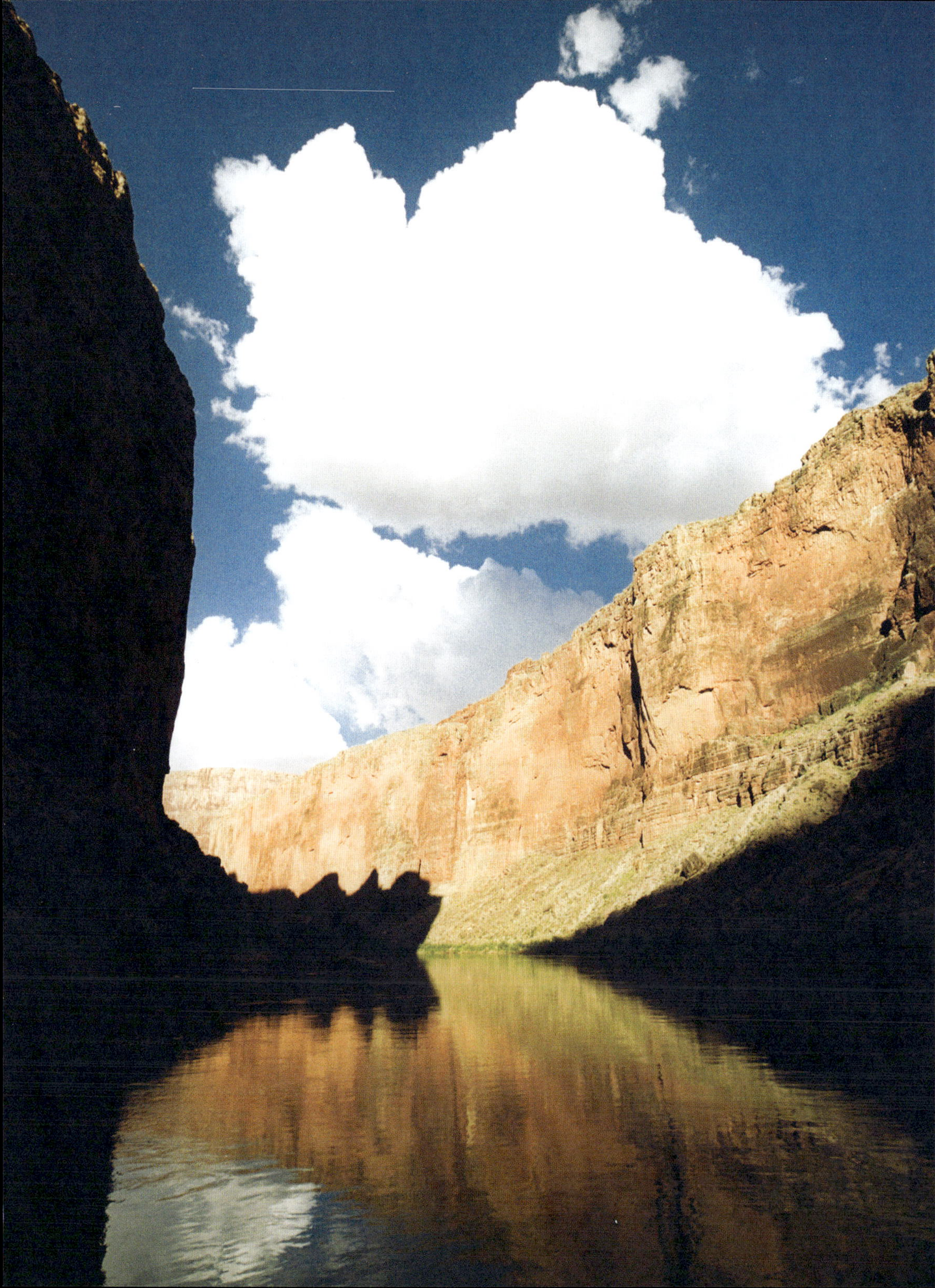

TOP EXPERIENCES / GRAND CANYON

Rapid-raft the Colorado River
GRAND CANYON

USA

Left to right: Out on the water along the canyon-banked Colorado River; Preparing to tackle the whitewater of Doris Rapid.

BEST FOR Unadulterated nature and adventure

Experience the Grand Canyon in a way very few people get to – on the water. Whether you join a group trip or win the lottery for a self-guided permit, this journey provides views, memories and stories to last any adventurer a lifetime. Discover the thrill of rafting while connecting with fellow travelers and epic nature along the way.

LEGENDARY RIVER RUNNING
There may come a time when you question your decision to whitewater-raft the Grand Canyon. It could be the moment your cell service cuts out for a week or, OK, three. It might settle in the first time you tuck into bed (which is, for the bold, a sleeping bag, sans tent). Or, it could hit you when you're introduced to the groover, a 'bathroom system' consisting of a bucket and sawdust. But, rest assured, all of these potential pit-in-stomach moments pale in comparison to the immense – and at times overwhelming – joy of being immersed in unadulterated nature.

Rafting the Colorado through the Grand Canyon has a legendary aspect to it. There's a reason people have been riding these rapids for centuries:

MOST MEMORABLE MOMENT

On a trip that necessitates so much time off, your senses are rewired to notice things differently: a rustling bush that could indicate an animal running past, the colors of the sky bruising into night, the sound – or lack thereof – on a nighttime float. Just being truly absent from devices and in the presence of such nature is a trip, in every sense of the word.

TOP EXPERIENCES / GRAND CANYON

to be a part of the time-honored tradition of river running, tussling with a force as raw and unapologetic as it ever was. You can almost imagine the Vishnu Schist – walls of craggy rock jutting out of the water – as home to our ancient predecessors. It is simultaneously rugged and pristine.

Soup-to-nuts tour companies like OARS and AzRA will ensure that you're well taken care of on prearranged group trips, whereas outfitters like Ceiba Adventures will help prepare all the food and accoutrements for self-organized expeditions of the lucky rafters who win the annual permit lottery.

TRAVEL AS MEDITATION

Creature comforts will be far from a concern, however, as you marvel at the splendor of a night sky so thick with stars that you'll need an eye mask to sleep outside. You may even find that what you first feared, you have come to value most. Opportunities to feel truly disconnected from the grind of modernity are increasingly rare. The most lasting gift of rafting the Grand is an ineffable constancy that ignores your to-do list, your meeting schedule, your needs. There, with the gush of 277 miles (446km) of river, you're undoubtedly confronted with perspective, your place in the order of nature and, perhaps, how small you are.

A typical travel itinerary has no place here. Instead, you adapt to the Grand. Wake up with the sun, read the water, work with its ebbs and flows to forge on, build a campfire, sleep, repeat. And it's a privileged existence if you can come by it. Here, you're suspended – physically and otherwise – and come out the other side changed for the better. Whatever your early trepidations or misgivings may have been, you'll come to dread one part the most: going home.

Clockwise from top left: Hop off the raft to explore narrow side canyons like Matkatamiba; Taking a riverside rest stop; Rafting the Colorado's winding course; A collared lizard on the bank.

–Annie Georgia Greenberg

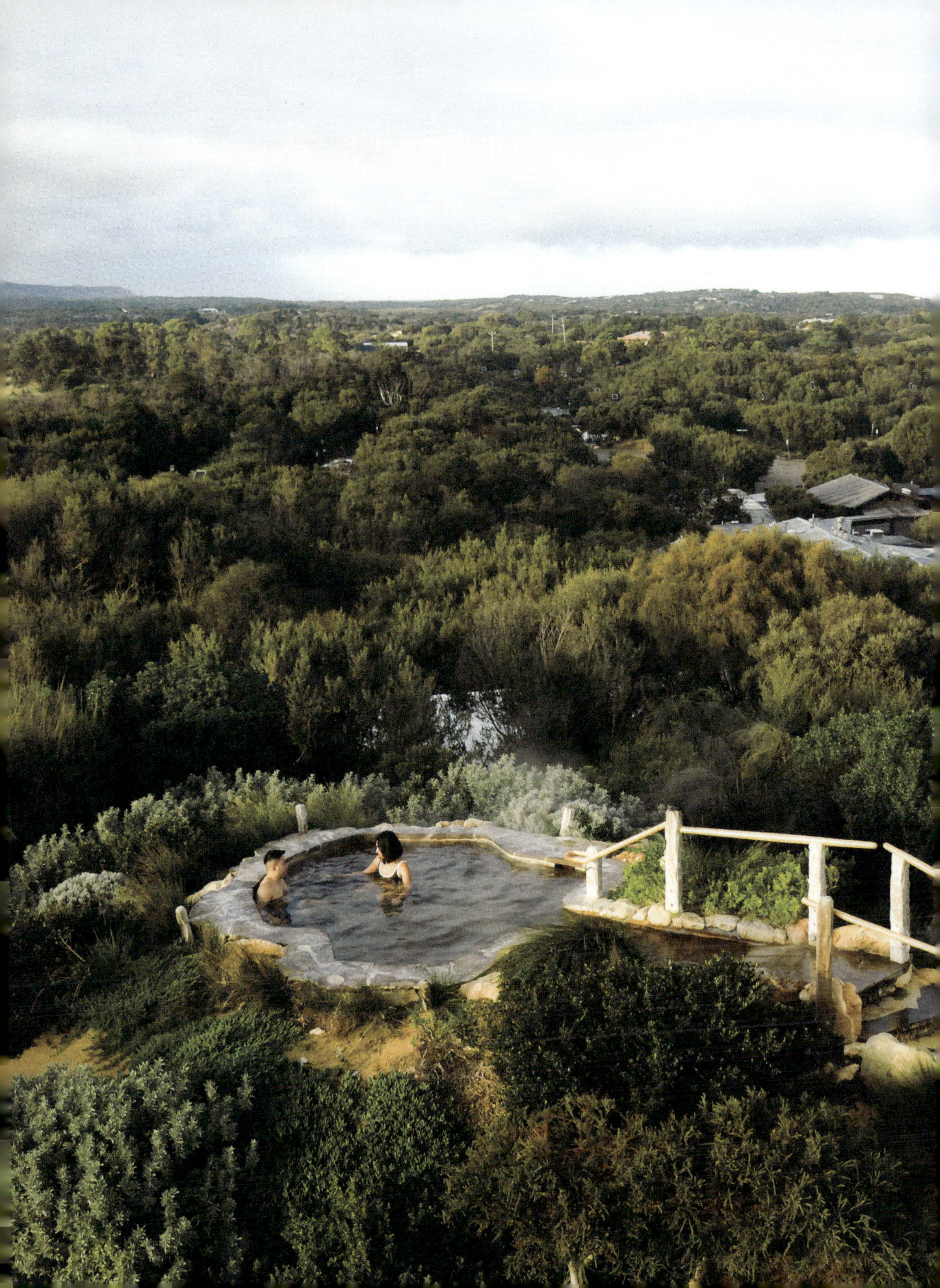

TOP EXPERIENCES / VICTORIA

Explore the Bathing Trail

VICTORIA

AUSTRALIA

BEST FOR
Open-air relaxation

Pack the car and grab your swimmers – Victoria's new Great Bathing Trail adds luxury and plenty of bubbles to the classic Oz road trip. Australia is rightly known for its thousands of miles of spectacularly photogenic beachfront, with towel-touting crowds flocking to Bondi, Manly and Noosa, but in the south a steamier bathing revolution is underway.

A NEW KIND OF TRAIL ADVENTURE

Buried deep underground, the Great Artesian Basin is an immense water reserve that covers more than a fifth of Australia – including large parts of Victoria. The southern state has tapped this subterranean aquifer to launch its Great Bathing Trail, a 550-mile (885km) driving route that connects historic and newly built hot springs, mineral springs and sea baths from the coast to the mountains.

And while luxuriating in steaming stone pools overlooking verdant farmlands and coastal heath is the star attraction, you can also combine relaxation with gentle hikes, yoga classes, illuminating First Nations experiences, and pit stops to graze produce sold at farm gates along the way.

The baths are open year-round, but the best time to head out on the road is during the cooler months, from March to November. A steaming outdoor hot spring makes a rejuvenating escape, even in the middle of winter.

Left to right: Taking the waters (and taking in the views) at Peninsula Hot Springs; Bathing in repurposed wine barrels at Metung Hot Springs.

BEST IN TRAVEL 2026 / 195

Clockwise from right:
Warm waters beckon at Peninsula Hot Springs; The Convent Gallery cafe in foodie-central Daylesford; Geelong's Eastern Sea Baths; Daylesford from above.

MOST MEMORABLE MOMENT

As twilight descends on the hilltop pool at Peninsula Hot Springs, the growing darkness heightens the senses. The air is alive with chittering insects and birds nestling down to sleep. Slide deeper into the water, and it rises to meet your chin. A slow exhale joins the evening chorus.

196 / BEST IN TRAVEL 2026

TOP EXPERIENCES / VICTORIA

SPRINGS (AND THEIR LUXURIES) IN EVERY DIRECTION

Driving west along Port Phillip Bay brings you to Geelong's Eastern Sea Baths, a sweeping crescent of saltwater that's been entertaining families since the late 1930s with its floating islands and slides. Further along the Great Ocean Rd is Warnambool's Deep Blue Hot Springs, renovated in 2021 to combine mineral-water rockpools with aromatherapy dips and glowing sensory pools.

North of Melbourne lies the mountain town of Daylesford, revered for its acclaimed dining scene and botanical gardens as well as the historic Hepburn Bathhouse, where bathers have been soaking in mineral-rich waters for 130 years.

To the east, perennially popular Peninsula Hot Springs has over 70 bathing experiences, including hot and cold treatment rooms, cold plunges, reflexology trails and an open-air theater with baths instead of seats. In late 2024, the springs introduced three new eco-lodges specially designed to improve sleep.

Alba Thermal Springs & Spa affords a more intimate bathing experience, with 31 small pools scattered across hills overlooking Bass Strait. Further east, Metung Hot Springs has the option to soak in a bath made from repurposed wine barrels, or indulge in a massage inspired by Indigenous Larn'wa healing techniques. And in the next few years, Phillip Island – a family destination beloved for nightly penguin parades – will welcome its own hot-springs facility.
–*Justin Meneguzzi*

BEST IN TRAVEL 2026 / 197

TOP EXPERIENCES / MEKONG RIVER

Cruise the Mekong River
VIETNAM & CAMBODIA

BEST FOR
No-hassle adventure

With its bounteous waters, banks of coconut palms and lush rice fields tended by farmers sheltered from the sun by their iconic conical hats, the Mekong Delta embodies the rustic beauty of southern Vietnam and Cambodia. In a place where life is so closely tied to the water, there's no better way to delve into the region's nature, culture and cuisine than on an epic river cruise.

TUCK INTO AN EASY PACE
The agricultural region around the vast Mekong Delta in southern Vietnam (and extending to Phnom Penh in Cambodia) is known as the country's 'Rice Bowl', contributing half of its rice and nearly 70% of its fruit. Time here is measured by the rise and fall of the river, and of the harvest cycle, as opposed to the ticking of a wristwatch.

Left: Mekong cruise excursions include gentle paddles through lily-strewn delta waterways.

A world away from big cities, there's a sense that little has changed here in the last few decades. Farmers still work the land with their gentle water buffalo, villagers use the downtime between harvests to make handicrafts, and fisherfolk live on the water, where the river's currents and nutrients nourish the fish stocked in nets suspended underneath their floating homes. Crisscrossed by thousands of kilometers of waterways, the Mekong Delta is a place ideally experienced by river cruise.

SAIL THE SIGHTS

Cruises usually begin or end in either Vietnam's Ho Chi Minh City (Saigon), Mỹ Tho (less than two hours to the southwest) or Cần Thơ (the delta's largest city), and make their way to Cambodian

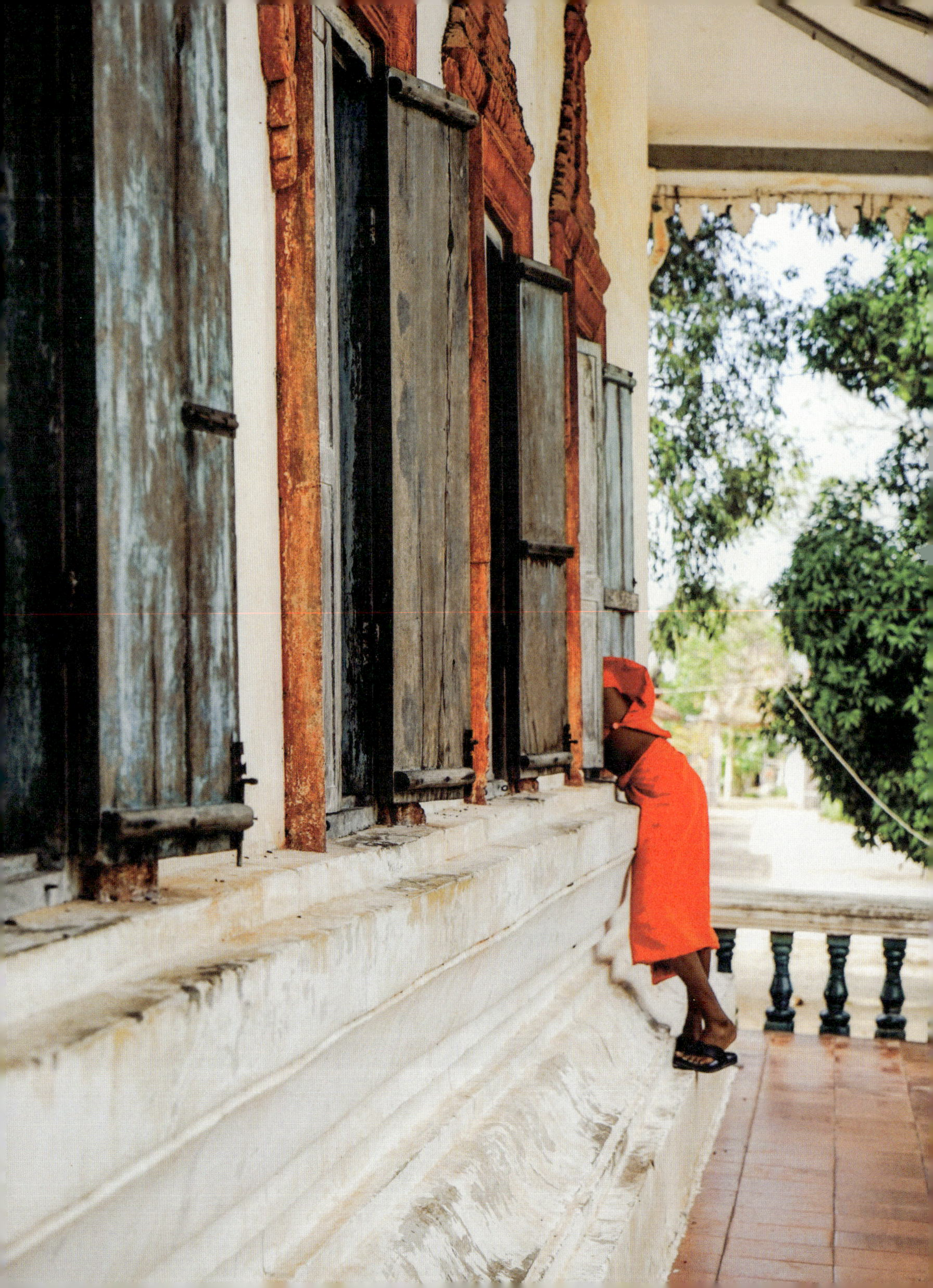

capital Phnom Penh, or on to Siem Reap, gateway to the fabulous temples of Angkor Wat. Expect pleasant days sailing the Mekong River and its tributaries, with shore excursions to charming riverside towns filled with colorful temples and lively markets, where residents blissfully go about their day.

River cruising encourages traveling low and slow, including shore excursions by canoe, bicycle, ox cart and tuk-tuk. Soak in the sights and sounds that are the delta: silversmiths' hammers ringing through a craft village, or thousands of birds chirping in a wetland preserve; a fleeting peek into stilt houses where people use river water to cook and do laundry, or a man climbing high into a sugar-palm tree to tap its juice for jaggery (a dark, unrefined sugar).

MIX IN SOME MOVEMENT

On shore excursions, canoes penetrate into dense mangroves where fronds of water-coconut palms form a canopy overhead. Boats glide along waterways completely carpeted by aquatic plants in an otherworldly waterscape of towering cajuput trees and pink lotus flowers, or amongst barges laden with fruit and produce in lively floating markets. Elsewhere, leisurely cycling trips along lush rice paddies lead to villages where locals still make most items by hand, from bowls woven from water hyacinth to earthenware hand-thrown with mud gathered from the riverbanks.

River-cruise ships are smaller than their ocean-going counterparts, meaning there'll likely be between 20 and 70 passengers on board, and plenty of

Far left to right: Cambodia's Wat Kampong Tralach Leu pagoda, near Phnom Penh; Harvesting Mekong Delta waterlily blooms.

Clockwise from right: Sampling street-food delights is a Mekong Delta highlight; Making rice paper in Mỹ Tho; A patchwork of Mekong Delta ricefields; Emerald everywhere in the delta's Trà Sư Forest.

MOST MEMORABLE MOMENT

Some of the best experiences come from visiting places with very few fellow tourists, like Cambodia's Kampong Tralach Leu Pagoda, to the north of Phnom Penh. Walking down the dusty path to see this tucked-away 300-year-old pagoda, surrounded by gorgeous murals, is one of those 'I can't believe I'm here' moments.

TOP EXPERIENCES / MEKONG RIVER

opportunities to socialize. Cabins and facilities also vary between cruise lines, from wallet-friendly three-star vessels to luxe five-star floating resorts. Meals thoughtfully incorporate the flavors and ingredients of each locale: river fish steamed with coconut for Khmer *amok*, bananas battered and fried with a drizzle of honey, or mango and papaya shredded for crunchy Vietnamese salads. Days follow a familiar pattern, with shore excursions typically starting early in the morning to avoid the heat, and relaxing afternoons spent lounging on the sundeck, curled up with a book or a cocktail as the soft pink glow of sunset descends.

On a river cruise, you can take in the beauty of the Mekong Delta in manageable bites. Active excursions break up slothful days. Noisy traffic is replaced by the quiet countryside. The every-shade-of-green provided by the omnipresent banana trees, coconut palms and Pantone-defying rice fields, as they change from chartreuse to forest to pistachio, lose their appeal over long hours on a bus. But from the seat of a bicycle or a quietly paddled canoe, they're nothing short of magical. Welcome to the very best version of the Mekong Delta.
–*James Pham*

TOP EXPERIENCES / ECUADOR

Ride horses in the Andes Mountains

ECUADOR

Follow the way of Ecuadorian cowboys – Los Chagras – on a life-affirming horseback ride through the Andes. During this short journey through Ecuador's 'Volcano Alley', learn the history of the country's evolving landscape amid a backdrop unlike any other.

BEST FOR
Sweeping views and would-be cowboys

HISTORY AND CULTURE MEET IN THE MOUNTAINS

High in the Andes Mountains, at around 12,000ft (3660m) above sea level, Ecuadorian cowboys – Los Chagras – have been roaming the region's majestic terrain for centuries. Known as the 'Spirits of the Highlands', Chagras are skilled horseriders, dedicated to their animals and to preserving the land.

The history of horseback riding in Ecuador began in the 1500s when the Spanish arrived, bringing horses with them. Locals quickly realized how well-suited these animals were to navigate the daunting and deadly mountains of the Andes. Horses replaced llamas and alpacas to become a staple in Ecuadorian life, birthing a pillar of this country's history and culture.

Today, you can ride amongst the Chagras, following their lead and charging (OK, ambling) across the Andean highlands with the awe-inspiring cone of Volcán Cotopaxi serving as a picture-perfect backdrop.

Left to right, from above: Wild horses graze the grasslands below the perfect cone of Volcán Cotopaxi; Ecuadorian Chagras (cowboys) ride out.

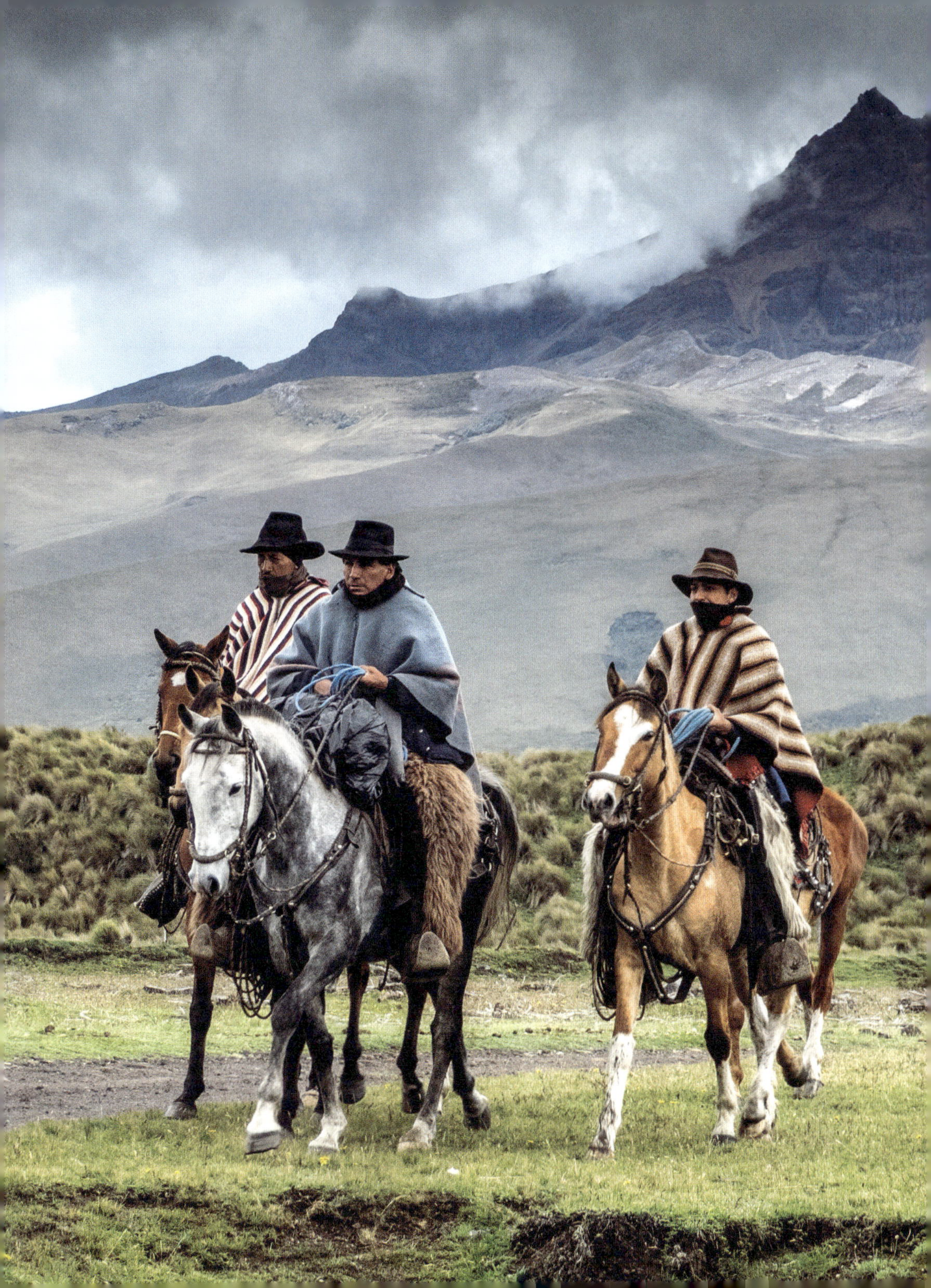

MOST MEMORABLE MOMENT

Getting to spend time in such a beautiful location, surrounded by volcanoes and wildlife, is a privilege. And to participate in a centuries-old tradition that can only take place in this extraordinary locale is nothing short of an honor. This is an experience to be relished and remembered: immersing oneself in an ancient culture in an authentic, tactile way.

TOP EXPERIENCES / ECUADOR

At century-old Hacienda el Porvenir, a working ranch and simultaneously rustic and luxe hotel sitting just 2.5 miles (4km) from the entrance of Parque Nacional Cotopaxi, guests are dressed in traditional Chagra-wear: vertically striped wool poncho, chaps and a brimmed hat (inexperienced riders should strap on a helmet). This is function, not fashion, designed to keep riders warm and protected from the elements.

VIEWS AND AN UNFORGETTABLE PAYOFF
Even if you've ridden before, climbing steep, uneven terrain requires a bit more focus than strolling along a flat trail. Having an experienced rider guiding you makes all the difference.

The circular route is gentle, and the ride deliberately slow, but you'll want to hold the reins tight to control the horse – stopping to eat grass is much too tempting. You won't be galloping on this two-hour trek; the horses and their riders stroll en masse and the mounts know the trails by heart.

The ride allows you to feel connected to the animal you're riding and to the ground you're traversing, offering an awareness that you're experiencing a way of life so essential and sacred that it's lasted for centuries. Making chitchat with fellow riders is as natural as the surroundings: the green, rolling slopes of the dormant Rumiñahui volcano.

Once you reach the Cotopaxi viewpoint, hop off your horse and sip on a cup of steaming mint-flavored tea made with *muña*, a regional herb; it's great for altitude sickness, which is handy at this height. From the lookout, you can see perfectly symmetrical Cotopaxi in the distance, towering above you despite the steady climb, while Andean condors soar in the sky.
–*Chamidae Ford*

Clockwise from top left: Snow-capped Volcán Cotopaxi; Riders clad in traditional ponchos; The 'Flower of the Andes' (*Chuquiraga jussieui*) in bloom; Reviving *muña* tea.

BEST IN TRAVEL 2026 / 207

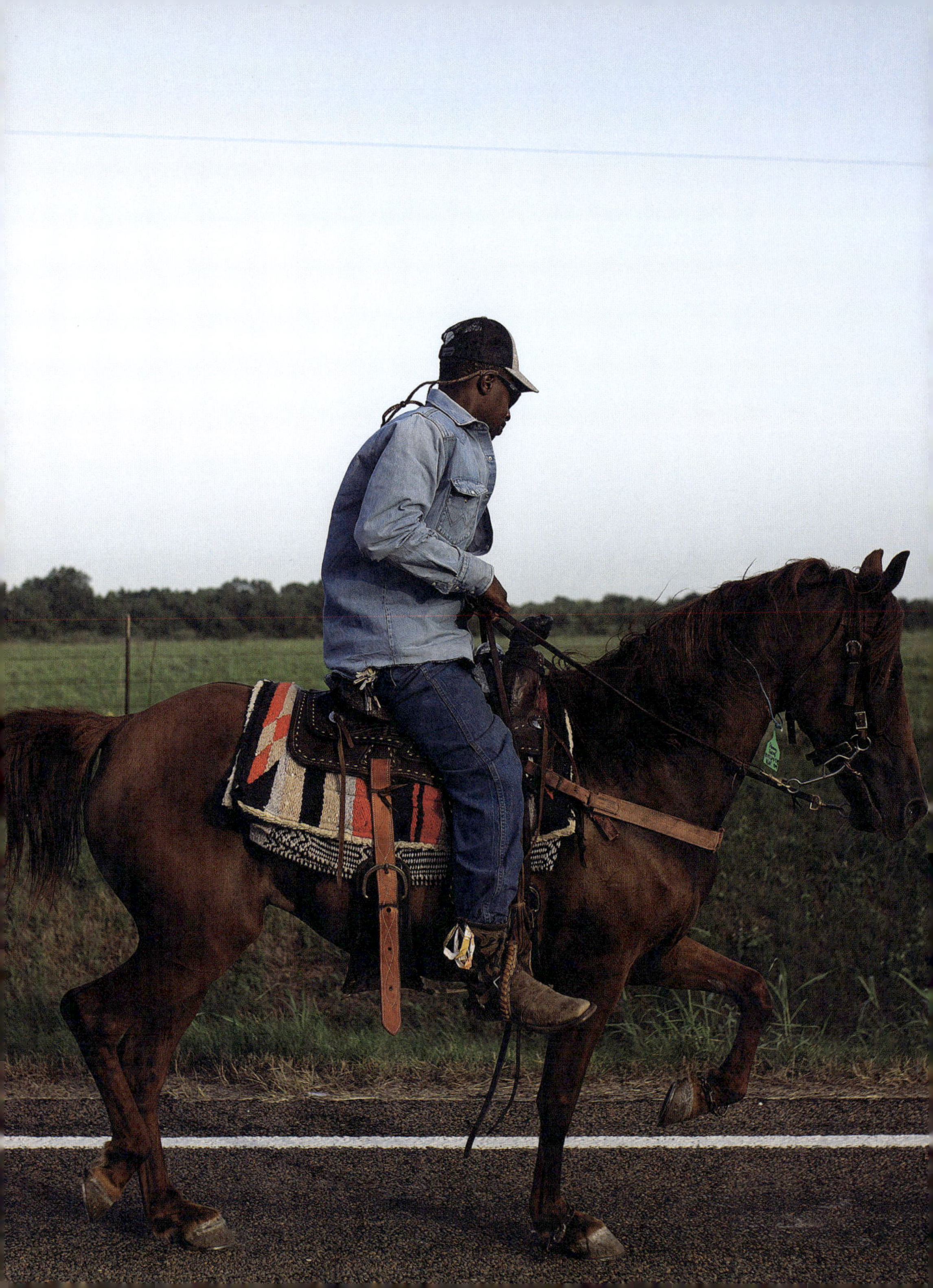

TOP EXPERIENCES / LOUISIANA

Take a Creole trail ride
LOUISIANA
USA

Left to right: Trotting out in Creole cowboy style; Feast on down-home Southern food at trail rides and in diners throughout Texas and Louisiana.

BEST FOR
Experiencing American roots

On the swampy plains and dusty trails of rural Louisiana and Texas, horses trot, trucks bounce to traditional zydeco music and cowboys ride in processions known as Creole trail rides. This fun, family-friendly tradition descends from the first US cowboys – but everyone's welcome to attend. Come to dance, see horses and to eat hearty Southern food.

LOUISIANA'S CREOLE COWBOY CULTURE
As early as the 18th century when France and Spain ruled Louisiana, free and enslaved people of African or Caribbean descent – known as Creoles – were among the first to herd cattle on horseback in what's now US territory.

Yet African American Creoles – an identity that persists today for descendants of these early inhabitants – have been largely left out of mainstream cowboy culture. For instance, Hollywood Westerns mostly starred white cowboys, and rodeos were often segregated. Fortunately, the image of a Creole cowboy is now not just more accepted, it's cooler than ever – and the best way to experience this underappreciated African American tradition is by attending a Creole trail ride.

TOP EXPERIENCES / LOUISIANA

WHERE HORSEBACK RIDING MEETS DANCE PARTY

Creole trail rides are community events held mostly in rural areas of northern Louisiana and eastern Texas, and to a lesser extent in other Southern states. If you go, you'll see hundreds of horseback riders decked out in cowboy hats, boots and matching crew shirts, trotting along country roads in a long procession for an hour or more. Joining them are pickup-truck-pulled wagons carrying non-riders and DJs, which are plenty of fun as they bounce to loud zydeco music – a traditional Creole genre characterized by an accordion and a *frottoir*, a wearable washboard instrument. The ride-along DJs also play hip-hop and country hits sung by African American stars like Lil Nas X and Beyoncé, who have helped popularize Black cowboy culture in recent years.

Once the riding portion of a trail ride is finished, the event culminates in a live concert at a hall, in a barn or outdoors in a field for a dance party that can stretch late into the night. Join cowboy-hat-wearing Creoles as they line dance and do the zydeco two-step – someone will show you the moves if you don't know them. To fuel your dancing, try Creole cooking, likely ladled out of giant pots from the back of a pickup truck. Popular dishes include seafood or meat gumbo; stuffed turkey legs; and a hearty concoction called cowboy stew, made with sausage and animal extras like cow innards, turkey neck and oxtail.

Although trail rides are most commonly attended by community members, visitors are welcome as long as they're respectful.

Left to right: The trail ride out on the road around Loreauville, Louisiana; Taking to the dance floor as a trail-ride after-party kicks off in Loreauville.

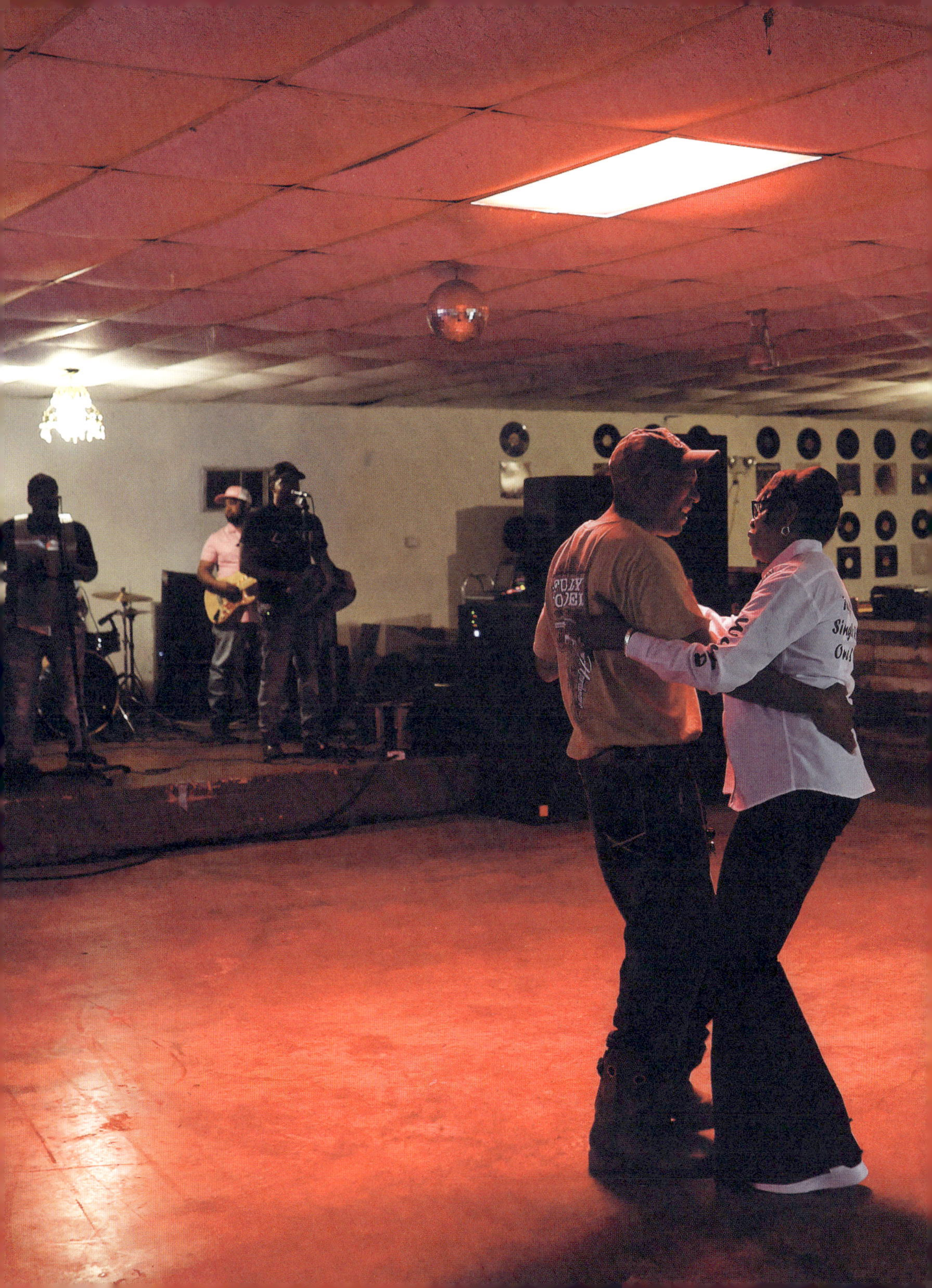

Clockwise from right: Accordion and *frottoir* players entertain trail-ride crowds with live zydeco music; A feast of smothered turkey legs; An expert trail rider puts his mount through its paces; Cooking up turkey wings for the cowboy crowds.

MOST MEMORABLE MOMENT

While on a trail ride, keep your ears open for Louisiana Creole, or Kouri-Vini, a language similar to French that's spoken by Louisiana Creoles. Kouri-Vini is definitely dwindling in popularity and, some argue, faces extinction. But passionate local scholars, writers and musicians are working to revive it by teaching classes, writing books and recording songs in the language.

TOP EXPERIENCES / LOUISIANA

FIND A TRAIL RIDE

Finding a trail ride does require an element of being in the know, but many are listed on the website Zydeco Events (zydecoevents.com/zydeco/trailride). Your best chance of finding one is from January to July. Some trail rides can attract thousands and last the entire weekend as people camp in trailers or tents. Tickets to get a spot on a wagon are usually purchased on site in cash, and don't usually exceed US$10 or US$20. Food and drink will be extra.

DRESS THE PART

Wear a cowboy hat if you've got one, and ideally long pants and boots so you'll be ready if someone invites you up on their horse. Bring your own drinks if you plan to imbibe during the trail ride, though there'll likely be beers for sale. If you're open to trying Creole cooking, bring some cash for that too – unless you're vegetarian, in which case a packed lunch is a good idea. Remember to stay hydrated (with non-alcoholic beverages, of course), as it can get burning hot under the sun.
–Joel Balsam

TOP EXPERIENCES / KERALA

Go on a culinary tour
KERALA
INDIA

BEST FOR
Gastronomic adventurers

TOP EXPERIENCES / KERALA

One of India's finest regional food scenes steps into the spotlight on a culinary adventure around bewitching Kerala. This is a place where fresh coconut fuels the kitchens, recipes are strongly rooted in tradition, and every meal feels like a feast-worthy celebration. Savor it all on an expert-guided food tour through this unhurried southwest state, as curious backstories emerge with every bite.

FOLLOW LOCAL FLAVORS

Best known for its vivid-green palms and its spice-growing mountains blanketed in swirls of shifting mist, Kerala is quietly putting itself on the map as one of the most thrilling culinary destinations in India. A food-focused journey to the country's southwest pocket not only reveals the secrets of Kerala's distinctive gastronomy, but also peels back the layers of a history where spices have always played a key role.

On any Kerala morning, breakfast might involve a lightly spiced, wafer-thin *masala dosa* (a crispy, potato-curry-filled crepe made with a spiced, fermented lentil-flour batter), served with velvety chutney and a stainless-steel cup of steaming *kaapi* (South Indian filter coffee). Turmeric, tamarind, cardamom, cinnamon and pepper are just some of the locally produced spices that infuse dishes here. All those palm groves also yield a wealth of coconuts, used in delicately fragrant stews and best mopped up with feathery *appam*, a rice-and-coconut-milk pancake; fish fresh from the Arabian Sea is served grilled, soaked with spice and wrapped in banana leaves. And within Kerala, local cuisine varies enormously, from the rich Mappila cooking of the northern Malabar region to the south coast's coconut-laden curries and the creative kitchens of Kochi.

Left: Served on a banana leaf, multi-dish *sadya* meals are a beloved feature of Kerala's Onam festival, but you can enjoy them here year-round.

MOST MEMORABLE MOMENT

A lovingly prepared Kerala sadya *(meal)* perfectly captures the region's food-loving soul. Enjoyed during the Onam festival celebrations (but easily found year-round), the feast-like sadya sees a parade of home-cooked side-dishes – thoran *(veggies stir-fried with coconut)*, aromatic rasam *(tomato and tamarind soup)* and mango chutney – served with rice and papad *(dough made from bean flour)* on a fresh banana leaf. Don't miss it.

TOP EXPERIENCES / KERALA

WHERE STREET FOOD, CULTURE AND ART INTERSECT

You could spend several weeks uncovering food stories all over Kerala, but among the most inspiring places to dive in is the ancient port of Kochi, where spider-like *cheenavala* (Chinese fishing nets) dot the landscape. With its beautifully evocative old quarter and thriving arts scene, this easygoing coastal city has grown into an under-the-radar culinary hub, where flavors from across India mingle. Kochi's street-food culture might not be as famous as that of Mumbai or Delhi, but local food has a background and specialities entirely of its own, especially around the lively, spice-trading Mattancherry district. Over the centuries, this compact pocket of Old Kochi has become home for more than 30 different communities from all over India.

One of the most captivating and special ways to savor Kochi's food scene is by joining a guided food walk such as those run by Kochi Heritage Project, a pioneering team devoted to celebrating, preserving and rediscovering the city's culture in creative ways. On an evening itinerary through Mattancherry, highlights might include sampling Konkani-style *goli bajji* (spongy fritters) and flaky Kerala *parotta* (layered flatbread) with beef curry, while also learning about the origins of Kerala's centuries-old love affair with rice, or seeing the intricate inner workings of an active spice mill.

However you end up digging in, Kerala's immense flavors are sure to linger long after you leave the region's tropical, golden-hued shores.

–Isabella Noble

Clockwise from top left: A houseboat on the Kerala backwaters; Frying crispy *paniyaram* dumplings; Browsing for fresh bananas in Kochi; Pair Kerala's curries with lacy *appam* (pancakes).

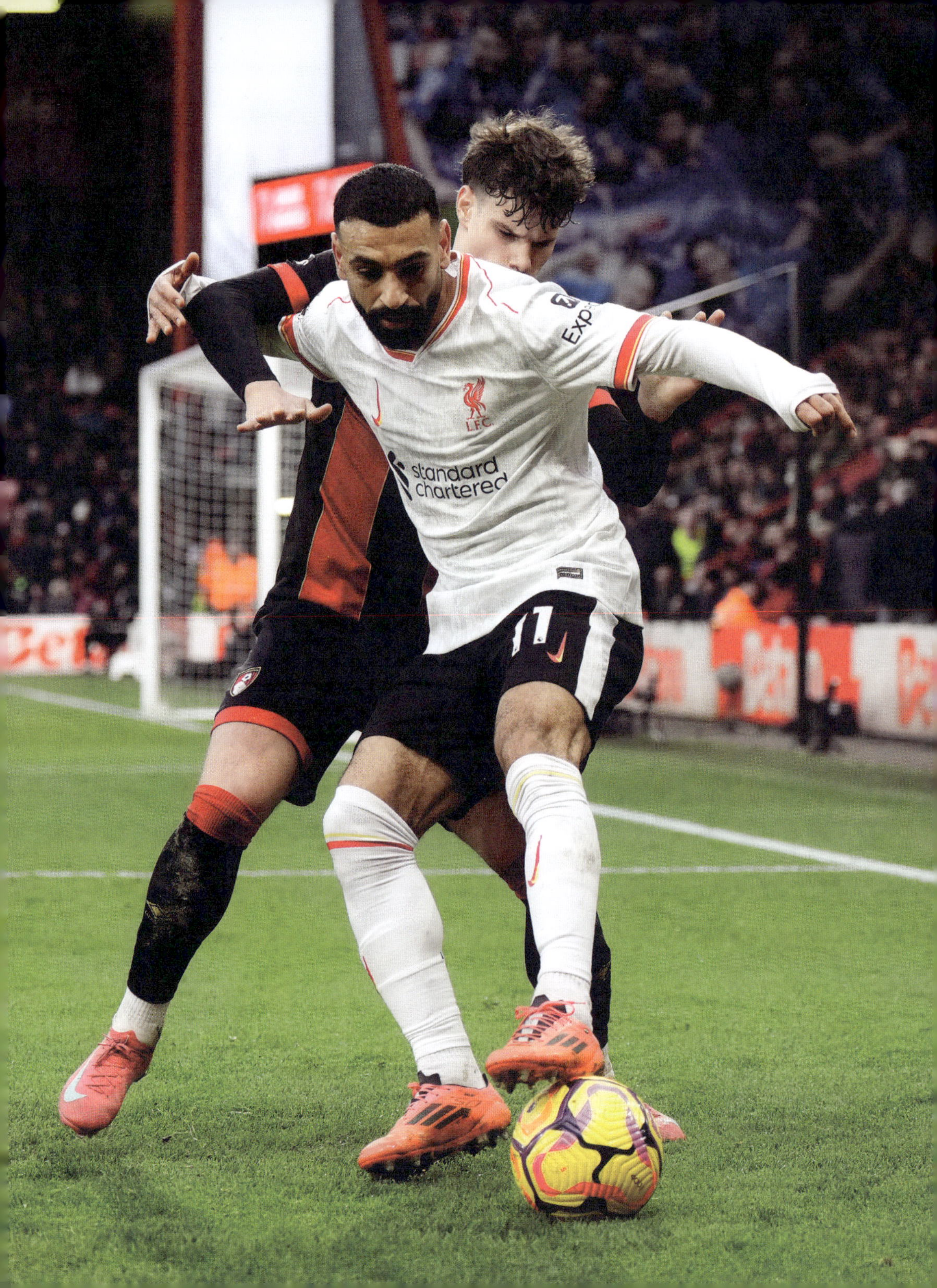
L.F.C.
standard chartered

TOP EXPERIENCES / ENGLAND

Attend a Premier League game

ENGLAND

Left to right: Bournemouth's Milos Kerkez battles for the ball with Liverpool's Mohamed Salah during a Premier League game; Liverpool fans display their team colors with pride on match day.

BEST FOR
Bonding over beers with fellow fans

For followers of football (not soccer, please, we're English), a pilgrimage to watch a Premier League match at one of England's football cathedrals is the ultimate sporting experience. Going to a match is not just visiting a stadium: it offers a unique window into the country's passions and character that you'd struggle to find doing anything else.

PREMIER LEAGUE PRIMER

Despite the international make-up of teams, coaches and owners and the worldwide TV coverage of games, the Premier League retains a parochial mentality. The only things the English seem to agree on is that they love their team, and that the referees are out to get them. Underneath the exuberant support, grudges are held for generations. Local rivalries are intense, as are traditional match-ups fizzing with historical animosity.

The Premier League comprises 20 clubs who are spread unevenly across England. Six are in London,

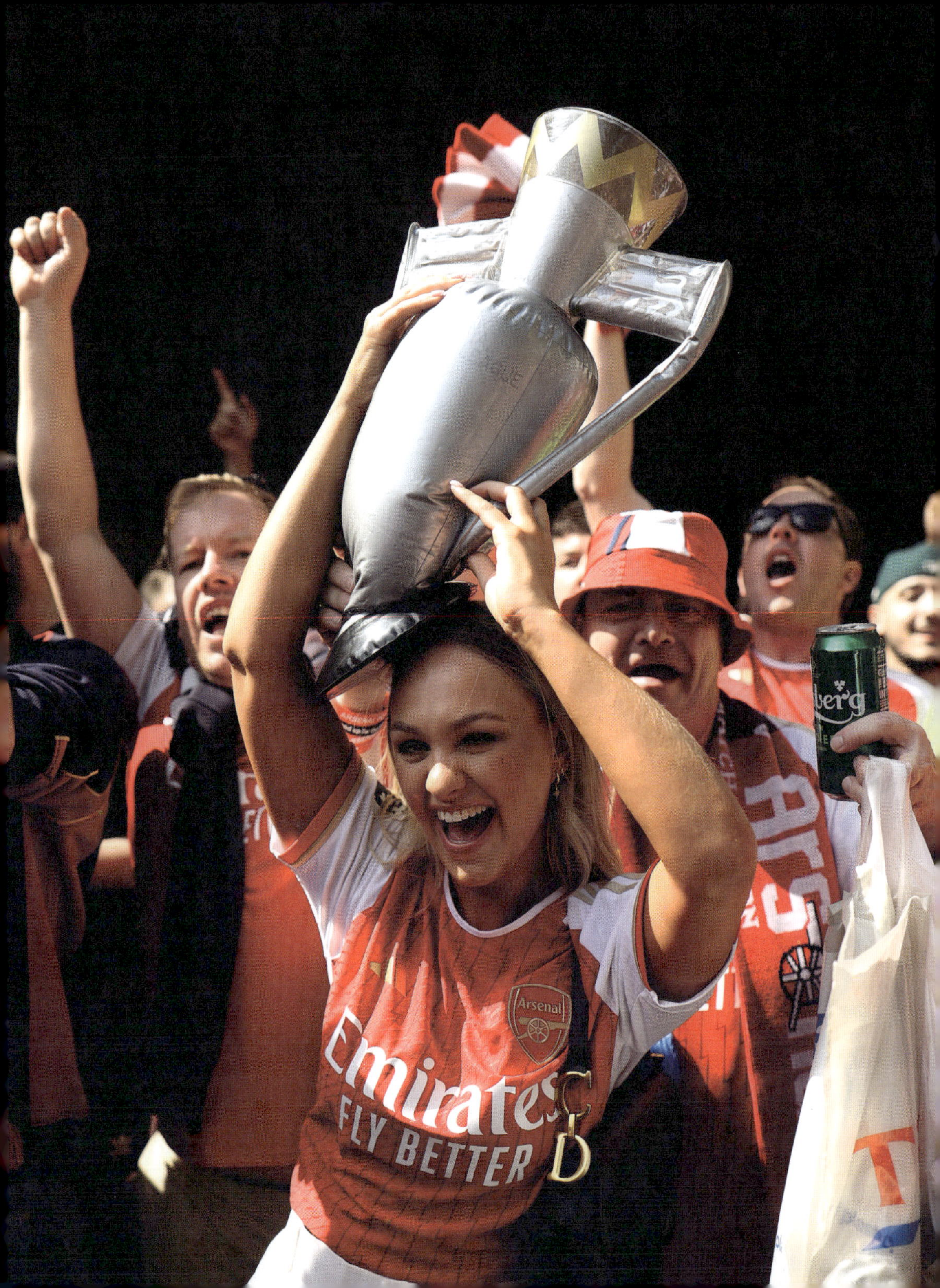
Arsenal
Emirates
FLY BETTER

including Arsenal, Chelsea and Tottenham Hotspur. The northwest is home to Liverpool, Everton and the Manchester rivals, United and City. Another four are in the Midlands, with the rest in other parts of England. Games take place most weekends from August to May, with occasional and very atmospheric midweek games under floodlights.

HOW TO GET TICKETS

The hardest part is scoring tickets. Seats are much sought-after and most games sell out far in advance. Start planning as early as you can with the club you're planning on watching. Clubs have membership schemes that give priority access; a local-to-you chapter of the team's supporters club may also be able to help. Buying a hospitality package is another (expensive) option. Reselling football tickets is illegal in the UK, so proceed with caution on secondary or reseller sites; buying off social media, Craigslist or a tout on the street is a recipe for a rip-off. In the days leading up to a game, keep an eye on club ticket-exchange sites; Reddit forums for each club are also a great source of tips. Face-value tickets will generally start at £45 (US$58) to £60 (US$76), but climb steeply from there.

Pre-match fun and beers can be had in pubs around the ground. At certain stadiums, things get noisy in the concourses or on fan-organized marches to the ground. For something to eat grab – if you can – a chicken balti pie, another English invention available at some clubs or, if you're in the north of England, chips (aka fries) smothered in curry sauce or gravy.

Once in the stands, you'll find that the biggest difference from watching on TV is that you're an

Far left to right: English football fans are famously fanatical, and Arsenal supporters are no exception; Fans in the stands as Brighton & Hove Albion host Liverpool during the Premier League rounds.

Clockwise from right: West Ham fans bring the band to the stands; Liverpool jubilation after a Premier League goal; Manchester United's hallowed Old Trafford Stadium; Hitting the pub before Arsenal play Aston Villa at London's Emirates Stadium.

MOST MEMORABLE MOMENT

The pandemonium in the stadium when a ball hits the back of the net for the home team is often accompanied by bear hugs and deafening yells. Depending on the team, there can be over 50,000 people all letting off steam in a moment of collective joy – which is celebrated with even more gusto if they're getting one over a rival team in the process. Warning: you may end up several feet from where you started, minus your hat, but with a few new friends.

TOP EXPERIENCES / ENGLAND

active participant, especially if you put your phone away and join in the vocal encouragement: you may find yourself learning some colorful new English words and sayings.

EMBRACE THE ENERGY

The game itself will be a lottery – classic or humdrum – but being there makes the details captivating. Players and officials emerge to a wall of noise which, depending on the match you're at and how the home team is faring, will ebb and flow during the game. The noisiest fans will probably be next to – and relentlessly taunting – the few thousand fans there rooting for the visiting team, who do their defiant best to be heard. As the tension rises during the game, you may notice just how worked up supposedly reserved English fans can get over the referee's decision-making. Indeed you might even question the sanity of the person next to you.

By the way, the Premier League is the tip of a vast footballing pyramid. There are dozens of professional sides, many of which attract huge crowds, playing in lower divisions that will be familiar if you've watched *Welcome to Wrexham* or *Ted Lasso*. There's also the thriving and fast-growing Women's Super League. Tickets for all of these are cheaper and easier to score than the Premier League. But we do get why the lure of a rainy night watching Manchester United, or hearing Liverpool's Kop in full voice, is strongest of all. After all, football's what England does best.
–*Tom Hall*

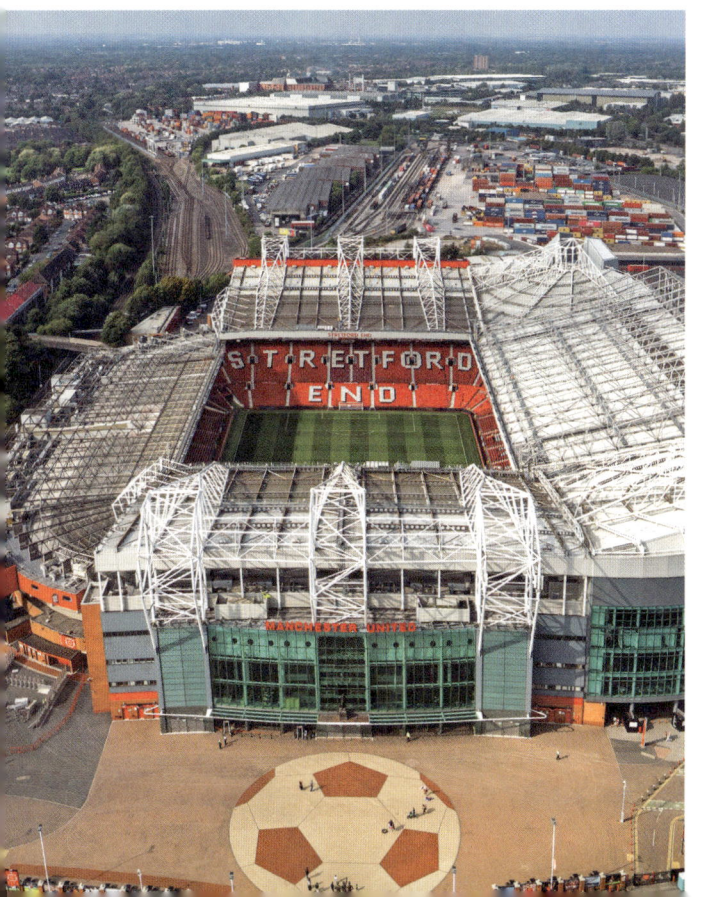

BEST IN TRAVEL 2026 / 223

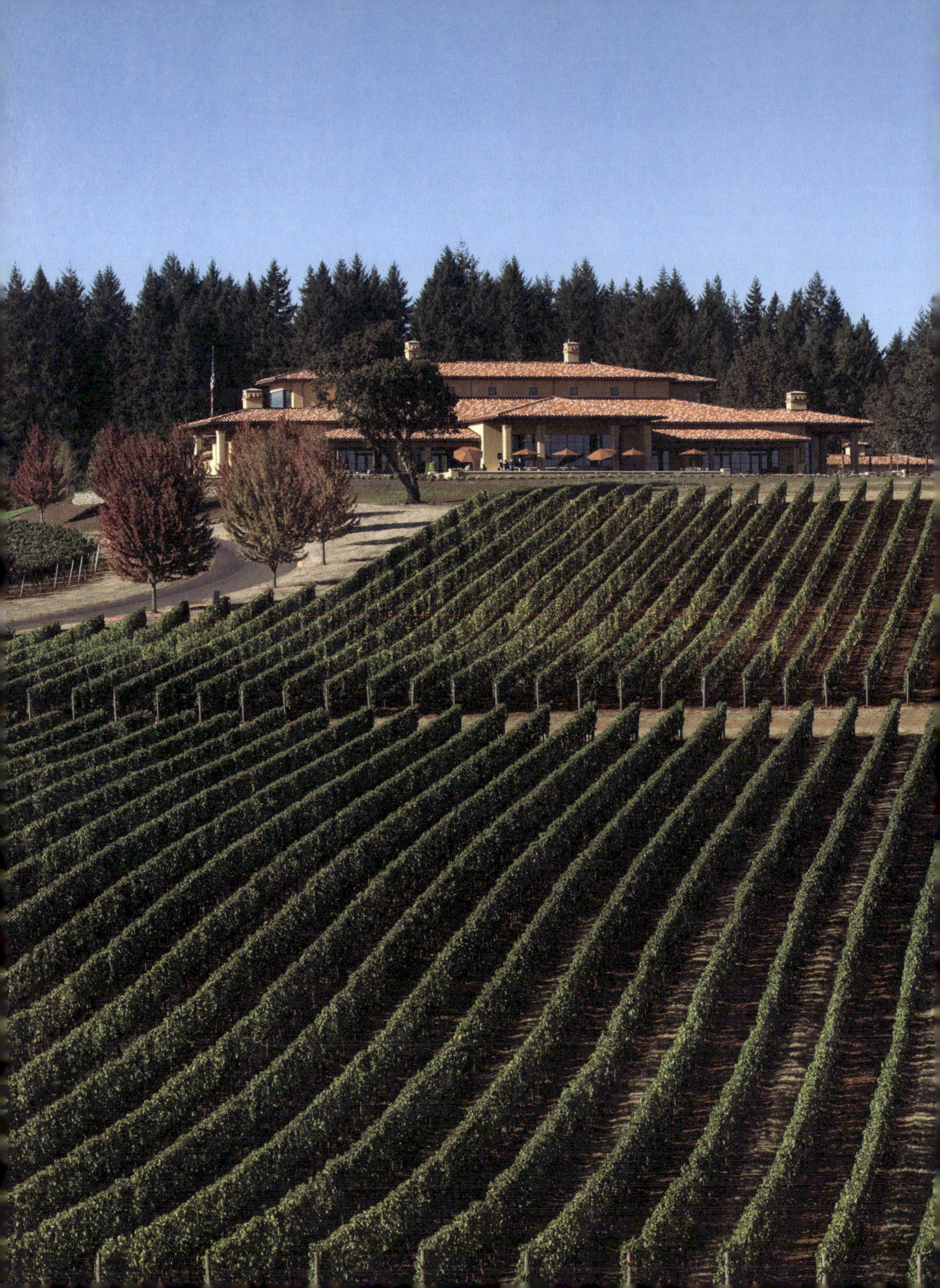

TOP EXPERIENCES / OREGON

Visit Willamette Wine Country

OREGON

BEST FOR
Farm-fresh produce and quaint country inns

USA

Reasons to visit the Willamette Wine Country are myriad: charming towns, beautiful and accessible vineyards (with relatively few visitors) and an abundance of chill. It's a literal breath of fresh air. The only question you'll ask yourself is: 'Why haven't I done this sooner?'

WINE COUNTRY IN ANALOG

Easily accessed from either Portland or Eugene and boasting fewer tourists than big-name wine hotspots, there are ample ways to find your bliss in this part of the US, whether on an afternoon visit or a long (extra-long) weekend of tastings. So why Willamette? The land here is fertile, alive and plentiful. Roadside inns, restaurants and towns are lovely and welcoming, without the tiniest bit of pretension. The hippy and hipster vibes here aren't a show: they're based on the simple understanding that living off the land is the best way to live.

You're not getting the sense of competition that one might experience in Napa or Sonoma, with multi-million-dollar, starchitect-designed hotel-spas owned by luxury conglomerates and boasting the latest design innovations. Here it's welcoming, warm and timeless. If you happen to feel like you're driving a 5-speed Fiat through Burgundy in 1976, so much the better.

Left to right: Serried ranks of vines near Dayton, Willamette Valley; Foraging for chanterelles near the Willamette wine town of Carlton.

MOST MEMORABLE MOMENT

Book a tasting at the Eyrie Vineyards in McMinnville. This is where Oregon's Pinot Noir production began, and the best place to learn about their 60-year history and perhaps try or buy an early vintage. After your tastings are done in the late afternoon, make your way to Humble Spirit for an early dinner of unfussy farm-to-table plates, from a top-tier burger to scrumptious fried chicken.

TOP EXPERIENCES / OREGON

STUNNING VIEWS, INCREDIBLE FOOD AND LUXE STAYS ON LOOP

The 'how' is as important as the 'why', so to make this perfect trip even more so, split your time between Newberg's Allison Inn and Spa and the Tributary Hotel in McMinnville. The entire Willamette Valley is 40 miles (64km) wide and 120 miles (193km) long, but from Newberg you can easily traverse a more manageable 50-mile (80km) circular route in two days, and taste the best of the region. Be sure to stop in Carlton where, within the space of only three blocks, you'll find dozens of tasting rooms – a veritable Pinot-palooza. Follow it up with dinner at the Blind Pig, where carnivores must order the French Dip sandwich (thinly sliced roast beef on a roll, with a side of jus or consommé).

For views and vistas, the wineries in and around the Dundee Hills are the most picturesque. And if imitation is the sincerest form of flattery, perhaps the best iteration of that maxim is French import Domaine Drouhin, opened by French vintner Joseph Drouhin after Eyrie Vineyards' Oregon Pinot Noir beat out Burgundy's best in a blind tasting at the 1979 Gault Millau 'Wine Olympics'. Joseph's daughter Véronique now runs the show in Dundee, and also makes some of the area's best Chardonnay.

Stop by other Dundee Hills wineries such as Domaine Serene, perhaps Willamette's most lauded and best-known producer, where you must prebook their rightfully in-demand full winery and cellar tour. Afterwards swing by Red Hills Market for a bite of something delicious – their storefront is pure Americana, while their menu features reimagined classics with an unexpectedly sophisticated bent: smoked-chicken pot pie and sweet potato pizza. You can even bunk there for the night in one of their two Market Lofts.

–Brekke Fletcher

Clockwise from top left: The grape harvest at Eyrie Vineyards, McMinnville; Farm-to-table food at Humble Spirit; Domaine Drouhin in Dundee; Pinot Noir grapes on the vine.

TOP EXPERIENCES / MELBOURNE

Savor the exciting food scene

MELBOURNE

AUSTRALIA

BEST FOR Foodies craving the taste of a place

Eclectic, energetic and experimental – there's good reason Melbourne's food scene is the envy of the world. This is Australia's cuisine capital, where the menu moves from the flavors of the Mediterranean to zesty Asian bites, detouring via the sweet spices of Africa – all served up in stylish yet affordable plates.

A GLOBAL SAMPLER

To get a taste of the famous Aussie café culture, take a wander through Melbourne's city-center laneways, bursting with boisterous, colorful and ever-changing street art. Opt for a takeaway ristretto (a local cold brew) or a piccolo latte at Maker Coffee before joining the line at Lune Croissanterie. Melbournians are obsessed with baked goods and after one bite of Lune's boldly flavored seasonal cruffins (croissant/muffins topped with popping candy, or stuffed with rum syrup and eggnog custard), you'll understand the addiction.

Thanks to a wave of immigration in the 1850s and then another burst in the 1960s, Italian and Greek migrants have brought their culinary know-how to the Victorian capital and its surrounding suburbs. In particular, the Italian influence on Melbourne's coffee and dining culture permeates the city, offering an overwhelming amount of choice. However, a visit to the stunning Il Mercato Centrale Melbourne, in the heart of the CBD, is an absolute must. This three-level marketplace is a culinary cornucopia of more than 20 vendors offering everything from fresh produce to simple yet delicious Italian dining. The Mediterranean theme continues at Mid Air, one of the city's premier rooftop bars and restaurants, with a menu that bursts with the flavors of Spain, Greece

Left: Melburnians are serious about their coffee, and everyone has their top spot, but Pellegrini's Espresso Bar is a longstanding favorite.

Clockwise from right: Try terrific tacos at Hotel Jesus; Enjoy Cameroonian delicacies at Vola Foods; Sip 'minimal interference' wine at Waxflower Bar; Snag a perfect pastry at Lune Croissanterie.

MOST MEMORABLE MOMENT

There's no shortage of incredible Asian cuisine in and around Melbourne. But it's Hanoi Mee Kitchen and Bar, tucked away in the bayside suburb of Port Melbourne, that should be on every culinary traveler's 'must-dine' list. Have your fill of the confit salmon in sesame cones and the green-rice-fried tiger prawns, but save room for the mouthwatering caramelized pork hock.

TOP EXPERIENCES / MELBOURNE

and Türkiye alongside outrageously gorgeous skyline views. And if the purse allows, book a table at Bottega to indulge in a delicious Australian spin on modern Italian cuisine.

CHEAT SHEET BEYOND THE CITY

Venture beyond the city and there are rewards aplenty. Jump on the 96 tram and head to the bustling, boutique South Melbourne Market (open Wed & Fri–Sun), where a pit stop at JuJu's Deli to fuel up on a crassly named yet incredibly delicious Chicken Schnitty Sanga (that's a chicken schnitzel sandwich, for the uninitiated) might be the most Australian thing you can ever do. You'll need to get your game-face on and fight the crowds for a tray of freshly shucked oysters at the market's Aptus Seafoods Oyster Bar. Take a more leisurely approach by grabbing a seat at Claypots Evening Star and indulge in, arguably, Australia's best seafood marinara.

Secreted away in the backstreets of West Brunswick, Vola Foods specializes in Cameroonian delicacies: the sweet sensation of fried plantains and the rich tomato-ey jollof rice will beckon you back for seconds. In Preston, the Falastini Food Truck serves up incredible Palestinian 'soul food'. Then, stop by the atmospheric Waxflower Bar nearby to sample their 'minimal interference' wine selection and treat your ears to their seductive soundspace before heading to Hotel Jesus in Collingwood, for some street tacos that will transport you directly to Mexico.
–*Chris Zeiher*

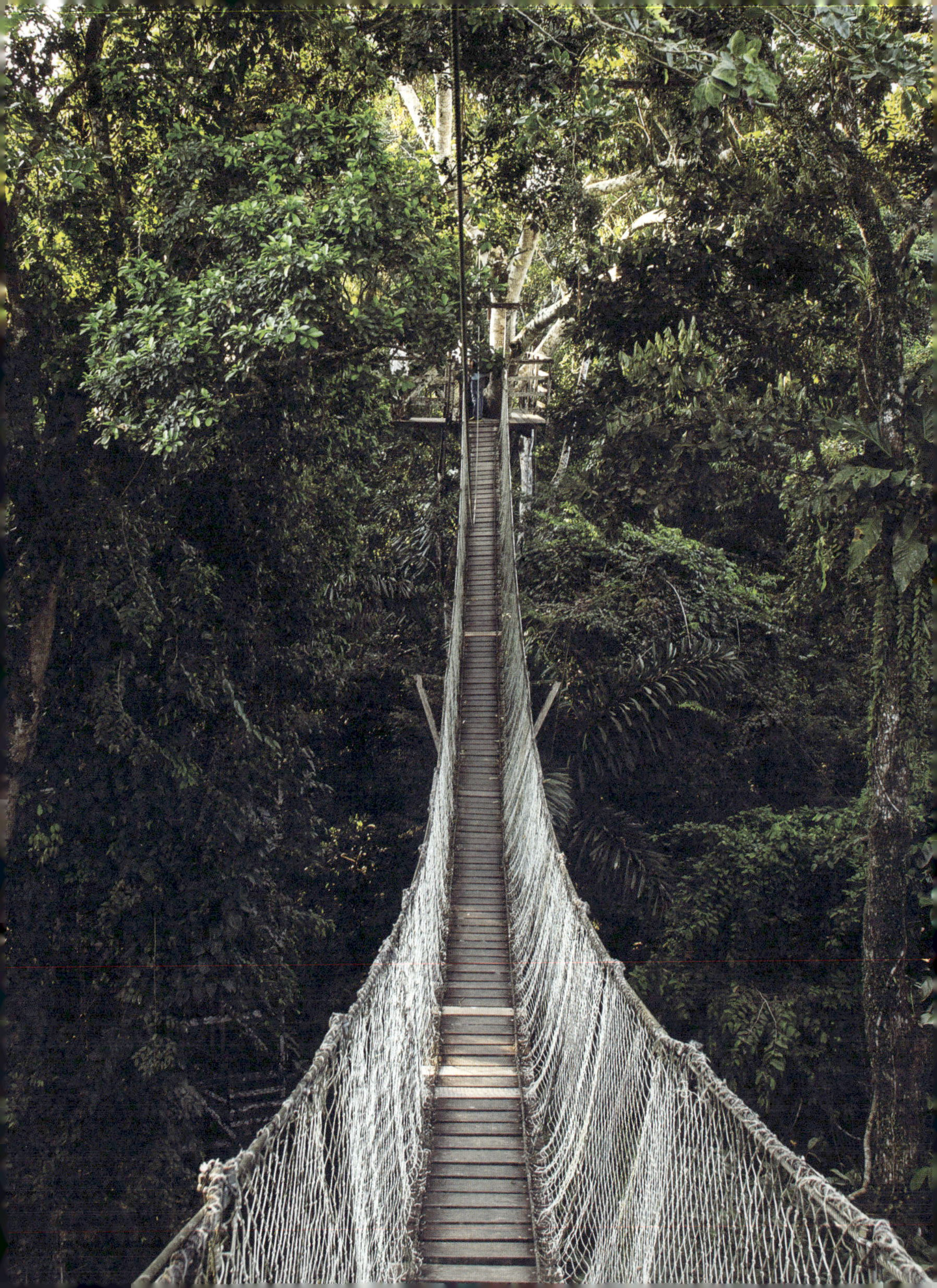

TOP EXPERIENCES / THE AMAZON

Become a citizen scientist
THE AMAZON

PERU

Left to right: Tiptoe through the treetops on the Reserva Nacional Tambopata's canopy walkways; A kaleidoscope of macaws at a Tambopata clay lick.

BEST FOR
Full-on jungle immersion

Roaring howler monkeys, rambling tapirs and scores of flamboyantly-feathered macaws all await visitors to the 1061-sq-mile (2748-sq-km) Reserva Nacional Tambopata in southeastern Peru. It's one of the world's last easily accessible virgin tropical rainforests and an emerging epicenter of a more hands-on, science-based approach to Amazon ecotourism.

WHEN TRAVEL AND RESEARCH SYNC
Crafted by tourism pioneer Rainforest Expeditions, the groundbreaking Wired Amazon program is designed to teach visitors about conservation by directly involving them in hands-on research. Trips within the Reserva Nacional Tambopata pair field biologists with citizen scientists eager to gain a deeper appreciation of the Amazon.

The World Wildlife Fund calls Madre de Dios, where Wired Amazon is based, one of the most biodiverse places on Earth thanks to its location on the southwestern edge of the Amazon, where nutrient-rich rivers spill down from the Andes. Madre de Dios has the planet's greatest concentration of bird species, as well as healthy populations of jaguars, tapirs and other large

BEST IN TRAVEL 2026 / 233

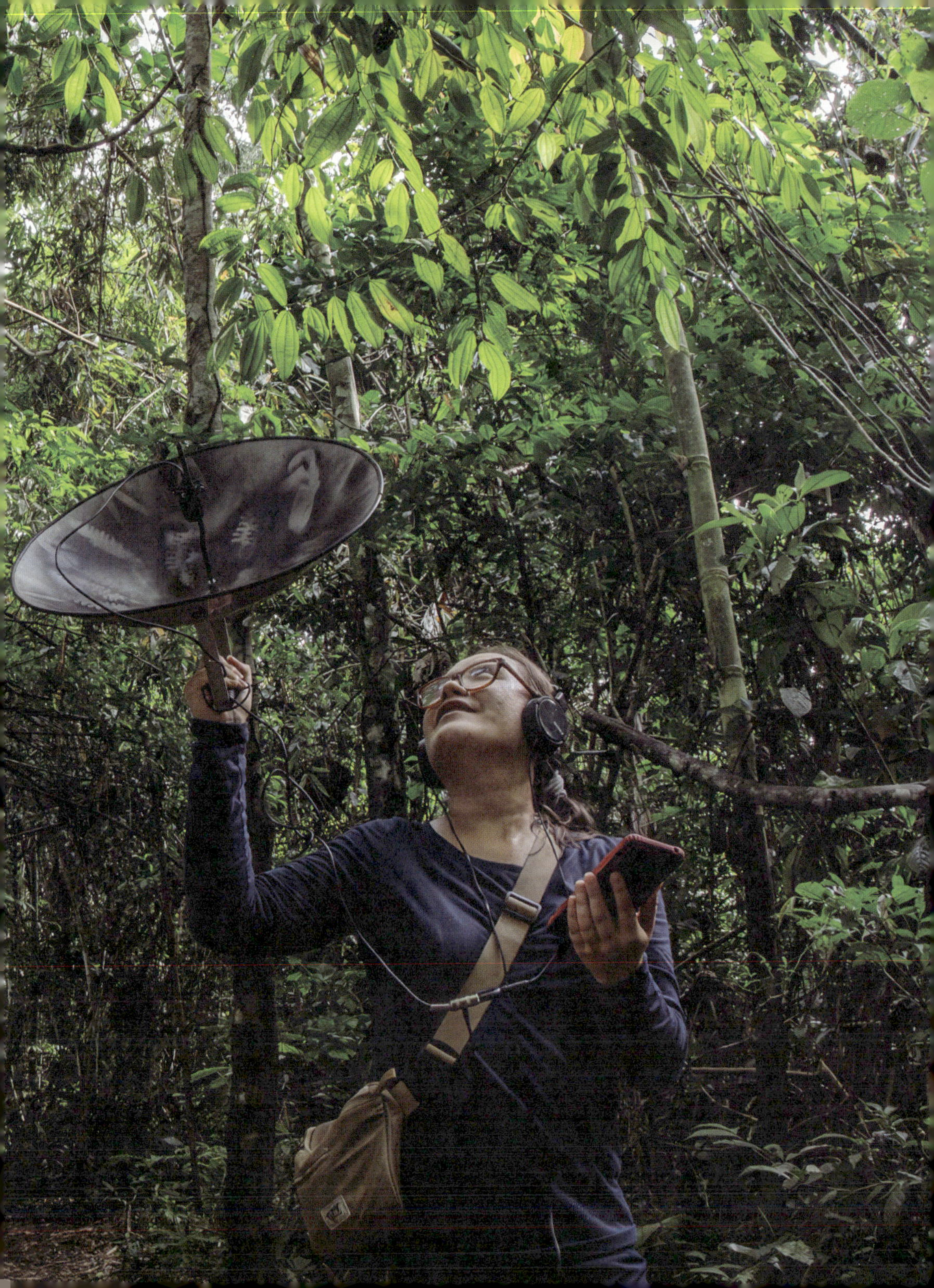

TOP EXPERIENCES / THE AMAZON

Amazonian mammals. Yet it also faces growing threats, including illegal logging and small-scale gold mining. The Wired Amazon project hopes to turn the tide on deforestation, working to protect the forest while also converting tourists into vocal ambassadors for it long after they visit.

Trips like these, based in citizen science, speak to the power of regenerative travel, one of the buzziest concepts in the industry right now, which is all about transformative experiences that leave destinations better than how you found them. What's more, many of the guides on these trips are former gold miners who now see the value of protecting this forest.

Not only does your money actively fund conservation, but your hands-on work adds to a growing body of research helping to protect Amazonian flora and fauna. What could be more win-win than that?

LEARN BY DOING

One day, head out with field biologists to place camera traps at strategic jaguar migration paths near one of the three Rainforest Expeditions lodges. The remote Tambopata Research Center is 2½ hours upriver from Puerto Maldonado, while Posada Amazonas is two hours upriver and owned by the Indigenous Ese Eja community. Another day, set light-traps in the ink-black forest to attract bugs, as part of an ambitious new program to discover unique species (some two dozen have already been identified here).

One incredible experience offered by the company involves tracking the health of Brazil nut trees (which need an intact ecosystem to survive), while another

Far left to right: A citizen scientist in the field, recording primate call-sounds for a bio-acoustics project; Jaguars thrive in the thick forests of Tambopata and the wider Madre de Dios region.

MOST MEMORABLE MOMENT

Tambopata is the best place on Earth to spot macaws in their natural habitat. Up to 500 of these large parrots gather at riverside clay licks each morning, in a rainbow of tropical hues. Birders and wildlife photographers wake well before dawn for the chance to arrive at first light and enjoy the spectacle.

TOP EXPERIENCES / THE AMAZON

project focuses on bioacoustics and recording the call-sounds of eight primate species. Visitors can sit in on myriad lectures discussing novel projects, including AI-enhanced artificial nests for endangered macaws, whose favorite nesting trees (the shihuahuaco) have been lost to the timber industry. This trip not only affords the opportunity to explore the Amazon; it also contextualizes the adventure through study and participation in dynamic preservation projects.

FUEL YOUR COMMITMENT TO THE PLANET

Other area operators are getting in on the action, too. Climate-positive hotel brand Inkaterra recently partnered with the Smithsonian Institution and USAID to develop a 390-sq-mile (1010-sq-km) biodiversity corridor to help empower local communities and create a viable economic alternative to illegal gold mining. Visitors are encouraged to help build out its inventory of regional flora and fauna, which stands at some 814 bird species, 365 types of ant, 313 butterfly species and over 100 mammals in the lands surrounding its two Tambopata jungle lodges and Amazon Field Station.

The fearless can go out at night in search of spiders, snakes, bats and caimans, whose eyeballs glow like marbles in the beam of probing flashlights. Wake early in the morning to stroll one of the Amazon's largest canopy walkways, which offers superb birding; or paddle through the tea-colored waters of oxbow lakes, including Lago Sandoval, in search of endangered giant river otters.

–*Mark Johanson*

Clockwise from top left: A Wired Amazon walk from Rainforest Expeditions' Posada Amazonas; Inkaterra's Reserva Amazonica; Paddling the Amazon; Citizen scientists planting.

BEST IN TRAVEL 2026 / 237

TOP EXPERIENCES / GRENADA

Party in the Caribbean
GRENADA

In Grenada, the parties will be too loud; they always are. You'll desperately search for a breeze to cool the constant perspiration from your forehead, armpits and, well, everywhere. But that won't be enough to call it. The celebration never stops; it moves from season to season. The biggest of the year is Spicemas, which takes place in August and culminates with a massive costumed bash through the streets. It's pageantry, it's Grenadian culture – and everyone is welcome!

Photographs by Chambers Media Solutions and Andy Johnson; Text by Alicia Johnson

TOP EXPERIENCES / GRENADA

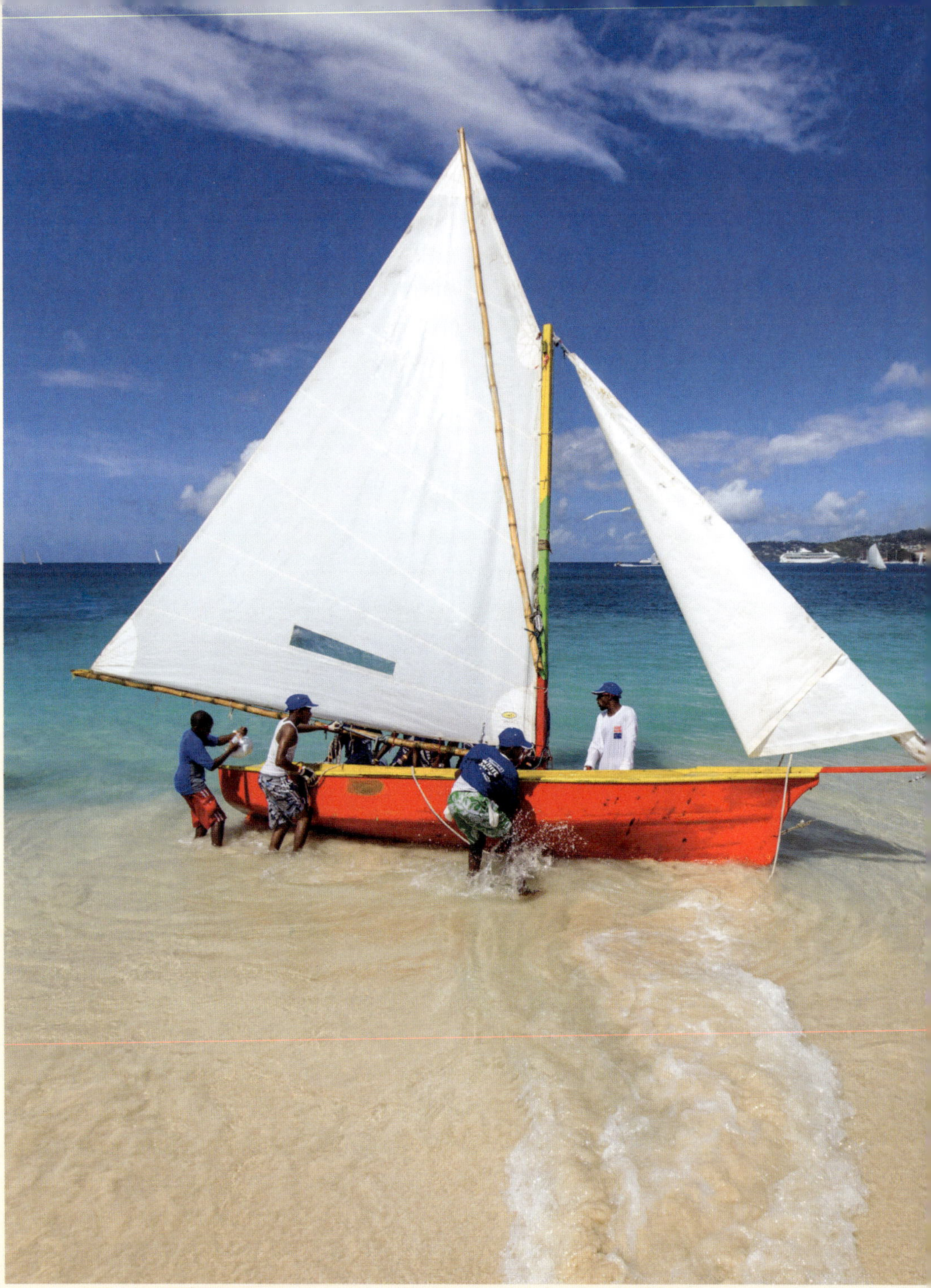

TOP EXPERIENCES / GRENADA

Previous spread: A good time on this Caribbean island comes with a sacrifice – your garments. But trust us, you won't regret a thing.

This spread: More than 20,000 people arrive for Spicemas, drawn in by the rhythmic melodies of soca (the 'soul of calypso'), dancehall and the heavy thumping of drums. Everything from plane tickets to hotels to pre-booked taxis is more expensive and sells out quickly – so plan ahead, and work in some time to see the island beyond the parties and parades.

White sands and clear waters at Grand Anse Beach make for the perfect cooldown after Carnival excesses. Visit St George's Market for fresh island-grown produce, and dip into the cool waters of Annandale Falls.

TOP EXPERIENCES / GRENADA

Grenada's promoters throw themed parties all year round, from the all-white LUSH on New Year's Eve to the Colors Fete marking February's Independence Day. Spicemas events include Pinknic and Ultra Gold, plus boat parties like the aptly named Rum Boat, or Legend Killa Day (hosted by Grenadian artist Mr Killa). Many are all-inclusive, with unlimited drinks and food. There's always a DJ and high-energy live performances.

But all fetes lead to Carnival Monday and Tuesday, when revelers parade the streets in colorful costumes, some outfitted with beaded headpieces or giant wings. Massive trucks with huge speakers blast the most popular songs of the carnival season. The sun is hot, you'll sweat, but that carnival spirit (and the rum) revitalizes.

242 / BEST IN TRAVEL 2026

BEST IN TRAVEL 2026 / 243

TOP EXPERIENCES / GRENADA

244 / BEST IN TRAVEL 2026

The highlight of Spicemas and a focal point of Grenadian heritage is J'ouvert, aka Jab. Taking place in the early morning of Carnival Monday, J'ouvert is as much about resistance as it is merriment. At the center of the celebration is the Jab Jab, a traditional carnival character and a symbol of defiance before and after emancipation. This character, above all others, has become synonymous with Grenadian culture. You'll find Jab Jabs everywhere, from music videos to stage performances, particularly during Spicemas.

J'ouvert revelers dress as Jab Jabs by covering their bodies in oil (motor oil for the purists, black paint or oil and charcoal for everyone else), donning devil horns and carrying chains to mock those who believed Black people were less than human.

The only thing better than covering yourself in oil and paint is covering others in oil and paint. It's the messiness of J'ouvert that gets everyone out of bed for this sunrise celebration. Consider wearing white to prove just how much mess is possible. Turns out, quite a bit. Worth it!

BEST IN TRAVEL 2026 / 245

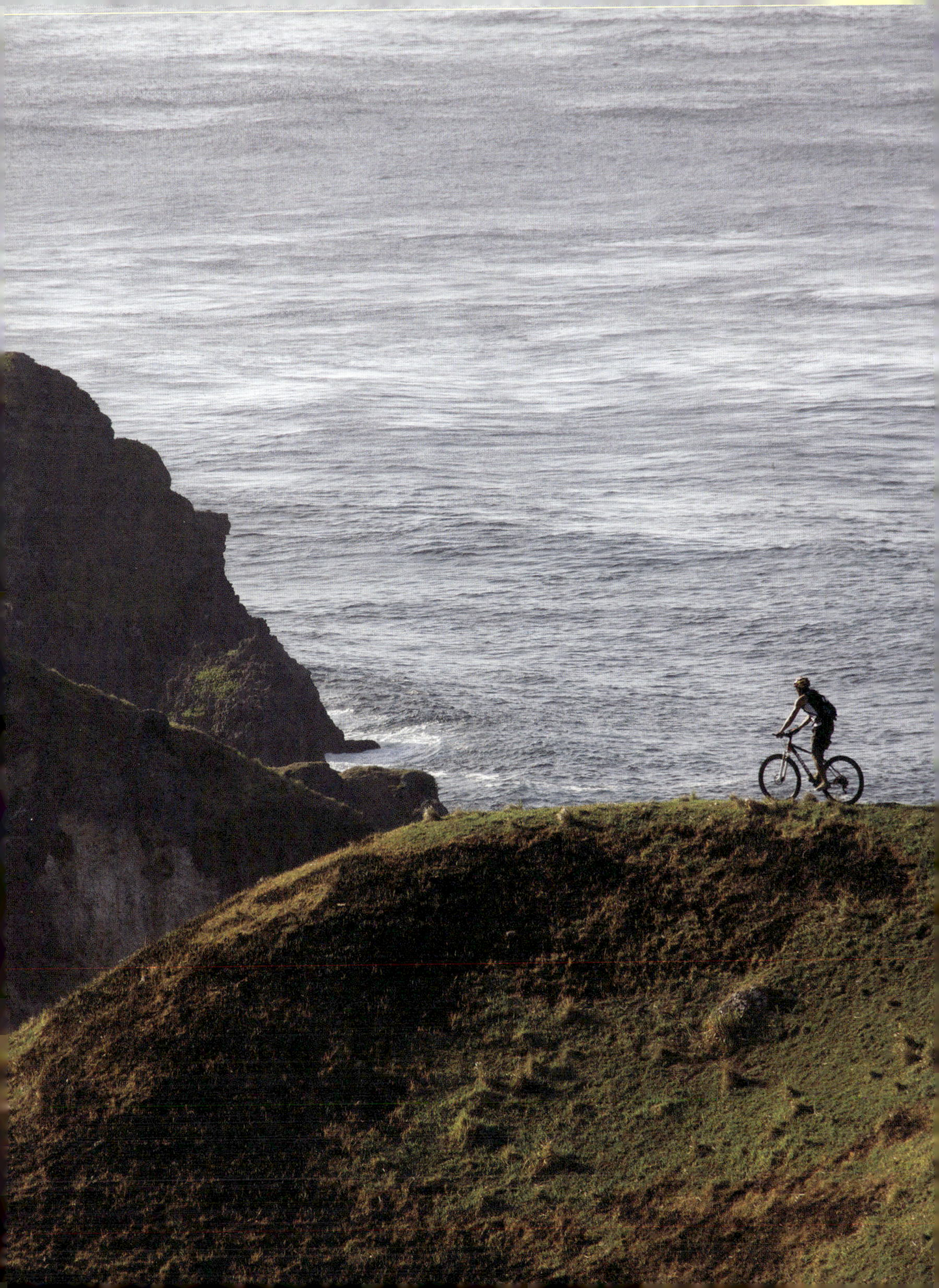

TOP EXPERIENCES / BATANES ISLANDS

See the sights by bike
BATANES ISLANDS

PHILIPPINES

Left to right: Biking the Batanes is the perfect way to channel the islands' go-slow vibes; Jump on a *faluwa* boat from Batan to see quiet Sabtang Island.

BEST FOR
Cyclists, walkers and solo questers

With rock-hewn landscapes, charming lighthouses, well-preserved culture and a crime-rate of zero, the Batanes group of islands in the Philippines is a universe apart. It may be the country's smallest province, but its wildly breathtaking scenery of rolling hills and seascapes will leave you feeling both insignificant and profoundly connected to the world.

BATANES BY BIKE

Batanes comprises three main inhabited islands: Batan, Sabtang and Itbayat (as well as smaller uninhabited isles). Unlike in the bustling cities, time flows slowly here. There's no need to rush and you'll be content to linger. As public transport is limited, van or tricycle tours offer the most convenience – but travelers who enjoy biking can discover sights for themselves. Every bend in the well-paved roads that hug the coast leads to otherworldly landscapes of grazing lands and endless blue waters, so it's best to soak in the natural splendor as slowly as possible.

Clockwise from right: Views of Mt Iraya on a ride from Basco, Batan's capital; Restaurants in Basco serve traditional Ivatan dishes, often cooked in banana leaves; Village life in the Batanes; Batan's rolling Racuh a Payaman (Marlboro Country).

MOST MEMORABLE MOMENT

Land, sea and sky meet in postcard perfection in Racuh a Payaman (aka Marlboro Country) on Batan Island. From the hilltop of a vast pastureland grazed by cows and wild horses, take in sweeping views of rolling hills and rugged coasts facing the Pacific Ocean. Breathe it all in.

248 / BEST IN TRAVEL 2026

TOP EXPERIENCES / BATANES ISLANDS

Rent a bike as soon as you land in the capital, Basco. Head first on a short cycle to Basco Lighthouse in Naidi Hills, to marvel at the views of Mt Iraya, then ride on to hop around the rocky shoreline of Chadpidan Boulder Beach. Pack up some lunch and plenty of water to spend another day looping the roads around north and south Batan. You'll visit lighthouses, churches, cute fishing villages, beaches and view-decks spread around Basco, Ivana, Uyugan and Mahatao. Consider bringing bikes on the *faluwa* (traditional boat) to explore Sabtang Island, seeking out stone houses built by the Indigenous Ivatan people (designed to withstand the harsh elements) and remote fishing villages on half-day trips or overnight stays.

TAKE IN A DELICIOUSLY SLOW PACE OF ISLAND LIFE

The Batanes Protected Landscapes and Seascapes are on the UNESCO World Heritage Tentative List for their unique natural features, from wave-cut cliffs to untouched white-sand beaches. This is also the only part of the Philippines where traditional stone houses still stand. The culture of the Ivatan people, who have resided in the Batanes for thousands of years, is remarkably well-preserved due to the islands' isolation from the rest of the country.

Biking around the Batanes may not be the longest in terms of miles, but the journey getting here, the remoteness and the untamed beauty will leave an indelible mark that lasts far beyond your stay.
–*Kara Santos*

TOP EXPERIENCES / BELGRADE

Experience the legendary nightlife scene

BELGRADE

SERBIA

*BEST FOR
Hidden clubs and underground beats*

Belgrade's nightlife is raw, electric and unapologetically wild. From riverbank clubs thumping till dawn to gritty underground bars pulsing with techno beats, Serbia's capital knows how to party. Cheap drinks, no-nonsense vibes and locals who live for the night make it Europe's ultimate after-dark playground. Sleep? Overrated. In Belgrade, the night is endless.

CULTURE BY DAY, DANCE FLOORS AFTER DARK
Few cities can match the pulsating energy of Belgrade by night. After dark, the striking brutalist architecture and quirky industrial spaces that make up the Serbian capital's distinctive skyline transform into the perfect gritty backdrop for a night of non-stop dancing, drinking and barhopping you won't forget.

Left: The ravishing riverfront in Belgrade, Serbia's buzzing capital city.

Belgrade sits at the confluence of the Danube and Sava Rivers, and nights out can easily start and end along the vibrant riverbanks. By day, industrial neighborhoods like Savamala showcase art galleries, creative spaces and cafes. By night, venues come alive – like KC Grad, set in a repurposed warehouse and hosting more than 200 music events annually, mixing industrial feel with cultural energy.

Over the years, even the city's port has transformed from an expansive industrial space into a banging cultural hub. A former cargo hangar here now holds the must-visit Hangar Luka Beograd nightclub, where the worlds of art and music come alive until the wee hours in a blend of non-stop electronic music and light shows. In March, the port's hangars provide the setting for the Illusion

TOP EXPERIENCES / BELGRADE

Festivals, a series of dynamic music and visual arts events drawing in headline acts from around the world.

TAKE THE PARTY TO THE WATER

These rivers also house Belgrade's legendary *splavovi* – floating nightclubs. Born out of the relative prosperity that followed the 1990s Yugoslav Wars, these floating bars and clubs have earned iconic status as party hotspots. Recently, many were relocated from the city center to the quieter Zemun neighborhood, just a 15-minute drive from Republic Sq. In summer, top picks include Leto, known for its pop, funk and R&B nights; or Lasta, where Sunday 'matinees' keep the party going all day.

Away from the water, the party continues across the city. Get a taste of Serbian tradition in Belgrade's *kafana* pubs, where food, drink and live music fuse perfectly. Classic dishes like *cevapi* (grilled kebab), buttery breads to die for, *ajvar* (roasted red-pepper dip) and pickles are the ultimate fuel for a long night. Head to Skadarlija, the historic bohemian quarter dubbed 'Belgrade's Montmartre', where pretty cobbled streets lead to iconic *kafanas* like Dva Jelena and Tri šešira. A popular hangout for impoverished Yugoslav poets and writers during the 20th century, Tri šešira was where famous Serbian poet Đura Jakšić could often be found raising a glass.

EXPLORE THE CITY'S SOUNDSCAPE

When you're suitably full, a short walk from boho Skadarlija gets you to Cetinjska. Originally a derelict brewery and massive

Left to right: Inside Sprat, one of many brilliant bars in the nightlife hub of Cetinjska; With options for all tastes, Belgrade's clubs are legendarily lit.

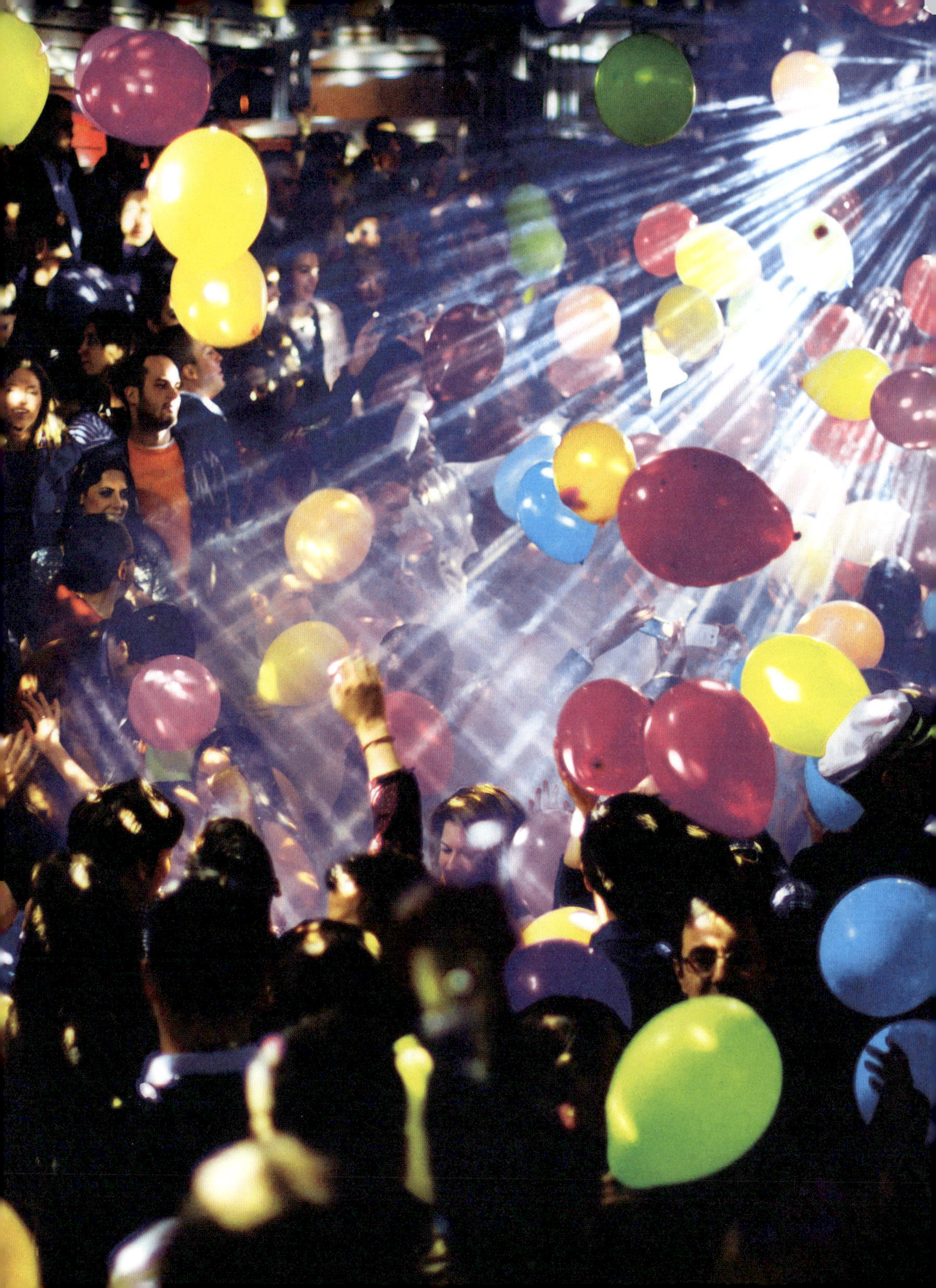

Clockwise from right: Nights at KC Grad offer a range of different flavors; Dorćol's Silosi, riverfront grain towers repurposed as an arts and events hub; KC Grad in full party-hard swing; Time to hit the bar at Cetinjska's Sprat.

MOST MEMORABLE MOMENT

At 3am on a cold October morning, rain comes down hard outside Karmakoma Club on the edge of town, but none of the club-goers care. They're not leaving. Acid trance pumps out from the speakers as the intimate crowd dances amid swirls of cigarette smoke. The party is nowhere near over. This is pure, hedonistic pleasure at its best.

TOP EXPERIENCES / BELGRADE

car park, this area has grown in popularity in the last decade and now thrives as a graffiti-covered nightlife hub. Bars like Berlin Monroe, Sprat and Polet have defined its late-night scene, offering a cool, underground vibe where locals party and DJs play every kind of music – from rock and ambient tunes to R&B and hip-hop.

Down the road, Belgrade's trendy Dorćol neighborhood is another great place to barhop. Dive into the city's excellent craft beer scene at top local spots like Gunners Pub, Krafter Bar and Das Boot, all serving a rotating list of affordable beers on tap. Cocktail bars are popular too, particularly the speakeasy Druid Bar (Instagrammers be warned: this is a 'no photo zone').

For those craving a heavier beat, Drugstore is a must. Set in a former slaughterhouse, this late-night club has developed cult status in the city: it kicks off around 2am, with the techno and electronic sets rolling well into Sunday morning. As with so many other venues in Belgrade, the club's industrial setting makes it easy to miss, so keep an eye out for the clubbers mingling outside.

If tickets sell out, neighboring Karmakoma delivers equally great trance and techno nights that will keep you out until well past dawn. Best of all, these venues are intimate and packed with locals ready to show you why their city is the beating heart of Europe's after-dark scene.
–Robyn Wilson

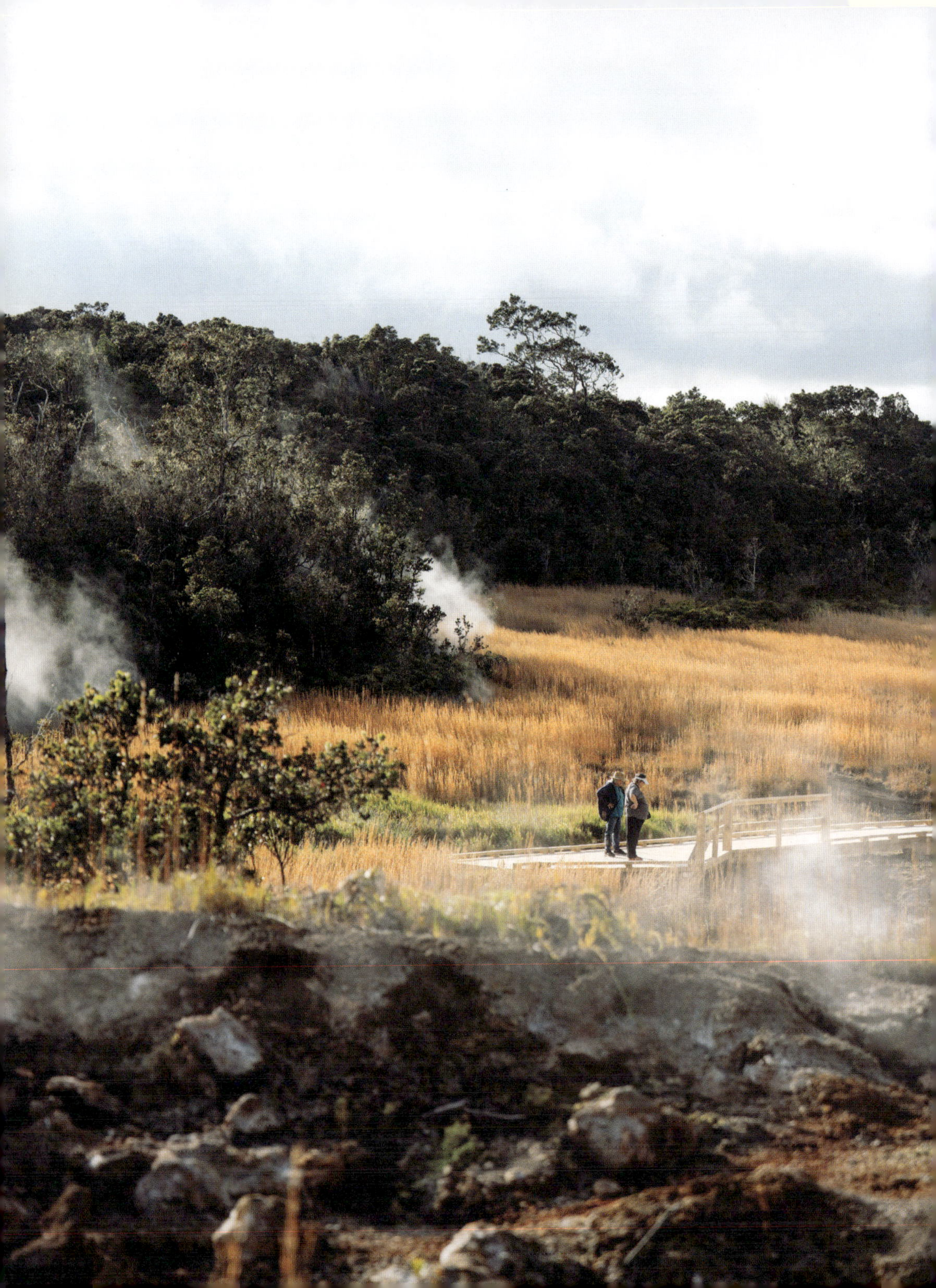

TOP EXPERIENCES / HAWAI'I

Stay at Hawai'i's Volcano House
VOLCANOES NATIONAL PARK

USA

BEST FOR
Lovers of lava and one-of-a-kind stays

Forged by volcanoes over hundreds of thousands of years, the ever-changing Big Island of Hawai'i is currently home to five: Kolaha, Mauna Kea, Hualālai, Mauna Loa and Kīlauea. For centuries, Hawaiians have honored these geological marvels by paying homage to Pelehonuamea (Pele), the Hawaiian goddess of volcanoes and fire.

A DIP INTO HISTORY

To this day, curious and cowed, people line up to see Kīlauea up close at the Hawai'i Volcanoes National Park, a UNESCO World Heritage Site and International Biosphere Reserve. Kīlauea holds the title of the world's most active volcano – its months-long 2018 eruption forever altered the island (and destroyed nearby residential areas).

The breathtaking sight of a fiery lava flow spilling into the ocean poetically exemplifies Hawaiian history and culture: living in harmony with nature means you honor its magnificence and understand its destructive powers. This is why it is customary to request permission from the goddess Pele before setting foot near her home.

One of the most unique and immersive ways to experience Kīlauea is a stay at the affordable, historic and stunning Volcano House (room rates can start at US$100/night), located within the island's beloved

Left to right: The Kūkamāhuākea (steam vents) in Hawai'i Volcanoes National Park; Traditional Hawaiian *hale* house near the steam vents.

MOST MEMORABLE MOMENT

If you stay here during an eruption, you'll witness the greatest show on Earth: the massive steaming crater-within-a-crater, Halema'uma'u, spewing lava as it has for much of the last quarter century. How active the volcano will be when you visit is subject to the whims of the Hawaiian deity Pele, goddess of fire and volcanoes. So ask her for admittance to increase your chances.

TOP EXPERIENCES / HAWAI'I

Hawai'i Volcanoes National Park. The original one-room structure, constructed in 1846, has been rebuilt multiple times. Now a 33-room lodge, rustic Volcano House has a decidedly 1960s Hawai'i feel in a setting that is nothing short of mind-blowing.

AN UNFORGETTABLE STAY

With its long history, well documented by the National Park Service archives, a stay at Volcano House is both fun and poignant. This is, after all, the same spot where Mark Twain bedded down in 1866, commenting that: 'The surprise of finding a good hotel in such an outlandish spot startled me considerably more than the volcano did.'

For those checking in today, Volcano House is a happy surprise, with unrivaled views of the Kīlauea caldera and the Halema'uma'u crater awash in an orange-red glow. There are, of course, risks when one is proximate to an erupting volcano. But both the National Park Service and Volcano House will keep you apprised of conditions and precautions that need to be taken.

Request a crater-view room to (potentially) witness spurts of lava from your window. Alternatively, Volcano House manages 10 camper-cabins and campsites, should that be more your speed. Non-guests can also stop by for a sunset meal at their restaurant, the Rim, or a drink at Uncle George's Lounge.

Awakening within this hallowed area's otherworldly beauty is an extraordinary and indelible feeling – one that can only be experienced in this otherworldly place.

Clockwise from top left: A tempting choice of trails from the Volcano House grounds; Taking a walk in the (national) park; The hotel buildings; Wild orchid along the Steam Vents Trail.

–*Brekke Fletcher*

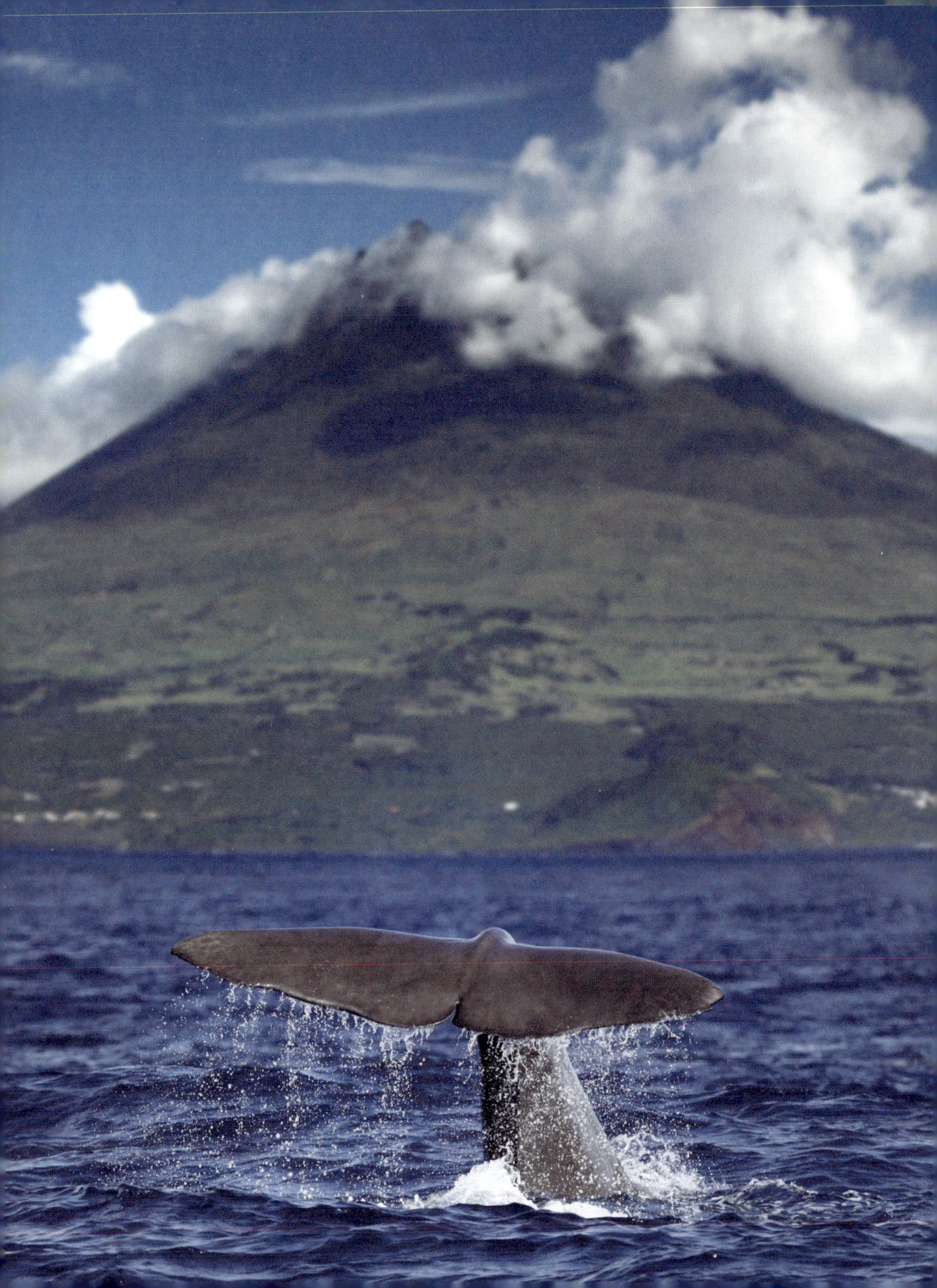

TOP EXPERIENCES / AZORES

Go whale-watching
AZORES

PORTUGAL

Left to right: A sperm whale deep-dives offshore of the Azores, backdropped by the Ponta do Pico volcano; Wild dophins skim alongside during a whale-watching tour.

BEST FOR
Ethical wildlife-watching

Although increased flight connections are making the Azores more popular than ever, nowhere among this island grouping is exactly what you'd call 'touristy'. Vast swaths of land dissected by well-paved roads running between tiny towns stretch out so far, it's easy to go a long way without meeting a soul (a human one, that is; cows are plentiful).

THE BEST BOAT TRIP YOU'VE NEVER HEARD OF
Occupying a tiny scattering of nine islands in the middle of the vast emptiness of the North Atlantic Ocean, the Azores are one of the best places on the planet to see whales and dolphins; sightings are almost guaranteed. Tour boats embark from most of the islands, but Ponta Delgada on São Miguel is the most popular departure port.

On board the boat, there's hope in the air, tempered by experience; as every wildlife-watcher knows, the potential for disappointment comes as part of the deal. Still, the excitement grows as the onboard marine biologist explains the possibilities of spotting the different species: dolphins, turtles, orcas, pilot whales and sperm whales, to name a few. Resist the calm shelter of the cabin and

Clockwise from right: Ponta Delgada on São Miguel, a hot spot for whale-watching boat trips; Local-grown produce on display; Striped dolphins surf the Azores' waves; A humpback breaches off Pico Island.

MOST MEMORABLE MOMENT

If you perch at the front of the boat, you'll likely see dolphins chasing each other and racing in front of you. You'll be so close that the sunlight will reflect in turns off the rippling water and the dolphins' slick skin as they dive in and out of the waves. It may be the closest you'll ever get to wild dolphins – don't be surprised if it's an emotional experience.

TOP EXPERIENCES / AZORES

spend your time on the boat deck if you can. You won't want to miss a moment. Dolphins, naturally friendly and prone to arriving without notice, often appear to race the boat and dive in front. But if the trip ends without any cetacean action, ask for a second go; most tour operators happily oblige free of charge.

TIME YOUR TRIP
Between April and early July, the whales are on their annual migration and there are more species in the surrounding waters, including the elusive orcas. But the ocean surrounding the Azores is teeming with life all year round and, yes, that includes those friendly dolphins and pilot whales.

The only thing that may stop you is the unpredictability of the weather, which is also a year-round feature, but less of an issue in the summer months.

With trips lasting more than three hours, there's ample opportunity to follow tips from the shoreline about where the wildlife has recently been sighted. Every time, passengers of all ages react with wonder, as childlike 'wows' are passed around the deck. No doubt, you'll wobble off the boat at the end with hundreds of pictures, a great story and hair full of windblown knots.

The rest of the Azores awaits, with its myriad verdant hiking trails, photogenic viewpoints, freshly caught seafood and local wine still carrying the salty tang of sea air. But nothing quite beats being out on the ocean, racing those chittering dolphins.
–*Annemarie McCarthy*

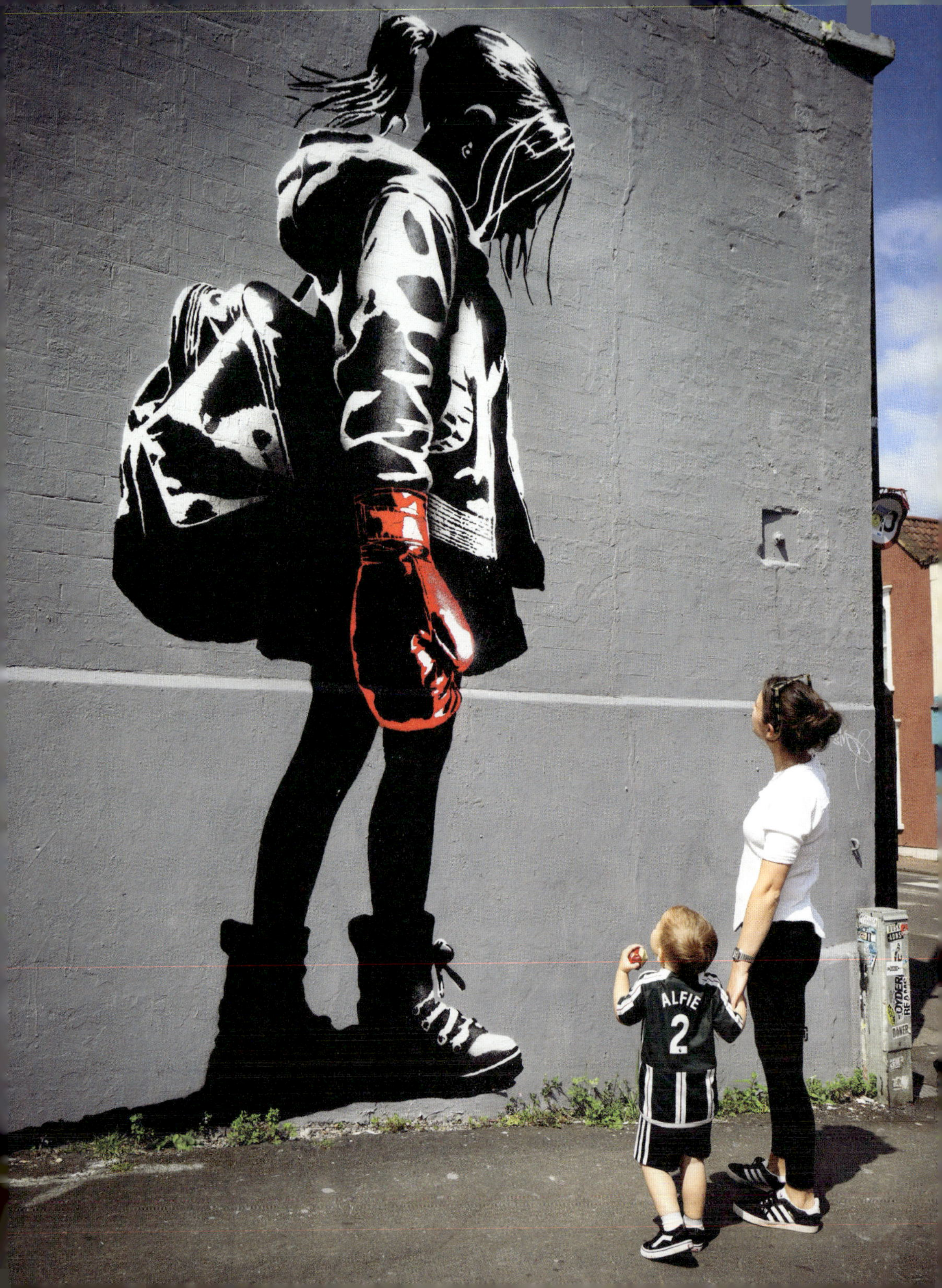
ALFIE
2

TOP EXPERIENCES / BRISTOL

Deep-dive into street art

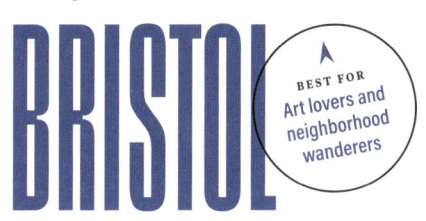

BRISTOL

BEST FOR
Art lovers and neighborhood wanderers

ENGLAND

It should come as no surprise that Banksy's hometown is a hotbed of color and creativity. Whether it's the rainbow row of houses high up on Cliftonwood Crescent or the eye-popping murals in counterculture enclave Stokes Croft, Bristol seems to burst with art from every pore. Put on your walking shoes and explore some of the best street art anywhere in Europe.

WATCH ART UNFOLD IN REAL TIME

No city in Britain uses its urban landscape as a canvas quite like Bristol. From shop facades to shipping containers, nowhere on these art-splashed streets is safe from a new mural appearing overnight.

One of the biggest joys of strolling through Bristol is the element of surprise: the most unremarkable street scene can reveal something unpredictable – Irony & Boe's cheeky seagull peeking around a terraced house corner off North St, for example, or Sophie Long's sublime flowers and hummingbirds flanking the windows above a coffee shop on Bedminster Parade.

Bristol's thirst for outdoor expression began in the 1980s, when hip-hop culture made its way over from the USA. Art and music intertwined through DJ crews and graffiti artists, with pioneers like Inkie and Robert '3D' Del Naja becoming a significant part of the city's counterculture scene. And from this movement emerged

Left to right: Goin's Stop Bullying, on the wall of the Spotted Cow pub in central Bristol; Live painting during Bristol's Upfest street-art festival. www.goin.art

BEST IN TRAVEL 2026 / 265

MOST MEMORABLE MOMENT

Some murals are harder to find than others, and finally discovering Banksy's Girl with a Pierced Eardrum *is a satisfying delight. Hiding at the end of a small dockyard alley on Spike Island, it's a playful take on Johannes Vermeer's 1665 painting* Girl with a Pearl Earring. *Enjoy the hunt!*

266 / BEST IN TRAVEL 2026

TOP EXPERIENCES / BRISTOL

the artist who would truly put Bristol on the global stage a decade later: Banksy.

The anonymous icon's distinct stencil work can still be found across Bristol; two of the more visible and accessible examples are *The Mild Mild West* in the Stokes Croft neighborhood, and *Well Hung Lover* on Park St.

GET TO KNOW THE AREA'S MOST INNOVATIVE ARTISTS

One of the most immersive ways to learn more about Banksy is through Bristol Street Art Tours' in-person tour around Stokes Croft every Saturday, or through self-guided audio tours at your own convenience. Some murals are easy to spot by yourself, but this fascinating tour takes you down dark alleys and up steep hills, uncovering some obscure early Banksy pieces while learning about Bristol's street-art lore from global graffiti art authority John Nation.

Back on North St, the best in modern Bristol's street art is showcased by the Six Sisters project, created by an all-female group of artists. The pieces incorporate intricate designs and bold splashes of turquoise, purple and hot pink above six ordinary shopfronts, and number among the city's most enchanting murals. North St is also home to Upfest, a gallery/store that's a great place to purchase a piece of original local art, and which shares its name with Bristol's biggest biannual street-art festival. Returning in 2026, the festival (in late May) is a wonderful mix of workshops, live painting, artist talks and street-art tours.

And if you're planning on staying a while, the Artist Residence – a quirky pop-art-strewn boutique hotel near Stokes Croft – makes an ideal base for exploring this gloriously creative city.
–James March

Clockwise from top left: Inkie's *See No Evil* on Nelson St; Irony & Boe's *Seagull* on North St; The Six Sisters project on North St; A Botanical Vandals mural by Graft on St Paul's Learning Centre.

BEST IN TRAVEL 2026 / 267

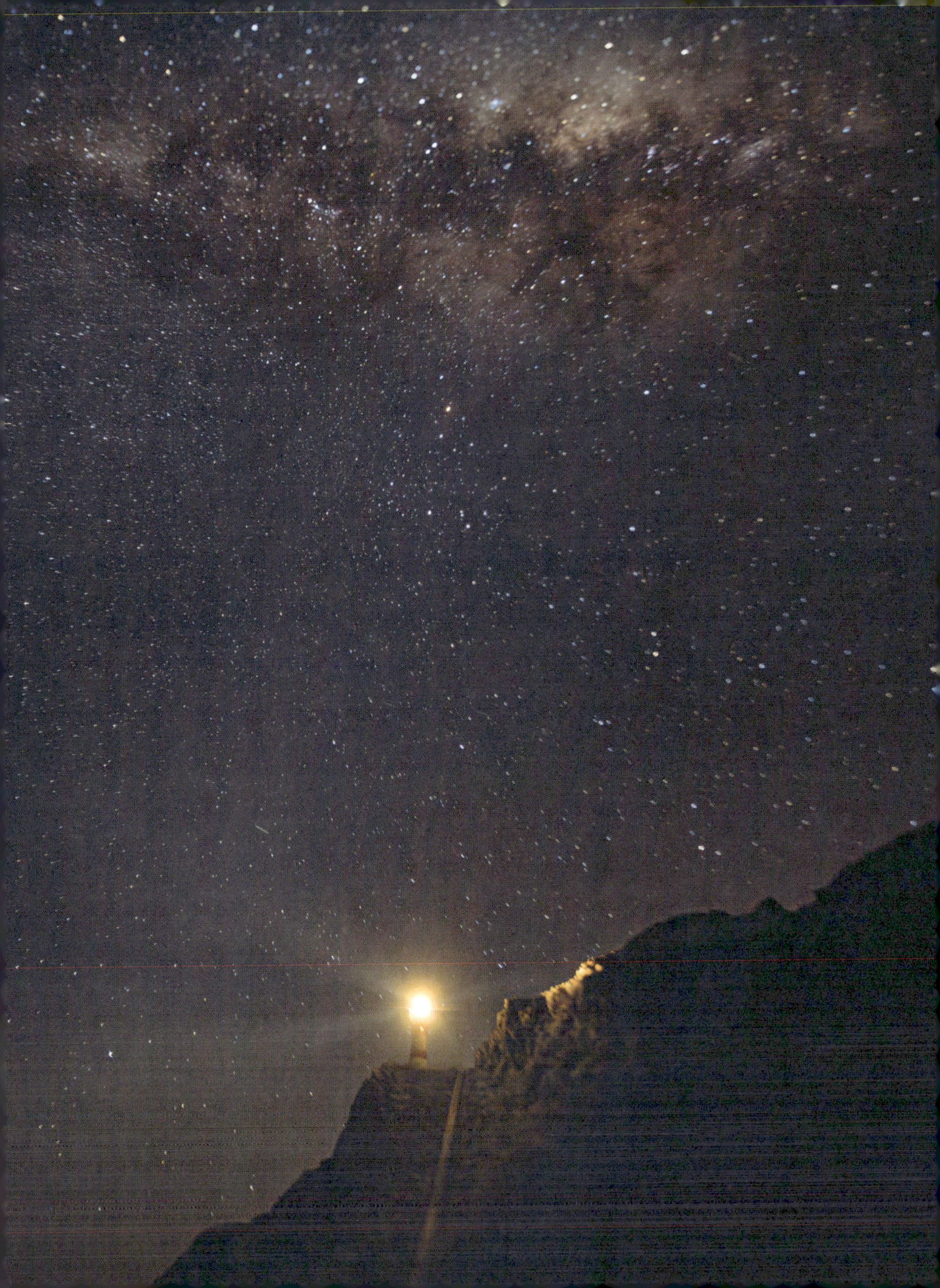

TOP EXPERIENCES / WAIRARAPA

Go stargazing
WAIRARAPA
NEW ZEALAND/AOTEAROA

Left to right: The Milky Way lights up the night above Cape Palliser Lighthouse; Rolling Wairarapa hills by day.

BEST FOR Bespoke astronomy experiences

Known for its clear skies and brilliant stars, New Zealand is on track to become the world's first 'Dark Sky Nation'. This is particularly evident in the Wairarapa – a region of vineyards and historic villages just outside of Wellington – where the stars have aligned to result in one of the country's most accessible stargazing experiences.

GO WHERE THE NIGHT SHINES
To become the world's first Dark Sky Nation is an audacious goal. In fact, it's a certification that doesn't even exist yet. But if it did, the first country in line to receive it (after tiny Niue in the South Pacific) would be New Zealand.

Already, Aotearoa (the country's Māori-language name) boasts nine certified DarkSky places (with 17 more working towards certification through Arizona-based DarkSky International), where light pollution is nonexistent or drastically limited. Amongst them are the South Island's

BEST IN TRAVEL 2026 / 269

TOP EXPERIENCES / WAIRARAPA

Aoraki Mackenzie International Dark Sky Reserve, one of the world's largest at 1686 sq miles (4367 sq km); and Tāhuna Glenorchy, one of the country's newest, having achieved certification in 2025.

FOLLOW THE STARS

But nowhere else in the country do the stars shine quite as brightly as they do in the Wairarapa, NZ's most accessible dark-sky destination. Situated just over an hour east of Wellington, most of the Wairarapa Dark Sky Reserve's 1415 sq miles (3665 sq km) is easily explored by foot, bike or car – but you don't have to leave your accommodation to experience its best feature. Instead, book a room at one of the region's countless countryside Airbnbs or lodges. An experienced astronomer from the tour company Under the Stars will bring their telescope and laser pointer right to you for a bespoke stargazing experience, with special packages (and pricing) available for smaller groups and couples.

If you'd prefer to situate yourself in one of the main centers, get away from the city lights at the Star Safari Observatory outside Martinborough. There, you can gaze out towards the galaxies using the largest telescopes for public use in the Wairarapa. And no stargazing trip to the region is complete without a stop at Stonehenge Aotearoa. On a 'Star Trek' here, you'll learn how the massive stone circle was constructed for the southern hemisphere's specific celestial patterns before seeing firsthand how it all aligns in the dark of night.

The best time to visit is in mid-June, when Matariki – a cluster of stars also known as the Pleiades – rises over the horizon. Its appearance in the early morning sky marks the Māori new

Left to right: Brooding skies over Palliser Bay; Hiking into the limestone chasm at Patuna Farm.

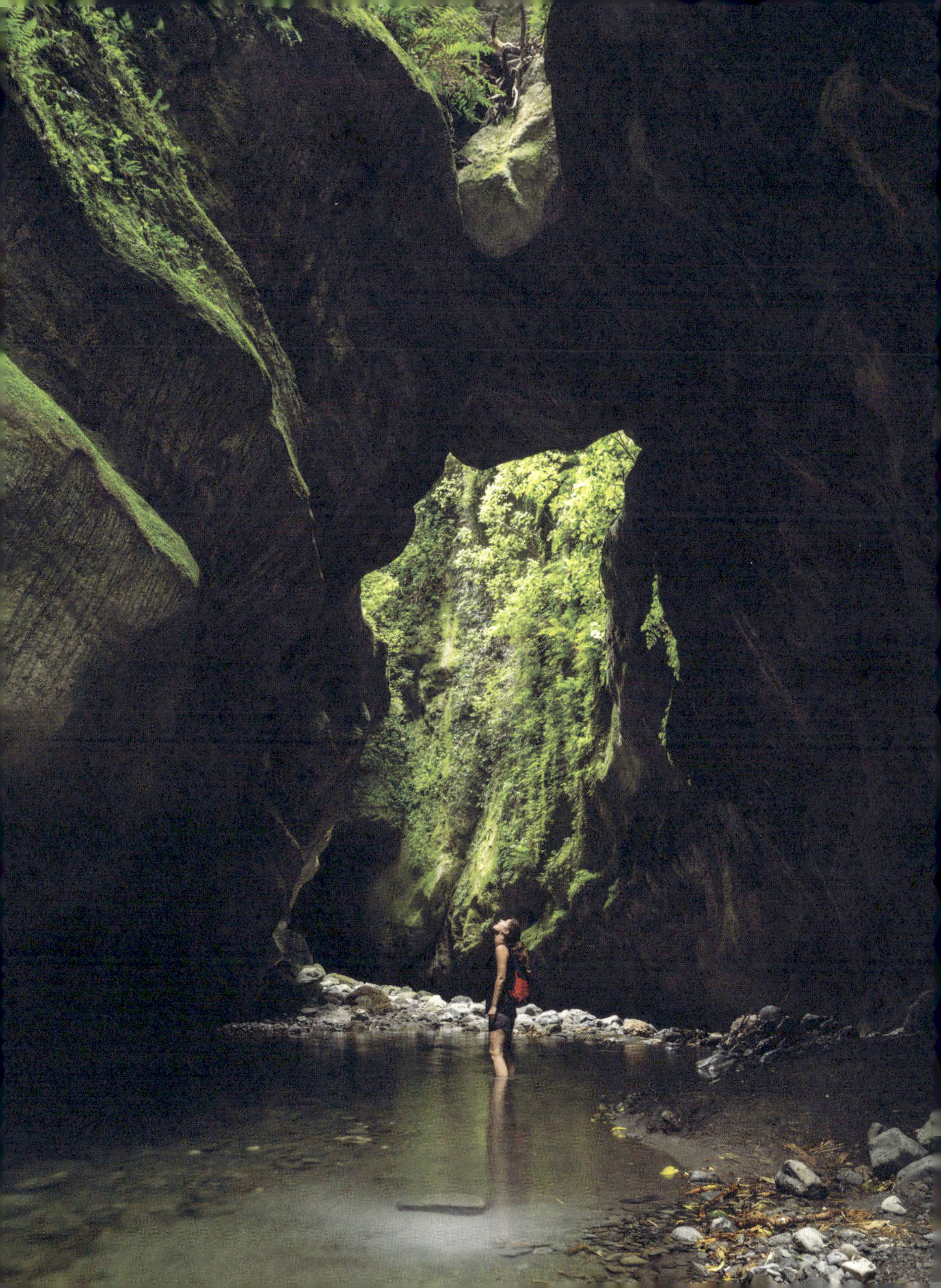

Clockwise from right: Victorian-era charm in Martinborough; Head out from the town to visit wineries and cellar doors by bike; Stonehenge Aotearoa; Perfect stargazing above the Rimutaka Crossing Memorial near Featherston.

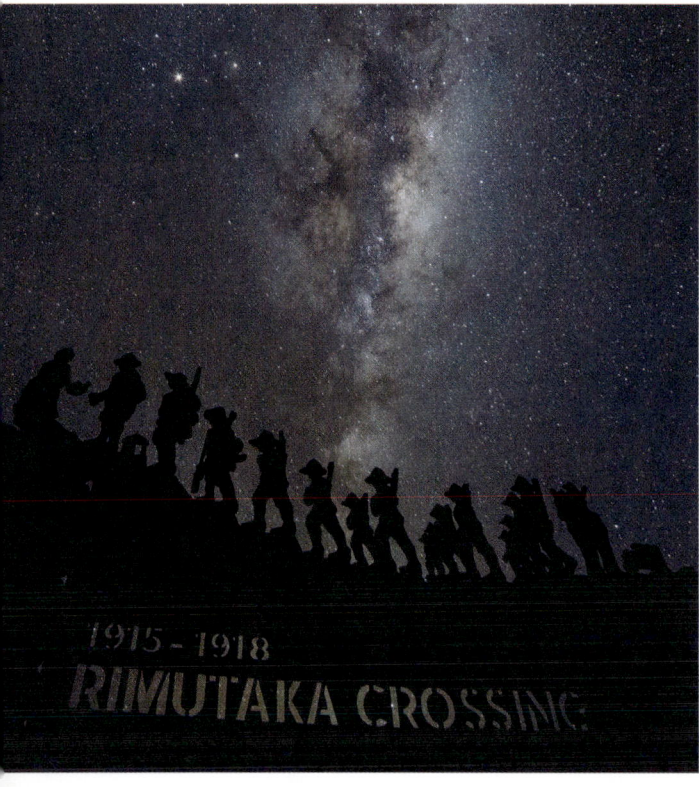

MOST MEMORABLE MOMENT

For every world-class attraction in New Zealand, there's one that reflects the quirkiness and curiosity of Kiwis. Case in point: Stonehenge Aotearoa. Gazing up at the night sky here, it's hard not to feel in awe of both the universe and the ingenuity of the Kiwis who built this strange structure.

TOP EXPERIENCES / WAIRARAPA

year and is celebrated throughout the Wairarapa with community festivals, markets, hāngī (meals cooked in underground firepits) and light shows. If you time a visit for Carterton Space Week in October, you can participate in an astrophotography or celestial navigation workshop.

BOOK YOUR DAYS, TOO

The Wairarapa isn't just an after-hours destination: its villages are a beloved weekend getaway for Wellingtonians. On any given Saturday or Sunday in Greytown – a scenic 75-minute drive northeast of Wellington through the Remutaka Ranges – the carefully preserved Victorian-era main street hums with visitors perusing boutiques and gift shops. In nearby Martinborough, oenophiles can cycle from winery to winery, with over 20 cellar doors pouring samples of the good drop, including Pinot Noir and Sauvignon Blanc.

For families, Masterton – the region's largest town – boasts a bird sanctuary and kiwi hatchery (Pūkaha National Wildlife Center); arguably one of the country's best playgrounds (Queen Elizabeth Park); and an art gallery, Aratoi, with a modern and Māori art collection that wouldn't be out of place in a much bigger city. It's tempting to pack your days with outdoor adventure, too: visit the seal colony and lighthouse at Cape Palliser, or hike through a hidden limestone chasm at Patuna Farm. Don't forget to nap, though. You'll need to stay awake when the night skies come alive.
– *Jessica Lockhart*

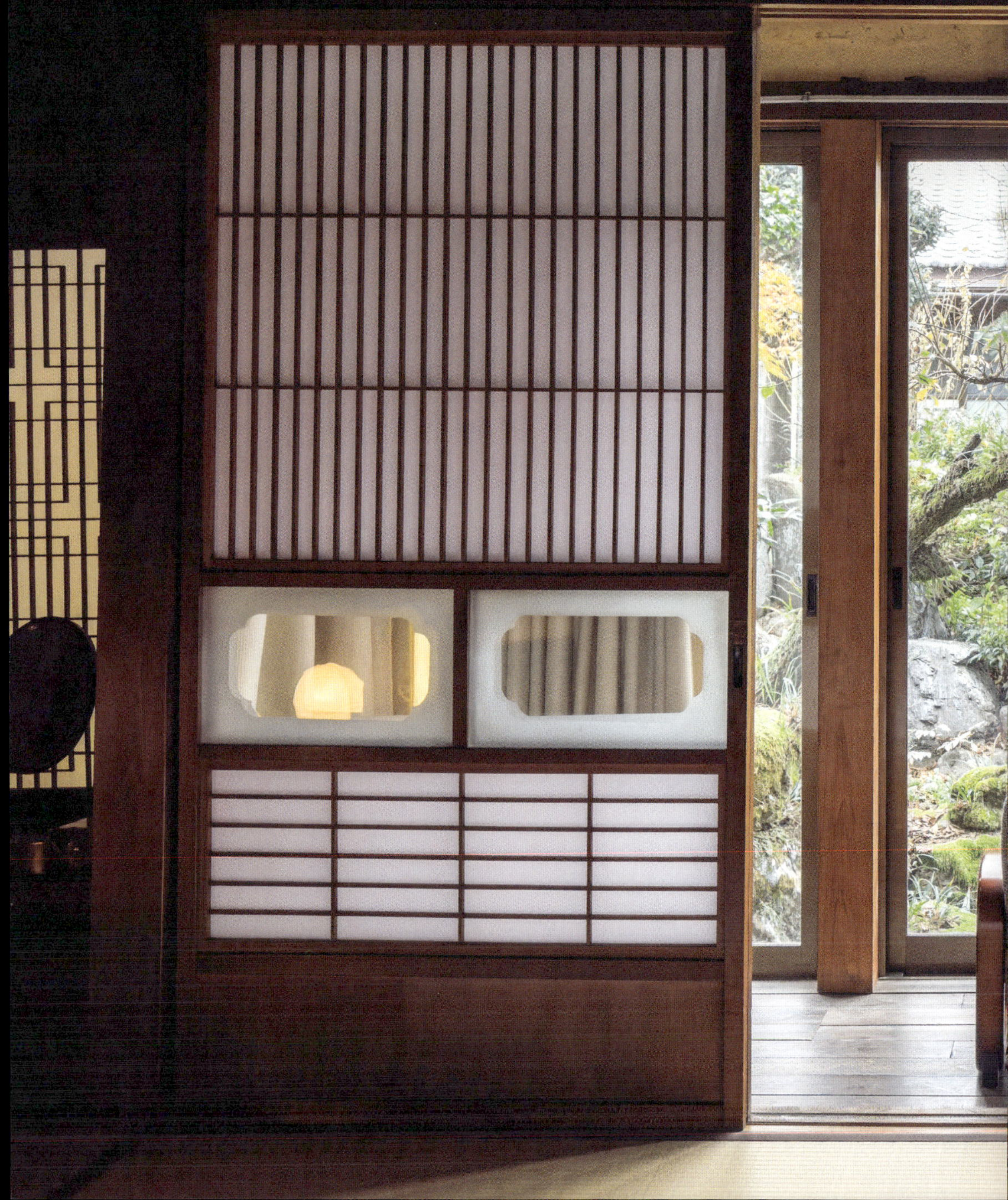

Ryokan (p168) like Matsuya, on the Nakasendō Way, were built along historic routes that date back to the Edo period.

ABOUT THE AUTHORS

Dubai born and raised, Natasha Amar has called Old Dubai home since the area was the heart of all the action in the city. She has spent countless evenings among the traditional houses of Al Fahidi Historical Neighborhood, pottering around the souks of Deira, and eating her way along the Dubai Creek – very much a living, breathing feature of the city. Through her submission in this book, recounting a walking food tour through Old Dubai, Natasha is keen to share the lens through which she views her delightfully diverse and culturally rich hometown.

Johannesburg-based Sophie Baker covered Kruger Shalati, the 'Train on the Bridge'. She has been on more than 40 safaris across South Africa, experiencing the wild in every way imaginable – from luxury lodges to remote camping and even a safari on horseback. Few experiences, however, compare to sipping champagne from her seat in an infinity pool on a suspended train deck, while watching elephants wade below.

Joel Balsam first heard about Creole trail rides while on a four-month RV road trip across the US South. The first one he attended in Calvert, Texas, was welcoming and fun – riding on a wagon, dancing to zydeco and filling up on cowboy stew. Joel has since attended another Creole trail ride, in New Iberia, Louisiana, and is passionate about sharing this exciting African American cultural tradition far and wide – including in this book.

Ray Bartlett has crisscrossed Guatemala and worked on numerous travel titles there, including his submission for this book on Quetzaltenango (aka Xela), which he often uses as a base for his Guatemaltecan adventures. When not on assignment, Ray lives near Boston, drinking far too much coffee and burning equally as much midnight oil. In addition to his travel work, he is a 'destination fiction' novelist, with one title set in Mexico's Yucatán and another in Japan.

Although based in Cleveland, Ohio, Laura Watilo Blake feels at home in Colombia, where she and her husband adopted their daughter in 2016. Since then, it's been her goal to explore the country's incredible cultural and geographic diversity, from the Caribbean coast to the Amazon River and everywhere in between. Cartagena, which she wrote about for this book, is one of her favorite places for street photography – its timeless setting offers new sights and experiences with every visit.

Lonely Planet editor Sasha Brady loves unhurried escapes. From her home in Dublin, Ireland, she enjoys regular weekend breaks to Tipperary, a short spin away, where she hikes the Galtee Mountains, collects farm-fresh produce from the markets and joins traditional music sessions from a cozy snug in a local pub. She also enjoys quick breaks to Utrecht in the Netherlands, to cycle its medieval streets and relax with a coffee by its sunken canals. She couldn't choose which destination she loved the most, so she decided to write about both for this book.

Australian Chloé Braithwaite is based on the French Riviera. A lover of urban design and architecture, she came across Eileen Gray's villa and fell in love with the history, the drama – and the woman herself. Having traveled the length and breadth of France, she can confidently say: there's nothing (and no-one!) else quite like it. When she's not exploring (and subsequently writing about) her adopted Riviera home, you're likely to find her nose in a book, planning her next trip away.

Karen Catchpole wrote about looking for jaguars in the Iberá Wetlands of northern Argentina. A full-time traveler through the Americas since 2006, Karen has spent years exploring Argentina – from Ushuaia in the south to Salta in the north. She's often in search of nature and the chance to see animals in the wild. When she reached the Iberá Wetlands, she knew it was unlike any other wild place in Argentina – and not just because of the big cats that live there.

Despite being based in New York City, Kelsy Chauvin is a national- and state-parks enthusiast. For this book, she reported on North Dakota's most famous reserve, Theodore Roosevelt National Park, where Kelsey was surprised to find both a wild geological wonder and a place that was transformative in the life of Theodore Roosevelt. With this piece, Kelsey accomplished a life goal of visiting all 50 United States and is now part of North Dakota's 'Best for Last' Club – and has the T-shirt to prove it.

ABOUT THE AUTHORS

Daniel James Clarke's love for slow, slightly offbeat travel – plus his persuasive friend Nicole – first brought him to Central Asia. Even as an amateur (and, admittedly, not overly fit) multiday hiker, he fell hardest for the remote, wild and unforgettable peaks, lakes and starlit sleeping spots of Tajikistan's Fann Mountains. Of all his travel experiences across 78 countries, trekking the Lakes Loop here fast became a favorite – one he wrote about for this book, and recommends to anyone seeking a truly epic backpacking adventure.

Jamie Ditaranto has always seen São Paulo's multiculturalism as one of its biggest assets. She grew up visiting family in São Paulo, Brazil, and for this book chose to write about her favorite neighborhood here: Liberdade – a characteristically Japanese district of the city with a colorful, eclectic attitude. As a secret anime fan and not-so-secret matcha lover, Jamie loves to explore Liberdade; every time she goes back São Paulo, she makes sure to visit to see the new shops and the street art.

Luisa Dörr is a Brazilian photographer whose work explores femininity, identity and human nature. In Bolivia, she immersed herself in the world of the Flying Cholitas, Indigenous Aymara women who have turned the 'fight/sport' into a symbol of defiance and empowerment. Guided by Marco, a social worker and Aymara activist she met on her visit, she came to understand the deeper struggles and triumphs of these women beyond the wrestling ring – in the streets, markets and protests of El Alto.

Brekke Fletcher wrote about wine tasting in the Willamette Valley, Oregon, and staying at Hawai'i's Volcano House hotel. Growing up on the US West Coast, Brekke (Lonely Planet's Senior Director of Content) spent her early years traveling with her family to Oregon and Hawai'i. Her recent and frequent childhood visits to both places have yielded life-long memories, including her selections for two of this year's best experiences.

When Lonely Planet editor **Chamidae Ford** was growing up, travel was a constant priority for her family – and that hasn't changed. She lives on the opposite (US) coast to her mom, and the pair have begun a yearly ritual of meeting in destinations across the world. For *Best in Travel*, Chamidae shares their 10 days exploring Ecuador, horseback riding through the Andes to catch a view of Volcán Cotopaxi. The trip has become a forever, one-of-a-kind, lifelong memory she and her mother can share.

After exploring nearly every corner of Vietnam, no coastal place has captured **Karla Foronda's** attention quite like Quy Nhơn. She fell in love with this quiet, undiscovered place, where fishing villages dot the coastline, empty beaches stretch for miles and the seafood is as fresh as it gets. Despite all her travels, Karla keeps returning, convinced that Quy Nhơn is one of Vietnam's last great coastal secrets – a secret she shares in this book.

Annie Georgia Greenberg is the Executive Creative Director at Lonely Planet, where she obsesses over photo, video and design. And, when she's lucky, she travels while doing all three. Always planning her next getaway, Annie is equally powerless to spontaneity and sleeping bags as she is to the thread count of five-star-hotel sheets. For *Best in Travel*, Annie wrote about her life-altering whitewater rafting trip through the Grand Canyon, an experience that left her in love with running rivers and with a number of river-guiding friends.

Tom Hall is a Lonely Planet staffer who wrote about the experience of attending a Premier League game. A lifelong Arsenal supporter and season ticket holder, Tom has misspent much of youth and adulthood following his team all over England and Europe watching thousands of matches, some of which have been enjoyable. Tom's family have been attending Arsenal games since the 1930s, when his maternal grandparents moved near the club's beloved old home in Highbury, north London. He continues the tradition going to matches with his dad, sons George and Harry and daughter Winnie.

Paula Hardy wrote about Tunisia and why this miniature North African country deserves more love, given the incredible variety of experiences it offers. Paula spent many teen summers on its golden beaches, and got to know the country well in her 20s as she shuttled back and forth from sanctioned Libya, where she lived at the time. Since then, she's reported extensively on the Maghreb for Lonely Planet. She likes being surprised, which is why she never gets bored of medina life.

Selena Takigawa Hoy is Lonely Planet's Destination Editor for Northeast Asia and lives in Tokyo, a busy city that requires plenty of energy. For respite, she likes to rove the Japanese countryside staying in hot-spring inns. She wrote about the experience of staying in a ryokan and the way it erases the stress of city life. Her favorite ryokan are in the beautiful but beleaguered Fukushima Prefecture, and her ancestral home of Shimane Prefecture.

Mark Johanson wrote about citizen science in the Amazon, as well as what makes Peru such a great place to visit in 2026. He's based in Santiago, Chile, where his favorite restaurants are all Peruvian. Mark escapes north to Peru whenever he can to hike past remote Inca ruins, dine on Nikkei (Japanese-Peruvian) cuisine, and drink superior pisco sours (shh, don't tell the Chileans!). The Peruvian Amazon, in particular, has always called to his inner nerd with its abundant opportunities for hands-on educational adventures.

After years of hearing her friends talk about the pageantry, wonder and fun of Carnivals throughout the Caribbean, Lonely Planet Destination Editor for the Caribbean, Central America, South America and Mexico, **Alicia Johnson** finally got a chance to experience (and write about) it herself. Aside from the infectious music and the deep history associated with all the revelry, watching Grenadians come home (sometimes after years away) for the country's annual Spicemas celebration truly moved her heart. Spicemas is an unforgettable experience that requires loads of stamina and energy. But, Alicia contends, it's worth it.

Anna Kaminski loves old-school Andalucían tapas bars where you have to elbow your way to the counter. She loves authentic, raw flamenco performances and dressing up in feathers, sequins and masks for Spain's biggest party, Carnaval. These are the things that prompted her to write about the Andalucían town of Cádiz for *Best in Travel 2026*, and which initially sparked her infatuation when she first set foot there as a young backpacker in 2005. Now privileged to live a mere three-hour drive away from Cádiz, Anna visits when she can, to walk barefoot along the seafront promenade and haunt the Peña Flamenca La Perla.

Stacey Lastoe finally made it to the place at the top of her travel wish list: Botswana. The trip surpassed every expectation as the wild, rugged landscape of the country revealed itself to her. The warm, welcoming Batswana were a huge part of what made Stacey fall in love with this remote destination in Africa. After seeing so many lions ruling the land, the Brooklyn-based Lonely Planet contributor maintains a healthy fear of the king of the jungle, but cannot wait to return to see them in action again.

Jessica Lockhart is Lonely Planet's Destination Editor for Oceania. Originally from Canada, she lives under the starry skies of New Zealand/Aotearoa, which is on its way to becoming the world's first true 'Dark Sky Nation'. Jess has seen the transformative effect that Māori-led tourism has achieved firsthand – and how North Island tour operators are leading the way in regenerative tourism. New Zealand may be at the end of the world, but it's also right on the doorstep of the South Pacific, where there are countless nations to explore, including one that Jess can't stop gushing about: the Solomon Islands.

James March hails from Birmingham, England, but is constantly drawn southeast to Bristol. His trips might find him exploring the underrated beer scene and enjoying more unconventional attractions like surfing (yes, really), but it's Bristol's artistic soul that James finds more alluring than anything else. Uncovering the city's street art (which he covers for this book) is a constant delight, even when it means traipsing up hills and crossing bridges from neighborhood to neighborhood. Every step is worth it.

Annemarie McCarthy is Lonely Planet's Destination Editor for Portugal and, by extension, the glorious Azores. She commissioned and edited *Pocket Azores*, the very first Lonely Planet guide to the islands. After reading about one of the most beautiful destinations in the world and working closely with local writers, she was not disappointed when she got to explore them herself for this book.

Born and raised in Melbourne, Australia, **Justin Meneguzzi** doesn't mind hitting the road with good snacks and better company. In a country known for its road trips, he's driven across much of the Australian coastline to lay down a

ABOUT THE AUTHORS

towel on far-off beaches – including the new spas that have popped up across Victoria, which he writes about for *Best in Travel*.

Laura Motta is a New York–based travel writer and editor who spent her childhood summers exploring Maine's lakes, beaches, mountains and backwoods with her beloved grandparents. Many years, soft-serve ice creams, boiled lobsters and mosquito bites later, she is still finding more to uncover in its borders. She wishes she were – and she just might be – sitting on a dock in Ogunquit drinking a rum punch right now.

Isabella Noble is a Spain-raised British-Australian based between Barcelona and Málaga. She has been spending time in India, especially the south, for more than 15 years, and wrote about the experience of taking a culinary adventure across Kerala. As a lifelong vegetarian, Isabella loves discovering new flavors and recipes among India's hugely varied gastronomies (though a fresh *masala dosa* will always be a firm favorite).

James Pham is Lonely Planet's Destination Editor for Southeast Asia, and for *Best in Travel*, he wrote about cruising the Mekong Delta. James lived in Cambodia for 10 years before moving to Vietnam 13 years ago. He's always been fascinated by how people are drawn to living on and by the rivers of Southeast Asia, and how closely their lives are tied into their environment, whether it's fishing, farming or handicrafts. He takes every opportunity to spend time in the Mekong Delta, where life slows down considerably and there's something new to discover nearly everywhere you look.

Kristen Pope wrote about the experience of tracking desert elephants in Namibia. She frequently writes about outdoor adventures and ways to connect with nature, and is always on the lookout for opportunities to see wildlife, whether viewing penguins in Antarctica, watching moose near her home in Wyoming's Tetons, or spotting desert elephants in Namibia.

Zinara Rathnayake wrote about Jaffna, a city in northern Sri Lanka flecked with palmyra palms, marshy lagoons and colorful Hindu shrines. Born and raised in Sri Lanka, Zinara grew up listening to the stories of her late uncle and aunt, who met in Jaffna, fell in love and got married in the 1970s. Her aunt raved about the sweet, juicy Karthakolomban, Jaffna's native mango variety. Decades later, Zinara often visits Jaffna with her husband Nathan, whose family's ancestral home in the historic city safeguards a large, centuries-old mango tree.

Nick Ray first came across the temples of Angkor in an encyclopedia as a young child, and decided he simply had to visit the one and only Angkor Wat. Little did he realize that Cambodia would become his home and Angkor a playground of sorts. Now, he describes Siem Reap as his spiritual home, and wrote about it for *Best in Travel*; no matter how many times Nick has visited 'Temple Town' and its incredible buildings, he always finds it a fascinating and friendly place to explore.

On **Simon Richmond's** first visit to Jeju-do, South Korea's beloved holiday island, he spent an enjoyable couple of weeks admiring the striking landscapes while hiking sections of the Jeju Ole Trail. He climbed to the summit of Hallasan, the nation's tallest peak, and connected with the friendly local people. In 2024, when he returned to research the latest edition of Lonely Planet's *Korea* guidebook, it was the island's thriving contemporary art scene as well as its superb range of cafes and restaurants that made him love it even more.

Brendan Sainsbury moved to British Columbia from the UK in 2004 after falling in love with a Canadian woman he'd met in Spain. He quickly fell for his newly adopted province too: a tall, muscular, physically well-endowed landmass significantly larger than his country of birth, but with only a small fraction of the population. After growing up in Hampshire, England, Vancouver felt slick, modern and infinitely more spacious, with a dozen mountainous Switzerlands radiating from its urban core. In 21 years of navigating the city's expansive hinterland, he still feels as if he's barely skimmed the surface.

Kara Santos is a leisure biker and motorcycle rider who enjoys exploring destinations on two wheels, mainly for sightseeing and food trips rather than clocking up kilometers traveled. For *Best in Travel* she wrote about cycling in Batanes in the Philippines. Kara has explored all provinces of her home country – a long-term travel quest, which took more than a decade, with Batanes being one of her favorites. Between freelance assignments, she enjoys biking and motorcycling in and near Manila, where she's based with her husband Art and their four cats.

Nasha Smith hails from St Lucia and has studied abroad in the US, as well as Wales, Belgium, Germany, Czechia, Spain, Greece and Italy – but nowhere compares to the West Indies. From the vibrant street-food scene in Trinidad to the volcanic landscapes of St Vincent, the French-Caribbean charm of Martinique, the spice markets of Grenada, the dancehall vibes of Jamaica and the rum-fueled parties in Barbados (the country she wrote about for this book), each island holds its own incomparable magic.

Phillip Tang first visited Mexico City in 2001 and has lived between there and Australia since 2011. He has researched and written dozens of guides and articles on Mexico and Latin America (including the Mexico City submission in this book), while eagerly building a repertoire of Chilango slang and poetic ways of swearing. A perfect Mexico City day for Phillip is mural-spotting in designer Roma, followed by sniffing out the local street-food scene in a far-flung neighborhood.

Kerry Walker wrote about the joys of Finland. Over the past decade, Kerry has developed an obsession with Nordic climes, and Finland is one of her all-time favorites for its phenomenal nature and lovable quirks. From Moomins to the Northern Lights, Sámi culture to salty liquorice, Baltic-shaped islands to the snow-frosted wilds of Lapland, Kerry has made it her mission to dive deep into the country and find out what makes one of the happiest nations on Earth tick.

From her home in London, **Robyn Wilson** has been exploring the Balkans for more than 15 years. For *Best in Travel*, she wrote about Belgrade's legendary nightlife, with its mix of underground clubs, lively *kafanas* (taverns) and riverside *splavovi* (floating lounges). Fascinated by the city's history, food and people, Robyn is drawn to the stories behind Belgrade's buzzing music scene and hidden bars. From *rakija*-fueled nights to early morning burek stops, she has experienced it all.

Barbara Woolsey has been living and working in Thailand for more than a decade. She first fell in love with Phuket in 2022 while studying at Chulalongkorn University, and recently wrote about it in Lonely Planet's *Pocket Phuket* – and this book, too. The island is her happy place, for writing on jungle balconies and going to electronic-music festivals (she also performs as a DJ around southern Thailand). Every year, Barbara aims to trade winter in Europe for dancing and sunning on Phuket's beaches – and these days, as a new mom, with her daughter in tow.

Fabienne Fong Yan was born and raised on Réunion. For this book, she wrote about her island's multicultural heritage and breathtaking landscapes, which she grew to appreciate even more while living abroad. Like many Réunionnais who move to mainland France for studies or work, Fabienne has spent much of her adult life away from her homeland – living and traveling across Europe and Asia. Now based in Paris, she returns frequently to reconnect with Réunion's striking scenery and rich cultural diversity, and to nurture her desire to write about her magical island as often as possible.

Born and raised in the picturesque Adelaide Hills, **Chris Zeiher** is a parochial South Australian, constantly advocating for Australia's bohemian southern state. Whether it's gallivanting around Kangaroo Island, skipping between wineries in McLaren Vale or going bushwalking in the Flinders Ranges and the Australian Outback, Chris is constantly exploring his former home state. Having been based in Melbourne for the last 20 years, Chris has also eaten his way around the city and watched its eclectic food scene evolve and explode. He shares his love of both the Flinders Ranges and Melbourne for *Best in Travel*.

A ferry ride away from **Angelo Zinna's** home base in Tuscany, Italy, Sardinia has been a great source of inspiration between guidebook assignments in Europe's far-flung corners. This marvelous Mediterranean island shows its most intriguing side during the off season, when crowds are absent and the atmosphere is most relaxed. For *Best in Travel*, Angelo has written about experiencing Sardinia beyond its most beautiful beaches and resorts.

PHOTO CREDITS

Back Cover: Jonathan Stokes/Lonely Planet, Chamidae Ford/Lonely Planet; **Cover Flap:** Fabiano Goreme Caddeo/Adobe Stock, Gilles van Winsen/Shutterstock; **4:** Daniel James Clarke/Lonely Planet; **6:** benedek/Getty Images; **9:** Christian Ouellet/Shutterstock; **12:** Kadagan/Shutterstock; **14:** Max Dickson/Lonely Planet; **15:** Max Dickson/Lonely Planet; **16:** Max Dickson/Lonely Planet, Max Dickson/Lonely Planet; **17:** Max Dickson/Lonely Planet, Max Dickson/Lonely Planet; **18:** Ed Gifford/Getty Images; **19:** Xeni4ka/Getty Images; **20:** Gonzalo Iglesias/Unsplash; **21:** Russell Johnson/Shutterstock; **22:** Christian Declercq/Shutterstock, Vitmark/Shutterstock; **23:** The Magical Lab/Shutterstock, AlexSava/Getty Images; **24:** Mark Parren Taylor; **25:** Mark Parren Taylor; **26:** Mark Parren Taylor, Mark Parren Taylor; **27:** Mark Parren Taylor, Mark Parren Taylor; **29:** Southern Lightscapes-Australia/Getty Images; **30:** Luke Shelley/Shutterstock, Andrew Bain/Alamy; **31:** Yury Prokopenko/Getty Images, Bjorn Svensson/Alamy; **32:** Old Town Tourist/Shutterstock; **33:** AlexeMarcel/Shutterstock; **34:** quintanilla/Getty Images; **35:** trabantos/Shutterstock; **36:** japatino/Getty Images, Philip Lee Harvey/Lonely Planet; **37:** DEA/Getty Images, Oscar Chamorro/Shutterstock; **38:** Manuela Lourenço for Lonely Planet; **39:** Manuela Lourenço for Lonely Planet; **40:** Manuela Lourenço for Lonely Planet; **41:** Manuela Lourenço for Lonely Planet, Manuela Lourenço for Lonely Planet; **42:** Angelo Zinna; **44:** Fabiano Goreme Caddeo/Adobe Stock; **45:** Angelo Zinna; **46:** Elisa Locci/Shutterstock, Gengis90/Shutterstock; **47:** Tore65/Shutterstock, Fabiano Goreme Caddeo/Shutterstock; **48:** Education Images/Getty Images; **50:** Jacob Boomsma/Shutterstock, Chris Martin/Stocksy; **51:** Bruce Montagne/Alamy, Laurens Hoddenbagh/Shutterstock; **53:** Romain Philippon; **54:** Romain Philippon; **55:** Romain Philippon, Romain Philippon; **56:** Romain Philippon; **57:** Romain Philippon; **58:** Romain Philippon, Romain Philippon; **59:** Romain Philippon; **60:** Severine Sajous; **61:** Michael Greenberg; **62:** Michael Greenberg; **63:** Michael Greenberg; **64:** Severine Sajous, Anastasia Kamysheva/Shutterstock; **65:** Severine Sajous, Jess Kraft/Shutterstock; **66:** Kyle Babb for Lonely Planet; **67:** Kyle Babb for Lonely Planet; **68:** Kyle Babb for Lonely Planet, Kyle Babb for Lonely Planet; **69:** Kyle Babb for Lonely Planet, Kyle Babb for Lonely Planet; **71:** Jessica Lockhart/Lonely Planet; **72:** Ethan Daniels/Shutterstock; **73:** Jessica Lockhart/Lonely Planet; **74:** The Asahi Shimbun/Getty Images, Jessica Lockhart/Lonely Planet; **75:** Jessica Lockhart/Lonely Planet, Jessica Lockhart/Lonely Planet; **76:** Joe Dube/500px; **77:** Andrew Castilo/Unsplash; **78:** Jeana Bala/Unsplash, Brianna Soukup/Portland Press Herald/Getty Images; **79:** Laura Peruchi/Unsplash, Cindy Hopkins/Alamy; **80:** Nikialex/Shutterstock; **81:** mehdi33300/Shutterstock; **82:** Chris Luengas/Unsplash; **83:** ItzaVU/Shutterstock; **84:** WitR/Shutterstock, Kamira/Shutterstock; **85:** Santiago Castillo Chomel/Shutterstock, Evan Ruderman; **86:** Thomas Bresenhuber/Shutterstock; **87:** Hemis/Alamy; **88:** Discover Lough Derg; **89:** Liam Murphy/Fáilte Ireland; **90:** Tipperary Tourism, Stephen Power/Alamy; **91:** Tipperary Tourism, Carsten Krieger/Tourism Ireland; **92:** Fabrizio Cortesi/Alamy; **93:** IngaL/Getty Images; **94:** traumlichtfabrik/Shutterstock, Fernanda Reyes/Shutterstock; **95:** Bruno Adrian/Shutterstock, Ingo Bartussek/Shutterstock; **96:** trabantos/Shutterstock; **97:** Jonathan Stokes for Lonely Planet; **98:** Shashh/Shutterstock; **99:** Kanujan Singarajah/Getty Images; **100:** Denis Costille/Shutterstock, Malcolm P Chapman/Getty Images; **101:** Wirestock Creators/Shutterstock, Oscar Espinosa/Shutterstock; **103:** Lauryn Ishak for Lonely Planet; **104:** Lauryn Ishak for Lonely Planet; **105:** Lauryn Ishak for Lonely Planet, Lauryn Ishak for Lonely Planet; **106:** Lauryn Ishak for Lonely Planet; **107:** Lauryn Ishak for Lonely Planet; **108:** Lauryn Ishak for Lonely Planet, Lauryn Ishak for Lonely Planet; **109:** Lauryn Ishak for Lonely Planet; **110:** Samira Kafala for Lonely Planet; **111:** ColorMaker/Shutterstock; **112:** Samira Kafala for Lonely Planet, Samira Kafala for Lonely Planet; **113:** Samira Kafala for Lonely Planet, Samira Kafala for Lonely Planet; **114:** Juan Tapias for Lonely Planet; **115:** Atosan/Shutterstock; **116:** Juan Tapias for Lonely Planet; **117:** Zoonar GmbH/Alamy Stock Photo; **118:** Juan Tapias for Lonely Planet, Jessyth Rivera/Shutterstock; **119:** Juan Tapias for Lonely Planet, Juan Tapias for Lonely Planet; **120:** Mark Read/Lonely Planet; **121:** BlueOrange Studio/Shutterstock; **122:** kriskit/Shutterstock, SariMe/Shutterstock; **123:** Mark Read/Lonely Planet, ArtBBNV/Shutterstock; **125:** Hien Phung Thu/Shutterstock; **126:** Simon Oostveen, Simon Oostveen; **127:** Simon Oostveen, Simon Oostveen; **128:** Russ Heinl/Shutterstock; **130:** Peter OHara/Getty Images; **131:** Ryan De Jong/Shutterstock; **132:** CoolPhoto2/Shutterstock, Nalidsa/Shutterstock; **133:** Lee Rentz/Alamy, Bob Pool/Shutterstock; **134:** Nelson Antoine/Shutterstock; **135:** Pelikh Alexey/Shutterstock; **136:** Mark Read/Lonely Planet; **137:** Mark Read/Lonely Planet; **138:** CatwalkPhotos/Shutterstock, Jefferyhamstock/Shutterstock; **139:** JM Travel Photography/Shutterstock, Gilles van Winsen/Shutterstock; **141:** Mark Read/Lonely Planet; **142:** Liz Carlson; **143:** Justin Foulkes/Lonely Planet; **144:** Liz Carlson, Wai Ariki Hot Springs and Spa;

145: iv4ngrigoryev/Shutterstock, Smith & Sheth; **148:** Bob Pool/Shutterstock; **150:** Daniel James Clarke/Lonely Planet; **151:** Daniel James Clarke/Lonely Planet; **152:** EJ Wolfson/Unsplash, Daniel James Clarke/Lonely Planet; **153:** Slava Auchynnikau/Unsplash, Daniel James Clarke/Lonely Planet; **154:** Natalie Naccache for Lonely Planet; **156:** Natalie Naccache for Lonely Planet; **157:** Natalie Naccache for Lonely Planet; **158:** Andrew Mongomery/Lonely Planet, Natalie Naccache for Lonely Planet; **159:** Natalie Naccache for Lonely Planet, Natalie Naccache for Lonely Planet; **160:** Kruger Shalati; **161:** Michele Spatari/AFP/Getty Images; **162:** Kyle Lewin, Michael Heffernan/Lonely Planet; **163:** Emma Shaw/Lonely Planet, Kruger Shalati; **165:** We are Content(s)/Centre des monuments nationaux; **166:** Françoise Huguier/Centre des monuments nationaux, Françoise Huguier/Centre des monuments nationaux; **167:** Françoise Huguier/Centre des monuments nationaux, We are Content(s)/Centre des monuments nationaux; **168:** Jonathan Stokes/Lonely Planet; **169:** Alla Tsyganova/Shutterstock; **170:** Adrian Gaut/Trunk Archive; **171:** Thomas Dashuber/laif/Redux; **172:** Trunk Archive, Markus Kirchgessner/laif/Redux; **173:** weniliou/Shutterstock, Asaba; **174:** Andrea Chiozzi/Shutterstock; **175:** Kumar Sriskandan/Alamy; **176:** Claude Huot/Shutterstock, Evenfh/Shutterstock; **177:** sma1050/Shutterstock, Thomas Retterath/Shutterstock; **179:** Fabian von Poser/Alamy; **180:** Daniel Falcão/Getty Images, si saber L/Shutterstock; **181:** Victor Moriyama/Redux, Freedomwanted/Shutterstock; **183:** Luisa Dörr; **184:** Luisa Dörr; **185:** Luisa Dörr, Luisa Dörr; **186:** Luisa Dörr; **187:** Luisa Dörr; **188:** Luisa Dörr, Luisa Dörr; **189:** Luisa Dörr; **190:** Raleigh Gambino; **191:** Raleigh Gambino; **192:** Raleigh Gambino, Raleigh Gambino; **193:** Raleigh Gambino, piola666/Getty Images; **194:** Ben Savage/Visit Victoria; **195:** Ben Savage/Visit Victoria; **196:** Natalia Vostrikova/Shutterstock, FiledIMAGE/Shutterstock; **197:** Corleve/Alamy, f.ield of vision/Getty Images; **199:** James Pham/Lonely Planet; **200:** James Pham/Lonely Planet; **201:** CravenA/Shutterstock; **202:** James Pham/Lonely Planet, James Pham/Lonely Planet; **203:** James Pham/Lonely Planet, Nguyen Quang Ngoc Tonkin/Shutterstock; **204:** Jonatas Neiva/Shutterstock; **205:** Sunart Media/Shutterstock; **206:** Sunart Media/Shutterstock, Helissa Grundemann/Shutterstock; **207:** Chamidae Ford/Lonely Planet, Zoltan Bagosi/Alamy; **208:** Stephanie Foden; **209:** Stephanie Foden; **210:** Stephanie Foden; **211:** Stephanie Foden; **212:** Lee Celano/The New York Times/Redux, Lee Celano/The New York Times/Redux; **213:** Stephanie Foden, Lee Celano/The New York Times/Redux; **214:** Sahana M S/Shutterstock; **216:** Shan Raheem/Shutterstock, Sudarsan Thobias/Shutterstock; **217:** Raja GamerXTC/Shutterstock, Miguel Moya Moreno/Shutterstock; **218:** John Walton/PA Images/Getty Images; **219:** Oli Scarff/Getty Images; **220:** Julian Finney/Getty Images; **221:** Matthew Peters/Manchester United/Getty Images; **222:** Justin Setterfield/Getty Images, Mark Leech/Getty Images; **223:** Liverpool FC/Getty Images, Thomas McAtee/Shutterstock; **224:** George Rose/Getty Images; **225:** Cannon Photography LLC/Alamy; **226:** Eyrie Vineyards, George Rose/Getty Images; **227:** AJ Meeker/Humble Spirit, Serge Chapuis/Domaine Drouhin; **228:** Sarah Pannell for Lonely Planet; **230:** Sarah Pannell for Lonely Planet, Sarah Pannell for Lonely Planet; **231:** Sarah Pannell for Lonely Planet, Sarah Pannell for Lonely Planet; **232:** Inkaterra Hotels; **233:** Carl Safina/Rainforest Expeditions; **234:** Louis Guillot/Rainforest Expeditions; **235:** Adalbert Dragon/Shutterstock; **236:** Carlos Gonzales/Rainforest Expeditions, Inkaterra Hotels; **237:** Inkaterra Hotels, Inkaterra Hotels; **239:** Chambers Media Solutions; **240:** Andy Johnson; **241:** Andy Johnson, Andy Johnson; **242:** Chambers Media Solutions; **243:** Chambers Media Solutions; **244:** Chambers Media Solutions, Andy Johnson; **245:** Chambers Media Solutions; **246:** Kara Santos/Lonely Planet; **247:** Joseph Oropel/Shutterstock; **248:** Luis G. Bayaras/Shutterstock, L. L. Lopez/Shutterstock; **249:** Arianne Grace Bautista/Shutterstock, Geela Garcia; **251:** vladimir-n/Getty Images; **252:** Mila Pantovic; **253:** Image Professionals GmbH/Alamy; **254:** KC Grad, Mila Pantovic; **255:** Bada1/Shutterstock, KC Grad; **256:** Michelle Mishina Kunz for Lonely Planet; **257:** Michelle Mishina Kunz for Lonely Planet; **258:** Michelle Mishina Kunz for Lonely Planet, Michelle Mishina Kunz for Lonely Planet; **259:** Michelle Mishina Kunz for Lonely Planet, Michelle Mishina Kunz for Lonely Planet; **260:** Henner Damke/Shutterstock; **261:** Marek Pelikan/Shutterstock; **262:** katatonia82/Shutterstock, wildestanimal/Shutterstock; **263:** Oleksii Piekhov/Unsplash, Andrea Izzotti/Getty Images; **264:** Colin Moody/GOIN for 'UPFEST PRESENTS', Bristol, 2024; **265:** Paul Box/REPORT DIGITAL-REA/Redux; **266:** Martin Booth, GRAFT; **267:** Steve Taylor ARPS/Alamy Stock Photo, Lee Thomas/Alamy Stock Photo; **268:** Hans Wagemaker/Alamy Stock Photo; **269:** Stewart Watson/Getty Images; **270:** James Coleman/Unsplash; **271:** Ed Goodacre/Shutterstock; **272:** Oliver Strewe/Getty Images, Wairarapa Dark Sky Reserve; **273:** Chash Gajanayaka/Shutterstock, mauritius images GmbH/Alamy Stock Photo; **274:** David Madison/Getty Images

INDEX

A
Amazon, Peru 233-37
archaeological sites
    Cádiz, Spain 37
    Mexico City, Mexico 83-5
    Peru 18-23
    Quy Nhơn, Vietnam 127
    Sardinia, Italy 43-7
    Siem Reap, Cambodia 135-9
    Tunisia 60-5
    Utrecht, Netherlands 110
architecture
    Batanes Islands, Philippines 247-9
    Maine, USA 79
    Siem Reap, Cambodia 135-40
    Eileen Gray's House (Villa E-1027), France 164-7
Argentina 178-81
art
    Belgrade, Serbia 250-5
    Bristol, England 265-7
    Jeju-do, South Korea 27
    Maine, USA 79
    Namibia 177
    Utrecht, Netherlands 113
    Wairarapa, New Zealand/Aotearoa 273
Australia
    Ikara-Flinders Ranges & Outback, South Australia 28-31
    Melbourne, Victoria 228-31
    Bathing Trail, Victoria 195-7
Azores, Portugal 261-3

B
Banksy 267
Barbados 67-9
Batanes Islands, Philippines 247-9
beaches
    Barbados 67-9
    Batanes Islands, Philippines 247-9
    Maine, USA 77
    Phuket, Thailand 102-9
    Quy Nhơn, Vietnam 124-7
    Réunion 52-9
    Sardinia, Italy 42-7
    Solomon Islands 70-5
    Tunisia 60-5

Belgrade, Serbia 250-5
boat travel
    Azores, Portugal 261-3
    Cartagena, Colombia 118
    Grand Canyon, USA 191-3
    Iberá Wetlands, Argentina 178-81
    Jaffna, Sri Lanka 100
    Mekong River cruises, Vietnam & Cambodia 198-203
    Old Dubai, UAE 154-9
    Peru 23
    Siem Reap, Cambodia 136
    Solomon Islands 75
Bolivia
    Flying Cholitas, El Alto 182-9
Botswana 15-17
Brazil
    Liberdade, São Paulo 39-41
British Columbia, Canada 129-34

C
Cádiz, Spain 32-7
Cambodia
    Mekong River cruises 198-203
    Siem Reap 135-9
camping
    Arkaroola Wilderness Sanctuary, Australia 31
    Tajikistan 151-3
Canada
    British Columbia 128-33
Caribbean
    Barbados 67-70
    Grenada 238-45
Cartagena, Colombia 115-20
caves
    Harrison's Cave, Barbados 68
    Palliser Chasm, New Zealand/Aotearoa 273
Colombia
    Cartagena 115-20
cultural experiences
    Belgrade nightlife, Serbia 250-5
    Cádiz Carnaval, Spain 32
    Carnival, Grenada 238-45
    cholita wrestling, Bolivia 182-9
    Creole trail rides, USA 209-13
    Crop Over, Barbados 69
    festival season, Grenada 238-45
    flamenco, Cádiz 37
    football matches, England 219-23
    Mamuthones, Italy 46

    Onam festival, India 216
    Ông Núi Temple, Vietnam 126
    ryokan accommodation, Japan 168-73
    Sámi culture, Finland 122
    Savosavo language, Solomon Islands 74
    Spicemas, Grenada 238-45
    street art, England 265-7
cycling
    Batanes Islands, Philippines 247-9
    Jaffna, Sri Lanka 101
    Martinborough, New Zealand/Aotearoa 273
    Mekong Delta, Vietnam & Cambodia 198-203
    Melrose, Australia 31
    Sardinia, Italy 47
    Siem Reap, Cambodia 138
    South Australia, Australia 31
    Utrecht, Netherlands 110-13

D
diving
    Islas de Rosario, Colombia 118
    Sardinia, Italy 47
    Solomon Islands 70-2
dolphins
    Azores, Portugal 261-3
Old Dubai, UAE 154-9

E
Ecuador
    Andes Mountains 204-7
Eileen Gray's House (Villa E-1027), France 164-7
elephants
    Botswana 17
    Kruger National Park, South Africa 162
    Namibia 175-7
    Phuket, Thailand 105
    Siem Reap, Cambodia 139
England
    Bristol street art 265-7
    Premier League football 219-23

F
family-friendly experiences
    Barbados 67-9
    Creole trail rides, USA 209-13
    Maine, USA 77-9

Theodore Roosevelt
  National Park, USA 49-51
Victoria Bathing Trail,
  Australia 195-7
festivals & events
  Cádiz Carnaval, Spain 32
  Carnival, Grenada 238-45
  Creole trail rides, USA 209-13
  Crop Over, Barbados 69
  Dakota Nights Astronomy
    Festival, USA 50
  Festival de Venado,
    Guatemala 95
  Festival of Carthage, Tunisia 62
  football matches, England 219-23
  Illusion Festival, Serbia 251-2
  Mamuthones, Italy 46
  Māori new year, New Zealand/
    Aotearoa 270-3
  Nallur Kandaswamy Kovil,
    Sri Lanka 98
  Onam festival, India 216
  Shell Money Festival,
    Solomon Islands 72
  Spicemas, Grenada 238-45
  Upfest, England 267
Finland 120-3
food experiences
  Cádiz, Spain 32-4
  Jeju-do, South Korea 27
  Kerala, India 214-17
  Maine, USA 79
  Melbourne, Australia 228-31
  Old Dubai, UAE 154-9
  São Paulo, Brazil 39-41
  Sawa, Tunisia 64
  Willamette Wine Country,
    USA 225-7
France
  Eileen Gray's House (Villa E-1027),
    Côte d'Azur 164-7

G
Grand Canyon, USA 191-3
Gray, Eileen 164-7
Grenada 238-45
Guatemala
  Quetzaltenango (Xela), 93-6

H
Hawai'i Volcanoes National Park,
  USA 257-9

hiking
  British Columbia, Canada 128-33
  Hawai'i Volcanoes National Park,
    USA 257-9
  Ikara-Flinders Ranges National Park
    & Outback, Australia 28-31
  Jeju-do, South Korea 25
  Maine, USA 78
  North Shore Mountains,
    Canada 132
  Peru 18-23
  Qhapaq Ñan, Peru 22
  Réunion 52-9
  Sardinia, Italy 47
  Solomon Islands 72, 75
  Tajikistan 151-3
  Theodore Roosevelt National
    Park, USA 51
  Tipperary, Ireland 88
  Tunisia 65
history
  Cartagena, Colombia 117
  Ecuador 204-7
  Hawai'i Volcanoes National Park,
    USA 257-9
  Mexico City, Mexico 81-5
  Old Dubai, UAE 154-9
  Peru 18-23
  Quy Nhơn, Vietnam 127
  Sardinia, Italy 42-7
  Tunisia 60-5
  Villa E-1027, France 164-7
horse riding
  Creole trail rides, USA 209-13
  Ecuador 204-7
hot springs
  Japan 168-73
  Lake Rotorua, New Zealand/
    Aotearoa 144
  Victoria Bathing Trail, Australia 195-7

I
Iberá Wetlands, Argentina 178-81
Ikara-Flinders Ranges National Park &
  Outback, Australia 28-31
India
  Kerala 214-17
Ireland
  Tipperary 87-91
Italy
  Sardinia 42-7

J
Jaffna, Sri Lanka 96-101
jaguars
  Iberá Wetlands, Argentina 178-81
Japan
  ryokan 168-73
Jeju-do, South Korea 25-8

K
Kerala, India 214-17
Kruger National Park,
  South Africa 161-3

L
Liberdade, São Paulo,
  Brazil 39-41
Louisiana, USA 209-13

M
Maine, USA 77-80
Mekong River, Vietnam &
  Cambodia 198-203
Melbourne, Australia 228-31
Mexico
  Mexico City 81-5

N
Namibia 175-7
national parks
  Acadia National Park, USA 77
  Glacier National Park, Canada 133
  Gwaii Haanas National Park,
    Canada 133
  Hawai'i Volcanoes National Park,
    USA 257-9
  Ikara-Flinders Ranges National Park,
    Australia 28-31
  Ichkeul National Park, Tunisia 65
  Isola dell'Asinara National Park,
    Italy 47
  Kruger National Park,
    South Africa 161-3
  Mt Revelstoke National Park,
    Canada 133
  Pacific Rim National Park,
    Canada 133
  Theodore Roosevelt
    National Park, USA 49-51
  Yoho National Park, Canada 133
Netherlands
  Utrecht 110-13

BEST IN TRAVEL 2026 / 285

INDEX

New Zealand/Aotearoa
  North Island 140-5
  Wairarapa 269-73
nightlife
  Belgrade, Serbia 250-5
North Island, New Zealand/
  Aotearoa 140-5

O
Oregon, USA 225-7

P
Peru 18-23
  Amazon region 233-7
Philippines
  Batanes Islands 247-9
Phuket, Thailand 102-9
Portugal
  Azores 261-3

Q
Quetzaltenango (Xela),
  Guatemala 93-6
Quy Nhơn, Vietnam 124-7

R
rafting 191-3
remote destinations
  Amazon, Peru 233-7
  Andes Mountains, Ecuador 204-7
  Batanes Islands, Philippines 247-9
  Botswana 15-17
  British Columbia, Canada 128-33
  Colorado River, USA 191-3
  Iberá Wetlands, Argentina 178-81
  Ikara-Flinders Ranges National Park
    & Outback, Australia 28-31
  Namibia 175-7
  Réunion 52-9
  Solomon Islands 70-5
  Tajikistan 151-3
Réunion 52-9
Roosevelt, Theodore 48-51

S
safaris
  Botswana 15-17
  Kruger National Park, South
    Africa 161-3
São Paulo, Brazil 39-41

Sardinia, Italy 43-8
Serbia
  Belgrade 250-5
Siem Reap, Cambodia 135-9
snorkeling
  Barbados 69
  Islas de Rosario, Colombia 118
  Jeju-do, South Korea 25
  Sardinia, Italy 47
  Solomon Islands 70-2
Solomon Islands 70-5
South Africa
  Kruger National Park 161-3
South Korea
  Jeju-do 25-7
Spain
  Cádiz 32-7
Sri Lanka
  Jaffna 96-101
stargazing
  Arkaroola Wilderness Sanctuary,
    Australia 31
  Theodore Roosevelt National Park,
    USA 50
  Wairarapa, New Zealand/
    Aotearoa 269-73
surfing
  Solomon Islands 70-5

T
Tajikistan
  Fan Mountains 151-3
Texas, USA 209-13
Thailand
  Phuket 102-9
Theodore Roosevelt National Park,
  USA 48-51
Tipperary, Ireland 87-92
Tunisia 60-5

U
United Arab Emirates
  Old Dubai 154-9
USA
  Creole trail rides, Louisiana &
    Texas 209-13
  Grand Canyon, Arizona 191-3
  Hawai'i Volcanoes National Park,
    Hawai'i 257-9
  Louisiana 209-13
  Maine 77-9

Texas 209-13
Theodore Roosevelt National Park,
  North Dakota 48-51
Willamette Wine Country,
  Oregon 225-7
Utrecht, Netherlands 110-13

V
Vancouver, Canada 129
Victoria Bathing Trail,
  South Australia 195-7
Vietnam
  Mekong Delta cruises 198-203
  Quy Nhơn 124-7
volcanoes
  Andes Mountains, Ecuador 204-7
  Jeju-do, South Korea 26
  Hawai'i Volcanoes National Park,
    USA 257-9

W
Wairarapa, New Zealand/
  Aotearoa 269-73
whale-watching
  Azores, Portugal 261-3
Whistler, Canada 130
wildlife
  Azores, Portugal 261-3
  Botswana 15-17
  Iberá Wetlands, Argentina 178-81
  Kruger National Park,
    South Africa 161-3
  Namibia 175-7
  Peru 23, 233-7
  Solomon Islands 72
wine
  British Columbia, Canada 130
  Cádiz, Spain 32-4
  North Island, New Zealand/
    Aotearoa 145
  Wairarapa, New Zealand/
    Aotearoa 273
  Willamette Wine Country, USA 225-7

X
Xela, Guatemala 93-6

Best in Travel 2026

Project Editors: Becca Hunt, Fionnuala McCarthy, Tom Hall, Polly Thomas, Brekke Fletcher
Copy Editor: Nicole Gull McElroy
Designer: Supriya Kalidas
Layout Designer: Jo Dovey
Publishing Director: Piers Pickard
Publisher: Becca Hunt
Art Director: Emily Dubin
Photo Director: Pia Peterson
Print Production: Nigel Longuet

October 2025
Published by Lonely Planet Global Limited
CRN: 554153
ISBN: 978 18375 8766 7
© Lonely Planet 2025
10 9 8 7 6 5 4 3 2 1
Printed in Malaysia

All rights reserved. No part of this publication may be reproduced, stored in a retrieval system or transmitted in any form by any means, electronic, mechanical, photocopying, recording or otherwise except brief extracts for the purpose of review, without the written permission of the publisher. Lonely Planet and the Lonely Planet logo are trademarks of Lonely Planet and are registered in the US Patent and Trademark Office and in other countries.

Although the author and Lonely Planet have taken all reasonable care in preparing this book, we make no warranty about the accuracy or completeness of its content and, to the maximum extent permitted, disclaim all liability from its use.

STAY IN TOUCH
lonelyplanet.com/contact

Lonely Planet Office:
IRELAND
Digital Depot, Roe Lane (off Thomas St), Digital Hub, Dublin 8, D08 TCV4, Ireland

MIX
Paper | Supporting responsible forestry
FSC™ C021741

Paper in this book is certified against the Forest Stewardship Council™ standards. FSC™ promotes environmentally responsible, socially beneficial and economically viable management of the world's forests.

NORTH
AMERICA

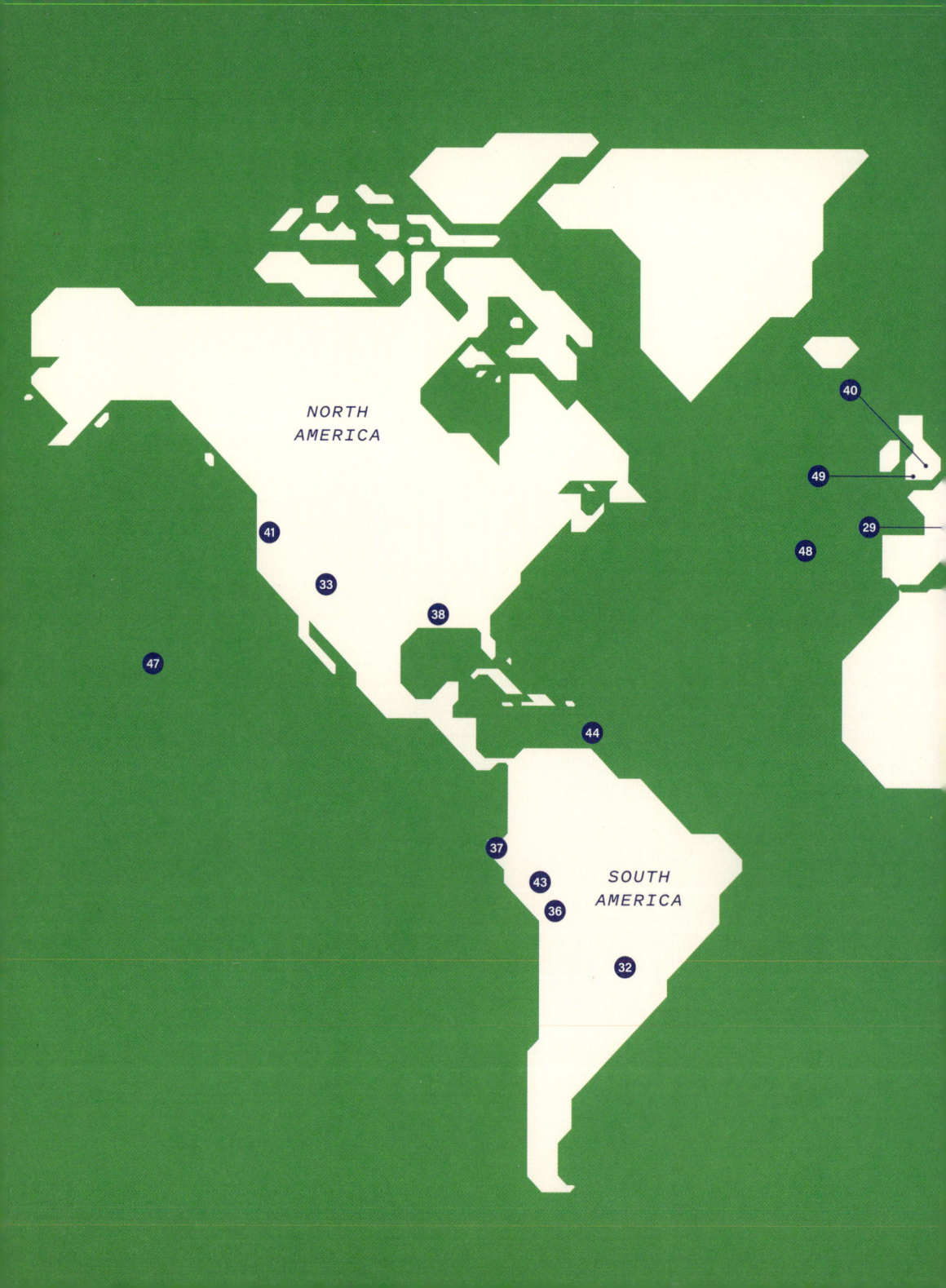

SOUTH
AMERICA

40
49
29
48
41
33
38
47
44
37
43
36
32